Chasing Lightning

Chasing Lightning

The Pursuit of Successful Living in America

Chris Moeller

Writers Club Press
San Jose   New York   Lincoln   Shanghai

Chasing Lightning
The Pursuit of Successful Living in America

Writers Club Press
an imprint of iUniverse, Inc.

For information address:
iUniverse, Inc.
5220 S. 16th St., Suite 200
Lincoln, NE 68512
www.iuniverse.com

ISBN: 0-595-21355-3

Printed in the United States of America

For my family
Who encouraged me to leave the nest,

For Brian and Jeanne
Who taught me how to fly,

And for Zoe, Olivia, Clark, and Heather
Who have yet to spread their wings

Epigraph

◆

Shamzara: A mystical, magical event or person that comes out of the blue, unsuspecting, striking like a bolt of lightning and forever changing your world for the better.

Introduction

❖

The unexamined life is not worth living

Socrates

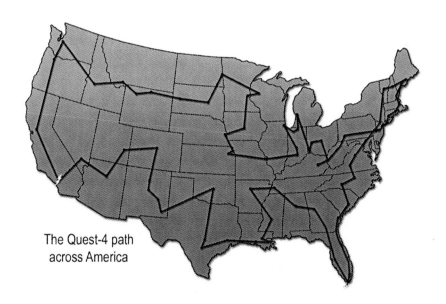

The Quest-4 path
across America

How do we go about finding our place in life and how do we know
when we get there? How is success defined in American today? Are my

definitions and that of my neighbor the same? Are we striving for the same things or are our paths completely different? And is there some way we can be helping each other along our way? Is it that people aren't really striving for "success" as society defines it but rather "successful living," that complete package of career, family, friends, happiness, and spiritual fulfillment?

These are just a few of the many questions that sparked the creation of the Quest-4 project and the book you are holding. At the beginning of 1998, my friend Brian Ardinger and I were both living in California leading "successful lives" as young, promising professionals. But something was missing; for some reason we felt restless and incomplete, like there was something more we should be doing. On outward appearances we seemed to have achieved success by society's standards (or were well on our way) but inside we felt we were off track.

We talked about these feelings with friends and family and found that we were not alone. There was a prevailing wind of confusion and discontent blowing through the lives of many of our peers. Many felt they were unhappy, or on the wrong path, or not sure where it was they were really headed. Brian and I took this to heart and decided to try to find out about this successful living in America by taking our questions on the road. So we left our jobs, stored our worldly possessions, and packed into a Jeep for a crisscross of America in search of answers.

During the course of our six-month journey we managed to hit every one of the lower 48 states and talk to people from all walks of life and backgrounds. Each time we got a fresh perspective of how people are facing the challenges of life and the many ways to do so. And with each encounter we came a little closer to understanding ourselves in the process.

This is a book about our journey, both the physical and spiritual. It is a modern day fable about the search for meaning and purpose. And while the book may be about our journey it could just as easily be about you, or your brother, or the person living down the street from you. We all face the same challenges in defining our version of successful living and we all take our own journeys.

Travel with us now as we set out to talk to your peers from across the nation. Our story begins on a lonely hilltop in the wilds of Wyoming and ends on a deserted highway somewhere outside of Las Vegas...

PART I

$\blacklozenge$

NEW BEGINNINGS

Alice was a little startled by seeing the
Cheshire Cat sitting on a bough of a tree a few yards off.

…"Would you tell me please, which way I ought
to go from here?"

"That depends on where you want to
get to?" said the cat.

"I don't much care where—" said Alice.

"Then it doesn't matter which way you go," said the cat.

"—so long as I get somewhere," Alice added as an explanation.

"Oh you're sure to do that," said the cat,
"if you only walk long enough."

Lewis Carrol
Alice In Wonderland

FOOL ON THE HILL

◆

*A journey of a thousand miles
must begin with a single step.*

Chinese Proverb

Even with nightfall rapidly approaching, the summer sun still beats down relentlessly, heating the earth beneath me and slowly baking my pale skin into tints of red. I sit unmoving in the circle of stones and stare at the fire, watching the flames kick and jump over the dead grass and lick up the twigs. It grows braver and bolder and overtakes the sticks and then the logs, erupting into a real fire. A slight breeze feeds the flames, and I notice it seems to be scaring off the mosquitoes as well. *At least that is one challenge I needn't worry about out here,* I think to myself.

Beneath me in the valley below a gentle stream flows over water smoothed rocks, adding accompaniment to the orchestra of nature sounds that abound around me. I listen to the calming sound of the stream, welcoming something to listen to, thankful I am left out here with *something* besides my own thoughts.

The setting sun casts long shadows across the clearing where I sit, the gnarled and twisted trees beside me providing the most bizarre and misshapen of the set. I find myself mesmerized by their complexity. If

only they were a bit less barren of leaves, then they would be able to provide a little more shade and relief from the sun over the coming days.
But then it's only two days. Surely I can survive *anything* for two days.

I close my eyes and let a breeze blow over me. Behind me the sun
must be beginning to set as the temperature is cooling off. The sounds
of nature take on a new quality in the dwindling light of dusk. An eerie
quality. Each is a bit more distinctive now, each demanding more attention and inspection. Whereas before they were simply background
noises, now they are the object of wonderment. What exactly is making
that noise, and is it getting any closer?

I open my eyes and see the fire leap taller. It cracks and sparks and
sends embers into the air. Now framed in darkness, its light competes
with nothing save the growing number of stars above. Its light now is
the writer, director, and producer of the show taking place in my clearing. It commands actors of shadows and choreographs them to writhe
and snake around my circle of stones. Dried up sage bushes, once harm-
less in the daylight, now seem menacing and ethereal. The rocks and
boulders at the edge of the clearing produce dark shapes of the most
maniacal creatures. All dance and flicker in the warm bath of yellow
firelight.

Lost in the fading sunlight and forged in the flames of my fire, my
mind begins to conjure up images and apparitions all around me.
Already my usually overactive imagination takes liberty with my surroundings, and this on just the first evening of the Quest. I can only
imagine what will happen once it has used up its energy source and the
deprivation of food and water comes into play. Will I be able to handle
it then?

Cross-legged in the center of the circle I close my eyes again and try
to sweep out my closet of thoughts. *Think of your breathing*, I tell
myself. *Concentrate on your breathing*. I inhale and exhale slowly, each
time taking a full breath of air. Inhale. Exhale. Inhale…

The crash of foliage to my left breaks my rhythm, and I throw my eyes open with a jolt. I stare into the dark hillside and listen attentively. My mind thinks of the knife Marcus gave me. It is lying just a foot or two behind me, right? I didn't move it, did I?

Again a noise. This time it is closer. I scan the hillside but see nothing. But there must be something there, for I can hear it moving through the brush. It's moving slowly and deliberately toward me. It can't be happening so soon. I tell myself. Not on the first night. Why would they come to me on the first night? I can't be ready now.

I crane to look behind me now and then slowly turn my head until I have looked all around the clearing. Nothing. Just blackness and shadows. Down below, the stream continues its song, crickets hum, frogs groan. And a few feet to my left something moves ever closer in the dark.

I turn back to the hillside, again starring into the firelight drenched shrubs and again thinking of the knife. I squint hard to see something, anything out there that could be making the noise. A bear perhaps? Or a coyote or a…rabbit?

My eyes focus and I see it crouched under a bush. It sits motionless and stares back at me. A rabbit. *Quick brave hunter, grab your dagger and thwart the evil intruder's advance.* Ha! I laugh at my own apprehension. Two hours from sunset and already I'm jumpy! I let out a chuckle then try to grab it back again. I notice a twitch from my rabbit visitor and don't want to frighten it off. *Don't worry little fella*, I think to myself, *there will be no knife play here. You are more than welcome to share the night with me. I could use the company.*

The rabbit seems to nod in understanding and takes a hesitant leap forward, coming within a few feet from the edge of my circle. There it stops again and stares up at me. How strange I must look to it sitting here in a circle of stones in the middle of nowhere—not nowhere, in his home—lit up by firelight. It brings a smile to my face just imagining what I look like through Rabbit's eyes. He wiggles his nose at me and takes another small hop in my direction.

Are you part of it Rabbit? Are you part of the Quest? Did they send you here to greet me?

Rabbit just sits and stares. If he knows anything about what lies ahead for me he is not telling. So we sit and stare at each other in silence. Two creatures brought together under a starry sky on a hilltop in the Wyoming wilderness. Both on a search for something, but only Rabbit knowing exactly what that is. Me, I'm still not quite sure I have a clue.

Rabbit is so close now I could easily reach out and touch him. His wide eyes gaze at me as if I might, and for a moment I think I'd do just that, reach out and touch his fur, remembering how soft rabbit fur is from holding baby rabbits at Bob Evans' Farm as a child.

It was a hot summer day just as this one had been, and after what seemed an endless drive in the family station wagon we had finally reached the farm. My brothers and sisters and I piled out of the car excited to see the deer and horses and pigs. But the highlight came when a farm hand placed a baby rabbit in my hands, so soft and delicate. Its rapidly beating heart gave my hands a faint vibration only adding to their shaking from excitement. "It's my turn!" One of my sisters, pushing against me to take the rabbit in her hands. But I held on for a second longer, unready to break the connection. When the rabbit was taken from me and place in Heidi's hands I beamed up at the farm hand and then my parents. I could still feel the tingling in my hands.

I think of reaching out to Rabbit now, but make no move to do so. It seems like such divine communication, he there and I here. Both alone but together, staring at each other in the dark. Besides, part of me thinks as soon as I reach outside the circle Rabbit will be gone. He will vanish, disappear. Of his own power or something more mystical I didn't know. I only know I want to keep his company.

I look at him a while longer and then close my eyes to concentrate on the sounds of the night again. When I open them a moment later Rabbit is gone. He has slipped away into the shadows much quieter than he had arrived. I glance around the clearing for him but find no trace of him. I wonder again if he has been sent to me. Was he here to check me out, to welcome me to the sacred place on the hill?

I find my mind filling with thoughts again. I think of Brian down in Sheridan and wonder what he is doing tonight and how he is spending his evening of solitude. Since this is the first time in over a month he has had a moment away from me and I from him, I'm sure he is finding the evening enjoyable. It's not easy being inside a box with another person for days on end, even if the other person is your best friend. I'm sure he is finding his own ways to use the evening to make sense of the past weeks' adventure.

In the time since we left Los Angeles a little over four weeks ago, a lot has happened. Enough to leave me with much to think about. The first leg has proven to be more than we expected, and we still have most of the country yet ahead of us.

As the fire wanes I add another log and stir the ashes. Slowly the log catches and the fire is going full force again. I settle back into the circle and the night, my thoughts already lost, remembering the decisions that brought me here…

CALIFORNIA DREAMING

◆

Good friends, good books and a sleepy conscience:
this is the ideal life.

Mark Twain

I sit staring at the computer screen, my mouse hand edging slightly on the pad bringing the image on screen into place. I have been working on the graphic all morning, slumped in front of the monitor, the stereo blaring behind me. The graphic is almost finished and I'm one step closer to payday. I lean back in my chair and stretch, a series of loud pops rifle off and I wonder if it is my spine or my chair. Above me the faces of friends and family stare down at me from glossy photos amidst a neatly packed desk of art and computer books, a poseable wooden art dummy, and a series of action figures—Spiderman, Wolverine, Beta-Ray Bill, Black Manta—that seems to be the norm for young computer programmers / designers. I reach into one of the large desk's cubbyholes for my coffee mug and lift it to my lips before realizing it's empty again. I place it back where I found it knowing it's highly likely that I'll only repeat the process again shortly after I let its lack of liquid slip my mind once more, concentrating intently on the task at hand.

That's me. Twenty-nine-year-old graphic designer. Mountaineer by birth, former resident of the People's Republic of China, new addition to the Los Angeles population. Movie buff, avid reader, sci-fi fan.

It's one of those moments that seem to come more frequently of late. A moment where I am suddenly aware of myself. Aware of where I am. Aware of what has brought me to this point; this point in time, space, and life. I am aware of the past and of the present and I contemplate the future. Time holds no meaning and all is together, blended up in the mixer of universal confusion.

A Talking Heads song plays out in my head:

And you may find yourself, living in a shotgun shack,
And you may say, this is not my beautiful wife, this....

I often try to write it off as fatigue or hunger pangs. But it seems to come too frequent these days to pass off so easily. I know deep down it's a different kind of hunger and fatigue, one of the soul. Some deep-seeded sense of confusion over life, over where I am and who I am and what I'm doing. It's a question of: Is this it? Is this all there is?

Sometimes I think it's an age thing. Something everyone experiences on the verge of turning thirty. But I also think this isn't it. I've heard too many people make comments about their lives now and then, people facing different challenges at different ages. No, it's just something that life throws at us once in a while to see if we're paying attention. It taunts us to try to make sense of it all, to try to define ourselves.

I look around the apartment and feel confined and constricted. I need some space. I notice some long unused paint brushes in the corner of the bookshelf. That's me, one-time art student with dreams of creating something big. A photo frame reminds me I was once a traveler of distant lands, an explorer of hidden wonders. All the things that make me who I am. All the things that demand attention and mix into the sea of confusion.

It seems simple enough. Find the answers. But it's never that easy. Seeking takes time. Time that can be spent being productive. Being responsible. Being practical. A new tune in my head, Supertramp this time:

But then they sent me away to teach me how to be sensible, logical, responsible, practical.
And they showed me a world where I could be so dependable, clinical, intellectual, cynical.

Music and the dance of life. Can I be so concerned with the steps that I'm stumbling all over the dance floor? Too concerned to look foolish trying to dance my own moves and instead hopping in the line dance with the rest of them.

Thoughts and questions that continue to haunt me. I get that crazy feeling again, a sense of being alone, different. Too many questions to be healthy. Too difficult to try to answer. It's best just to push them down into the murky holes of the mind and concentrate on the tasks at hand. But the questions scream out to be heard, they grow in strength and volume each time they surface. What I need is distraction. What I need is space.

The phone rings and I jump. I push back from the desk and the chair rolls out of control across the hardwood living room floor. I step out of it and toward the phone as the answering machine begins to pick up and greet the caller with, "Hello you have reached…"

I reach the phone before the answering machine manages to scare away whoever is on the other end of the line. "Hello?"

"Hi, it's me." A familiar voice calling from San Jose.

That's Brian. Childhood friend, eternal optimist, worldly gentleman, *Lucky Charms* consumer, Macintosh advocate, MBA, one time entrepreneur, and current hi-tech marketing consultant. Since moving back to the states from an extended stay in Hong Kong we have managed to talk quite frequently, taking advantage of the first time in over a decade we have lived anywhere close to one another. Since he moved away to Nebraska when we were kids we have been on opposite sides of the country or world. He in the midwest, me in the south. Me in Asia, he on the East coast. He in Asia, me in California. But now we had both landed in the same general area, he being reassigned to San Jose in northern California and me living in sunny Southern California in Los Angeles. Just a hop, skip, and a jump away.

"Hey, how's it going?" I ask, trying to push previous thoughts from my mind and beginning to pace around the apartment with the cordless phone. The pacing is a habit I picked up somewhere along the way. I can't seem to sit still while talking on the phone and usually begin to walk around immediately after hello. I often wonder if the person on the other end can tell, if they can hear the footsteps or perhaps the changing echo and reverberation of my voice as I stroll from room to room.

"Great. I'm just about finished with my last project for the year and looking forward to the break. How about you?" Brian asks.

"Good, good. I've just about finished the graphics for the CD Rom presentation I'm working on," I say, now standing in the living room once more and staring at the images on the computer in the corner. "I just have a few finishing touches to add then I'm good to go." Then from the kitchen, "So I got my ticket. It's one of those new electronic deals. I fly out on...got a pen? Okay. My flight leaves Friday afternoon arriving at 5:15 in San Jose."

"Southwest, right?" Brian asks.

"Yep. You are going to pick me up?" I ask.

"Sure. I..." Brian pulls the phone away from his mouth and I hear him say something away from it. "Oh, hey Chris, somebody just stopped by my cubicle looking for me. I gotta run. I'll talk to you later, okay?" Brian says in a hurry.

"Okay. Talk to you later. Bye." And with that he hangs up, leaving me holding a dead line and standing in the bedroom. I walk back through the kitchen and dining room and place the phone back in its cradle. I remember several things I meant to tell Brian when he called next and make a mental note to tell him when I see him over the weekend in San Jose.

I sit back down at my computer desk and look at the images once more. On it are several CD Rom screen designs a client has commissioned for a project they are pitching to one of their customers. The designs are finished, only needing a once-over to check to see that everything is perfect and ready for delivery. I hover over mouse and keyboard, hesitating to start to work again. As if on cue a faint grumble and moan comes from the depths of my stomach, reminding me to look at the clock. It's 1:30. I worked through lunch again. I look at the computer then out the window behind me. Outside the sun is shining down, almost as if mocking the snow and cold weather other areas of the country experience as we move into the first days of winter. I've found many faults with Los Angeles since moving here, but the daily doses of sunshine and severe lack of winter is not one of them. Continue working or lunch break in the sun? My stomach voices its opinion and my decision is made for me.

I stand from my computer and click the mouse to put Hal, my trusty Macintosh sidekick, to sleep. I sit down on the sofa to put on shoes and head for the door, pausing briefly to pick up a black duffel bag containing my Roller Blades. That's me: amateur roller hockey player, part-time athlete.

I head out the door and seek out distraction at Venice Beach.

VENICE BEACH

◆

Life is all memory except for the one present
moment that goes by so quick you can hardly
catch it going.

Tennessee Williams

Venice Beach is crowded for a Tuesday afternoon. Not that I am surprised. It seems every time I visit the beach it is packed with people running, biking, skating, shopping, eating, and performing on the streets. I often wonder where all the people come from. They can't ALL be tourists can they? And yet here on a sunny afternoon could they be people playing hooky from work? Or maybe out-of-work actors and actresses on parade hoping to be discovered.

I skate along the strand, the sun beaming down on me and a light wind at my back helping me along. I make it about a quarter mile from Venice Boulevard when I think about the sunscreen I had in my car and forgot to apply to my quick-to-burn skin. With an abrupt circle stop I move to the side of the track and consider going back to the car. But the car is far behind me and yet another bikini clad model-wannabe just skated by, assuring me forward is the direction I want to go. Beautifully tan hard bodies in bathing suits here in the last throes of December. I smile and remember what I like about L.A.

The beach to my left is sparsely populated. A few surfers take to the waves and a handful of camera-toting tourists stroll along the shore for prime photo opportunities. But for the most part it sits primarily unused. The waves crash and retreat from the shore, seeming not to mind the lack of crowds, rhythm delighting in solitude.

On my right as I head north on the strand the shops and restaurants are busy. I turn off the strand and onto the boardwalk—which, incidentally, is not made of boards at all but cruddy asphalt, pocked and marred with holes that have been haphazardly refilled. The transition from the smooth concrete surface of the strand to the bump and tumble boardwalk is a harsh one and I catch myself from spilling into a back massage stand (fifteen minute massages, just twenty bucks, come one come all). I skate further north along the boardwalk, passing by stalls of faith healers, psychics, painters, advocates for the use of hemp, a tin can sculptor, musicians, a man sculpting mermaids out of sand. Each call out to me with warm greetings as I coast by them on my skates. On passing I hear them turn their attention to others behind me, greetings, friendly hellos, invitations to browse.

All around me is a United Nations of faces: Asian, African, Hispanic, White, Native American. People on foot, on skates, on bikes. People walking dogs, and children, and boyfriends and girlfriends. Yuppies stride alongside skater punks, beach bunnies and policemen. Venice seems to represent the whole of America in all its spice and flavors.

I see the green awnings of the Fig Tree Cafe and roll in. The waitress gives me a table in the front corner of the patio, perfect for Venice's most popular activity of people watching.

I was first introduced to the Fig Tree shortly after I moved to LA. An old friend from college and long time L.A. resident brought me down soon after my arrival to the city. I was immediately taken in by the friendly wait staff, beautiful view of the beach, and prime location. And the food was good too.

"Hi, my name is Sydney. Can I get you something to drink?" Sydney smiles from behind loose tangles of black hair that have escaped her hair beret. She has the friendly disposition of someone who either just got on shift or truly loves her job.

"Hi Sydney. Actually I already know what I want to eat," I say closing the menu and handing it back to her. In the short time I've lived in the area I have already been here enough to know what it is I like. "I'll have an iced tea and grilled vegetable sandwich please."

"Great, I'll be right back with your drink." She smiles again and spins on her heels to head back inside.

I bend down to loosen the buckles on my skates as Sydney brings me my tea. Sitting back in my seat, tea in hand, I settle into the scene. The boardwalk bustles with activity and L.A. passes by in front of my table. Front row seats to the afternoon of other people's lives.

Watching the sand and surf and people strolling about, I find life's collection of mysteries remain with me. I begin to wonder if my fellow beach goers ever have questions about life. *What is their story?* I think to myself. *Independently wealthy? Freelancers like me? Tourists on vacation? So many people here with so many stories. The artisans with the stalls for instance. Are they currently at work doing their job selling their art and talents? Or is this just a daytime hobby and their real work begins in the evening? How is it that they can live by simply setting up shop at the beach and giving massages? Are they happy with who they are?*

I'm not sure why the questions come. But now as Sydney delivers a massive sandwich the questions are there as if part of my lunch, just waiting to be chewed up and digested. Again a feeling of uneasiness spreads around me. I should be happy with where I am, enjoying the moment. But something was missing, something tugging me in an unknown direction. As I start on my lunch I wonder about Sydney's story. And when she stops by my table to ask if I needed anything else, I look up in mid-chew and consider my reply. *Yes,* I picture myself saying, *could you answer a few questions? Are you happy with the way your life is going? What roads led you to stand before me here today?*

"No, I'm fine." I say instead. "Thank you."

Half the sandwich disappears and I begin on the second half when something at the table next to me catches my attention. Two blonde women have sat down and placed orders and are engaged in an animated conversation. I try to turn my attention back to my food and the parade on the boardwalk, but something from the next table keeps snatching me back.

"I'm telling you the guy is such a success. You are going to love him." Blonde A says leaning into the conversation.

"I don't know, the last person…" Blonde B volleys back.

"Yes, Susan," (*Ah, so her name is Susan*) "but we're talking major success story here. And besides he's definitely your type." Blond A continues.

Major success story. What does that mean? He's heavyweight champion of the world? The richest man in the world? Maybe he's the head sales rep for ABC pharmaceutical company here in southern California. Perhaps he's an actor who got his big break. Or could major success story mean he knows how to hold down a relationship, how to please a woman, how to say the right things at the right time. But then if that were the case why would he be available and need Blondie here to fix him up? Success can be such an ambiguous word.

I begin to turn to look at the table again, still envisioning what "type" Susan would be prone to fall for when Sydney interrupts me mid turn.

"Here's your check. I'll take that whenever you're ready. Have a nice afternoon." She says, slipping a small leatherette bill holder onto the table beside my plate.

"Thanks. You too." I answer back. She walks off and I finish my glance toward Susan, awkwardly catching her gaze as Blonde A is standing to take a momentary leave—cigarette, phone call, toilet break, I don't know. I turn back to my sandwich unable to finish it. Instead I sit there in the strange circumstance of sharing a moment in the life of a complete stranger. Susan at the table to the right of me with her own thoughts, me at my table with mine. The few feet between our tables might as well be several miles, as I'm sure there is to be no more contact between our worlds. A stolen glance, a curiosity in their conversation and in Susan's world. I sit and stare out at the beach and wonder if she does the same.

A hundred meters down the boardwalk a camera crew is setting up. Yet another movie or television scene of another buxom beauty in another red convertible driving down the street in Venice where cars aren't really allowed to drive. I glance around to see if there are any "stars" attached to the scene, knowing that if there were I would be sure to spot them. Seeing movie stars in L.A. is easy once you have the knack for tuning into them. You have to know what to look for, to know how to use your eyes. They can go to great lengths to blend into the crowd, and when you see them in three dimensions without the glossy sheen of a magazine cover or of the colossal scale of the silver screen they can seem quite ordinary indeed. But once you get your eyes adjusted to compensate for these real life differences you tend to see them all the time. It's like how you never noticed that one particular model of car on the road. But as soon as you decide to buy one they appear to be every-where. Stars begin to pop up in grocery stores, and shopping malls, and restaurants, and film shoots down at Venice beach. But not today. An unknown beautiful person is the center of this shot. Perhaps one of the stars of tomorrow.

I fish out my wallet and pay the bill as Blonde A returns to Susan's table. I consider for a moment hanging out a while longer to eavesdrop into their conversation a bit further but think better of it. Susan can deal with the matchmaking of her friend well enough alone, she needn't be bothered by the presence of a stranger at the next table. I stoop over to buckle up my skates and head back out to the beach.

At the strand I turn north and head toward Santa Monica, skating a little faster than before in order to work off my lunch and try to shake the weird uneasy feelings that still linger. *What in the hell could possibly make me feel down on such a beautiful day?* I toss the question over and over in my head, skating faster and faster to try to let it drop. It doesn't.

Is it guilt? Dissatisfaction? I move faster and further, I always feel motion makes things clearer, and if it doesn't it will at least delay the moment of impact. I try this method now, blurring my thoughts in a wave of sights, sounds, and momentum. I swerve in and out of passers by, hop puddles of sand on the track, and stay focused on the rapidly approaching pier and Ferris wheel on the horizon. I'm on a race with the devil, striving to beat out my inner demons and leave them behind me in the sand. Reaching the pier I skate into the tunnel beneath it, suddenly engulfed in the cool shadows. I stand up and stretch, coasting under the pier and into the bright sunshine of Santa Monica beach, past baby strollers and speed walkers and joggers. The momentum dies, and I drift to a halt and pull off to the side slightly out of breath. I succeeded in leaving the demons behind once again and smile up at the sun. The sea air smells of salt and mustard and cotton candy and sunscreen. The music of the Ferris wheel is in concert with the laughter of children and adults alike. Inside the demons rest. Outside I turn around and head for home.

ARRIVAL

◆

Of all paths a man could strike into,
there is, at any given moment, a best
path which, here and now, it were of
all things wisest for him to do. To find
this path, and walk in it, is the one
thing needful of him.

Thomas Carlyle

I see Brian's face in the crowd immediately as I exit the plane. He spots me even quicker, as always the lone redhead in the crowd. I bee line for him around a hugging elderly couple and step past a family of four, one child still asleep in her father's arms, the other excitedly looking around the airport. Even a routine 45 minute flight to San Jose must be an adventure for them. I reach Brian and we exchange a guy hug. It's the kind of hug men give to show affection without showing too much affection. One arm, slightly wrapped around the side of the other just far enough to provide a few good, strong slaps on the back. Very brief, very gruff, and quite innocuous.

"Hey man, welcome to San Jose!" Brian greets me looking at my carry-on for a brief moment as if considering offering to take it for me but thinking better of it.

"Thanks. It's good to be here. So how's your day going?" We begin to stroll toward baggage claim, I follow cryptic airport signs and Brian's lead.

"Let's, ah, talk about that later." Brian sighs, the look on his face already confiding that he has had another rough day. I am sure I'll hear about it, so I change the subject.

"Any big plans for the weekend?" I ask expectantly.

"Well we've got a dinner invitation to PJ's, but besides that it's pretty open. Down here." Brian points to a series of escalators that head down into the baggage area. We are spilled out into chaos. People line the walls at rental car agencies to pick up cars while in the center of the room large clumps of passengers await their baggage. Some faces are long and tired, obviously having traveled further than my own 300 miles. But everybody has the settled expression of acceptance, each knowing what was in store traveling so close to the Christmas holiday.

We pace back and forth along the carrousels looking for my flight number to pop up on the LED screen. Finally it appears at the end and a stream of flight 947 baggage begins to trickle out onto the conveyor belt. Brian and I watch silently as the luggage falls and begins its trip around the room. We're not without things to say, just comfortable with the silence. A large black duffel bag drops to the carrousel, a bright red strap stretched across the middle. Stitched cross it in big black letters read MOELLER. A gift from my mother last Christmas.

Brian takes over my carry-on bag as I reach down and haul the new bag to my shoulder. We turn to make for the elevator behind us and up into the parking structure. We reach Brian's car, a snow white BMW 318, black leather interior, sunroof, and best of all: heated seats. Sure, most people in California would never use them, but I love them. Plop down in the seat and adjust the temperature to fit your tastes. The car is

Brian's present to himself for a job well done. In his tenure at Dataquest he has steadily climbed the corporate ladder and made a name for himself. Now he has a desk at the corporate headquarters and a title of Senior Marketing Consultant. Thus the car to fit the title. A hi-tech consultant pulling up to consult a hi-tech Silicon Valley company in a low tech Nissan Sentra such as the one I drive would not do. I tease him about the car all the time, and he always replies with statistics on owner satisfaction, reliability, and resale value. But I know the truth. He's at a place in his life where he can enjoy the spoils of his labor and is young enough to do it, so why not.

As we head out of the airport I immediately adjust the temperature controls for my side of the car. Outside it may be a cool 58 degrees but inside I sit in a balmy 70.

"So how are things in L.A.?" Brian asks while I play with the dashboard controls.

"Good. The project I just finished was a lot of fun, I enjoyed it. It's funny though, I've been feeling weird about things of late."

"Weird how?"

"It's hard to explain. I feel like I'm missing the boat or something, like something is off. I feel I'm still looking for the magic of life."

"What do you mean?" Brian asks.

"The magic, you know, that thing that comes out of the blue. The great epiphany, the magic, the abracadabra, the kaboom, zap, shazam—"

I stumble for a moment to collect my thoughts. "I'm looking for what I call *Shamzara*, that mystical, magical event or person or thing that will come into my life unexpectedly and hit me like a bolt of lightning, forever changing my world into something wonderful. I know it's crazy, and my logical side tells me I'm insane to even think about it. But the truth is that deep down I'm still waiting, still expecting something like that to happen."

"And you think you're going to get this in a bolt of lightning?"

"Think? No. Hope? Maybe. It's the weird conflict of logic versus fantasy, of expectation versus reality. It's my mythical Shamzara, my moment of complete clarity and happiness. I'm thinking maybe it's just some age thing. A life transition that naturally occurs with the coming of 30."

"Maybe. Maybe not. Maybe it's something else."

"Well what about you. How's life up here treating you?"

"We may be experiencing similar things. I don't really think I'm in search of Shamzara as you call it, but there's been stuff going on with me as well. But let's save that for dinner, it's a long story."

I'm intrigued and want to ask questions but let it drop for now. I discover I'm hungry too and think I can wait till we get to a restaurant somewhere to pick up where we left off.

We pull into the parking structure for his apartment complex and park the beemer. I lug my duffel from the trunk and toss it into one of the complex's shopping carts kept conveniently by the elevator. Out of the elevator and onto the third floor we head down the open air hallway and into Brian's apartment.

The apartment is spacious, sparsely furnished, and severely overpriced in true Silicon Valley fashion. Two bedroom, two bath, kitchen and living room. Though Brian has lived here for over 5 months there are still unopened boxes from the move scattered here and there. In the far side of the living room sitting on the vacant floor that will serve as my bedroom lie a few opened boxes of Christmas presents. I walk by, kicking them out of the way and against the wall and drop my bag to the floor behind the sofa seat.

"Where's JoJo?" I ask Brian, inquiring as to the whereabouts of his new roommate.

"He's actually gone for the weekend to visit some relatives. I think he's back on Monday." Brian says from inside his bedroom. He comes back out wearing a more casual set of clothes, shedding his work attire in the closet. "So...dinner? What do you feel like eating tonight?"

"I don't care. Why don't we head somewhere where we can just hang out for a while, eat, and have a few drinks. Pizza perhaps?" I smile because it seems I always suggest pizza. It's just one of the few foods I could eat every day. Convenient and tasty, just pick it up and eat it. Lucky for me Brian likes it just about as well.

"Okay, let's head into Sunnyvale then and we'll try this place a friend suggested." Brian slaps his pockets to check that he has everything—wallet, check; keys, check—and then we head for the door.

Sunnyvale is one of the little cities that make up the Silicon Valley area. The area actually reminds me a lot of the Mid-West: plenty of mini-malls and shopping plazas, car dealerships and fast food restaurants. The cities in the area—Sunnyvale, Mountain View, Cupertino, Palo Alto, Redwood City, San Mateo, Foster City, Belmont, San Carlos, Menlo Park, Los Gatos, Santa Clara, Milpitas, Fremont, and maybe a few others depending on who you ask (no one really knows what geography defines the Valley)—all have a little flavor of their own, adding them to the pot that becomes the Valley. At the center of Sunnyvale is Murphy Street, two city blocks long and lined with shops, bars, and restaurants. The downtown area seems to have successfully warded off the attacks on its businesses by nearby shopping malls, unlike many of its Mid-Western counterparts. Perhaps it's because their competition is in the form of a mall just at the end of the street, bringing customers to the area instead of away from it. Whatever the reason the downtown merchants still get their fair share of the area's dollars and on this Friday night business is booming.

Brian parks the car in the mall parking lot, and we walk down Murphy Street. We pass by Fibbar Magee's, where Brian often meets his co-workers for drinks after work, and several other bars and restaurants, all beginning to come alive with weekend revelers. Toward the end of the street Brian points to an Italian restaurant across the road. "That's it," he says.

"*Gumba's*?!" I say looking at the sign. "What a great name for a restaurant. What gumba named that?" I'm sure "gumba" has some significant meaning in Italian, but for me it always meant an idiot. *What the hell are you doing you gumba?* Or *Good job you gumba!* I think of the many times I've used it in good fun. And now some gumba was going to make me a pizza.

We enter the restaurant and see we are still a bit ahead of the dinner crowd. We get seated right away at a table by the door and next to the pizza chefs where we can see our pizza and everyone else's being prepared. Our waitress is old school, gruff and impatient. She hands us our menus and demands our drink order before we have time to open them. Somewhat intimidated, I ask for a pitcher of beer glancing over at Brian who gives me a nod. She spins and walks off without another word. Brian and I quickly open our menus and choose a pizza so as to be prepared to order once our friendly waitress returns. She plops the pitcher and two frosted mugs onto our table, takes our order, and leaves as quickly as she came.

I take the pitcher and pour out two glasses, offering one to Brian. We raise the glasses, clink them together in toast and swallow some beer down. The perfect beginning to a weekend.

"Okay," I set my glass back on the table. "Now back to the job situation. What's up?"

"I don't know what's up," Brian begins. "I just feel like I'm at an impasse and I'm really frustrated over it. I want to do something more, be it start my own business or go somewhere else. I feel like no matter how much I contribute here it really doesn't matter much. It's helping the company's bottom line but it really doesn't have any impact on other people's lives. It's like you're only as good as your last project, or what you did last week. The human element of it seems to be missing. I want to go out and do something that has more of an individual impact, something to test myself and push myself to do something more." He leans back in his chair and exhales slowly. I can see now what he meant earlier, he really did have a lot on his mind.

"So I don't know what I want to do, I'm pretty frustrated. At this point I'm thinking of leaving. The money's good and everything but it's not fulfilling me personally. I'm not jazzed when I go into work and I want to feel that."

"Wow. Glad to see I'm not the only one messed up here."

"You're not. Me either. I've actually talked to a lot of my colleagues here who are doing well in the corporation, in their careers, and found that many of them aren't happy. Why is that? Why is everybody so frustrated with what they're doing, if what they have is supposedly good. I'm having a conflict with that. Look at me: I have the international experience, I've come back to the US—which I wanted to do—I've got the great job and everything else. So why am I not happy? There's something going on here that doesn't make sense. I'm finding I don't feel good about who I am or what I'm doing any more."

The words hit me flat on and my stomach sinks. In a few words he has summed up and brought to light the strange feeling that has been hanging over me for the past months.

"This is really strange," I offer. "These last few days I've been thinking about the same things. It seems like life should be wonderful. I'm living in L.A., the weather's perfect all the time; I'm doing freelance and I'm my own boss, I go to the beach whenever I want. And yet every time I go out during the afternoon I feel guilty." I let out a weak laugh and Brian joins me with one of his own. "I feel like I shouldn't be doing that, that I should be at work. Or I should be doing something with and for other people. Something just seems off."

"I think I know what you mean." Brian says.

"Sounds like it. It's the whole life thing. Am I doing what I want to be doing? Am I living where I want to be living." I take another pull from the beer giving Brian the chance to interject or take his turn at speaking. He just looks on and waits for me to continue. "I look at others and where their lives have taken them, and I wonder if that is what I want. You know, the family, the house, the PTA." Immediately a picture of my brother's family forms in my head: engineer, great wife, beautiful kids, house.

"But who says you won't have that or that you even really do want it?" Brian says, a bit of beer foam clinging to his upper lip.

"I know. Maybe I do, but then again maybe I don't. I always thought I did though. And the job thing. Is this it? Am I a web designer? Is that what I'm meant to be? Or is there something else out there that I'm missing, some path that I should be on?" I say as I watch the pizza chef throw a chunk of dough into the air, watching as it grows wider and flatter in his well trained hands.

"I guess that's kind of the same for me," Brian says. "I feel like there's more to life than the corporate cubicle. I want to be out there making an impact. The job is great, the people I work with are great, the work is even interesting, but I feel there is something else I should be doing. And I definitely should be doing it somewhere else. I guess I'm just not a California guy."

"That may be, but you sure have a sweet life here Bri. You're the poster child for young success stories. Sure you can give it all up?" I chide him, but part of me really wonders about his thinking on this.

"Give what up? The job? The money? I can get all this elsewhere, and probably somewhere I would be happier living. What is success worth if it isn't making me happy?" Brian says.

We both stare off for a while thinking about our own direction. The restaurant has grown more crowded and a couple is waiting outside for a table.

"Like we said, " I break the silence. "We're not the only ones that feel this way. There must be so many out there that are just as confused as we are. So how did they find their path? Are they happy? Do they feel successful?"

"A large portion of people I've talked to seem to be just not satisfied with what they're doing." He says.

"Yeah. I've heard it from a few of my friends too. Melissa—I don't think you ever met her—has just been promoted at the restaurant where she works and is staying on even though she hates working there. And my buddy Tom is going to business school to study something he doesn't like just because it will help his career. He's already told me he doesn't really want to go but feels compelled to. Why? All in the name of success." I feel a bit flustered thinking about my friends. Two similar situations and two people that have never spoken to each other about it. Would it help them, I wonder, help to talk to someone in the same boat?

"Maybe I need to just quit," Brian says, mostly to himself. "I need to say: Okay, take charge of your life and do something about it. If I'm not satisfied, no matter what society says I should be satisfied with, it's not working for me. Maybe I need to go out and figure it all out. It's a big step. A huge step. But at this point I'm definitely frustrated enough to do it."

The pizza arrives steaming at our table. Hot, thin, New York style with mushrooms and green peppers. Brian and I both dig in, hungry from beer and conversation and comfortable with the lack of pleasantries of proper dining etiquette. I bite carefully at first, testing the temperature of the cheese. Too often I jump too eagerly at the pizza only to burn the roof of my mouth and ending up spoiling the meal with dead and dying taste buds. This pizza is of perfect temperature.

"You know," Brian says behind a mouthful of food, "someone should go out and study this. Like you said there must be a lot of us. It could be an age thing. Or a renaissance in society, or maybe it's a millennium thing. Somebody should go interview people about their definition of success, the choices they've made, the paths they're on, and if they are really, truly happy."

"Yes, and no multi-million dollar CEOs or Bill Gates or the like. Real people from down the street. The people whose struggle you can relate to. And…" I stop chewing and look at Brian. Brian is staring at me, a smile creeping over his face that I am sure is mirrored in my own. It's obvious we are thinking the same thing. A light-bulb has clicked on. Somebody should do this. And that somebody should be us.

"We should do this." I say it. Brian says it. I'm not sure where it came from but it was there. It was voiced. The thought electrifies us with excitement and we jump a little in our seats.

"We should just get in a car and drive across country and talk to people!" Brian says. I can tell he's already planning a route in his head.

"A quest. That's what we need. Just like a vision quest, or a 'walk-about', we'll go out into the world searching for answers. We'll seek out the wisdom of our peers and let the winds take hold of us and show us the world." I'm talking more to myself than to Brian now. The *Voice Inside* is talking. It's telling me to do this, to take the Hero's journey, to go out and seek the hidden treasures of wisdom and slay inner dragons.

"But we need to share it," Brian continues. We are both talking faster and more animated now. "We need to be able to let others in on it."

"Yes. We can set up a web site and put everything we learn up on the Internet as we go along. Invite others to join us on the quest. Hah!" Now it's my turn to make mental plans as the web site structure and format begins to take shape in my head.

"Man, this is great! It just feels so right. I mean, I really *feel* like we need to do this." Brian says.

And I can see it. He is lit up with excitement over the idea. Whereas before he was all but slumped over the table and talking in a low voice, he now is animated and jumping. And he isn't alone. I too feel more alive. Whatever cloak of confusion hung over us before was gone now. In an instant we were on a quest. We are ready to go out and seek answers to the questions that plagued us.

The pizza is gone before we notice it. In our excited state we eat and talk and drink until the meal is over, and we sit with empty plates and busy heads. The waitress comes over and asks us if we'd like anything else. Brian looks over my shoulder at the growing lines of people, and before we can even answer the waitress has put our bill on the table. We both pull out our wallets, count and drop bills to the table and are out the door in seconds.

On the street we bounce past the line of people and head north, not really sure where we are going but just happy to be in motion. In motion. That is exactly what I need to clear my thoughts and settle things. To jump in a car and get in motion. The thought of it brings yet another smile to my face.

"So what now?" I ask Brian.

"Let's find some place to sit and chat some more, try to flesh this out a bit." He says and spots a coffee shop on the corner. "Up for some coffee?"

"Always." I answer, following him into the small cafe.

A mocha and a vanilla cappuccino join us at our table, both of us having fallen victim to the specialized coffee craze Starbucks has unleashed on the nation. We sip them and make plans. Brian talks about leaving his job. I talk about finishing up projects and clearing my calendar. The caffeine mixes with the alcohol in our system and lifts us into a frenzied euphoria. Everything we say seems right on and perfect. Plans fall into place. We toss ideas back and forth and watch them grow and build and spawn new and better ideas.

"We need a center for our quest. Something to start from, a leaping off point that people can relate to." Brian says. I understand where he's coming from. The ambiguous *thing* we had been discussing, the emptiness or confusion would be hard to explain to others. We need something more grounded to start from that would lead into the meat of the issue.

"Success." I say, my mind drifting back to Venice Beach. "We keep saying it. Everyone says it. But what the hell is it? How do you define it? That is our center. Everyone must have their own definition, their own ideas about what that means. Maybe that is what sets us all apart, what brings us to what it is we want out of life."

"Good," Brian picks up the conversation. "That's where we'll start. We'll try to define success as we strive more to find the secrets of successful living. What leads one person to contentment and happiness and leaves another struggling to find their way? What is the key to the pursuit of successful living?"

The anchor is set. We now have something to tie our ideas around. Midnight falls behind us and we find ourselves back at Brian's apartment. Maps and calendars and pages of notes are strewn about us as the planning and talking goes into the early morning. We scribble ideas, figure out routes, and sketch out web site schematics. But eventually the buzz of excitement and caffeine wears down and we drop off to sleep, leaving us to dreams of the adventure. We wake in the morning to…

REALITY

◆

Once the "what" is decided, the
"how" always follows. We must not
make the "how" an excuse for not facing
and accepting the "what."

Pearl S. Buck

Reality.

Brian gets up first and comes into the living room en route to the kitchen. From my place on the living room floor I can hear his footfalls across the carpet. I've always been one to take a floor over a sofa, it seems to offer a better night's sleep. People's sofas vary in degrees of comfort and you never know what you're going to get. With the floor you always know.

I hear the ping, ting, jingle of cereal being poured into a ceramic bowl. The sound echoes off the bare walls of Brian's vacant apartment. Footsteps again and Brian is sunk down into the sofa enjoying a bowl of breakfast cheer.

"Morning." I grumble from behind the two seat sofa.

"Good morning." Brian answers back. "Sleep well?"

I throw back the covers and climb up the back of the empty sofa seat and hurl myself over and down onto it. Reclining comfortably and facing Brian on the other sofa I feel a little more awake.

"Yeah, I guess so. Lots of things bouncing around in my head though." I say scratching my head.

"I've been thinking about it too." Brian says, still munching on frosted flakes.

"Do you think it's crazy? I mean, what we're thinking about doing. Maybe we should think about this. Can we afford to do it? And your job…" I'm talking as if continuing the conversation from last night, the eight hours of sleep in-between never have happened.

"Is not what I want to be doing with my life." Brian finishes my statement for me, though not the same way I had intended. "You said it yourself last night that this is what you needed. I don't see how we can afford *not* to do it."

He was right and we both knew it. But in the light of day we began thinking inside the box again. Thoughts of how such a hole in our resume would appear to others began to creep in.

"Four years in management, yes, yes. Ah, work for a respectable company, freelance for some big name clients. All good and fine. And…eh, what's this?"

The Suit leans in to look closer at my resume. I gulp and feel my swallow catch in my Adam's apple. The glasses slide down to the end of Suit's thin nose.

"Six months on the road without a job. Six months! And just how do you explain this Mr. Moeller?!"

I sink into the uncomfortable wooden chair as much as it will allow and think of a way to respond as Suit taps his pen anxiously on the Desk.

"I thought so. Good-bye slacker!" he says and pushes a large red button on his desk. A platform under me opens and I fall into blackness, forever banished from the shiny fluorescent corporate world.

"Chris…" Brian says, jarring the image from my mind.

But the thoughts continue. The strain on our savings accounts, the extended leave from our lives, all things logical and respectable and normal that we didn't consider the night before. In the newness of the morning we view our crazy idea from a new perspective. A perspective not from within but from outside, from the eyes and opinions of others.

It's not easy to take a stand and tell the world you have no idea what you're doing here. We're taught that you play the game or you will be labeled a radical. Conform or be ostracized. In life as in school we're told to ask questions but taught or conditioned not to; but to instead accept what is shown us to be the proper order in a chaotic world, what is given us as the truth and reality. After all, the unknown can be a scary place, you would have to be insane to try to find answers out there.

But while others may indeed deem us insane for taking such actions, it seems so genuinely right for us to do so, and logistics be damned. We both could afford it if we budgeted right, we reasoned. And the timing could never be better. We both knew we were on the verge of a transition, a life change. But into what and where we didn't know. Wouldn't it be much better to go into the transition armed with the knowledge such a quest could provide? And if we felt so compelled to take up the quest, shouldn't we say let others be damned?

"The hell with it, let's do it!" I say leaning forward and sitting on the edge of the sofa, reeling from the mental breakthrough. "But we need to change this itinerary," I say pulling the road atlas on the floor closer to me. The map of the entire United States is open. "If we take the northern route first…"

I am thinking from inside again. The Voice Inside is speaking and I am listening. Inside the living room the pieces of the puzzle begin to fall into place.

We continue planning for the duration of my visit. By the time I leave to go back to LA and Brian heads home to Nebraska for his birthday, the structure of the quest has been laid out. We would leave the end of June, the day after my thirtieth birthday. We would travel up the coast first—through California, Oregon, and Washington—then head east through the northern half of the states, up the coast through New England, down the coast to Florida, and then back through the Southern states returning to Los Angeles by the end of the year. The trip would be six months in total. This itinerary would allow us to avoid bad weather and see each area at its best weather-wise.

The budget takes us much more effort than the itinerary. Perhaps it's the attachment of fun and excitement to the trip routing versus the worry associated with depleting funds and savings. But we manage to come up with a way to make the trip feasible. Gas requirements and the price of fuel we cannot control, so we don't even try. To curb expenses we decide to crash at friends' and family's homes whenever possible and to camp at national parks when the home-stay option isn't there. Hotels, we decide, would be the last resort. As for food, pizza and Taco Bell are always viable cheap alternatives for us both if the local diners prove too pricey.

We plan out equipment requirements, packing space, camping needs, everything that can be thought of ahead of time. If one of us didn't think of it the other did, working in perfect unison. Two men on a mission.

The next few weeks seem to float by. We have a purpose again, something to commit ourselves to and invest our energies in. Brian calls me in L.A. the next week beaming about the positive responses he has been getting about our idea on the home front. Both family and friends, including the co-workers he told before heading home for his holiday, have had nothing but words of encouragement and support to offer. I tell him I have had much of the same, my voice betraying the surprise I felt at getting nothing but positive reaction.

Shortly after coming back to L.A. I had given my family a call. I did the usual asking about the weather, the family, my nieces, and everyone's health before bridging the subject of our quest. I was pretty sure my parents would accept it. After all they should be used to my crazy stunts by now and have grown to expect them. They've seen photos of me on camel back in the Thar Dessert of India, elephant back in the jungles of Thailand, and amidst rioters in Southern China. So this should be mild in comparison.

And yet when I spilled the plans over the phone I was surprised all the same at the extent of their positive responses. My father's comment still echoing in my ears: "It's a great idea Chris. Take your time and figure it all out. After all, I think we have it all backward in this society. I think you should be retired young while you have the time to enjoy everything and then work when you get older." A great concept for me at the time, but I don't think he's ready to make public policy just yet.

With all the people I tell I expect some cynical remarks or deterrence from making the trip. But I receive none. Perhaps I'm just not asking the right people. I'm not sure why I expect the obstacles, maybe it is just a reflection of my own cynicism or own hesitation. But why was I hesitant? The quest seemed to hold all the things I crave: travel, adventure, knowledge. And the doubts and questions I've had of late, aren't they alone big enough to warrant a search for answers?

I take a mental assessment of things I want to explore on the quest, drawing up a checklist in my head. Is there some place out there where I would prefer to live? Is there something else I should be doing with my life, something that I've forgotten over the years. My current work is enjoyable, but is there more I should be doing with my life? Is there some way to contribute more to the world around me? And if so, how do I go about finding it? How do others find their path and stay on it? And finally, is there a lightning storm on my horizon, a mystical force that is seeking me out and ready to alter my destiny? Is there the place, job, and woman of my dreams just around the corner waiting for me to go looking?

They are all questions I feel compelled to answer. My personal quest in the heart of the public one we were ready to undertake.

WHAT'S IN A NAME

◆

The most important thing about getting
somewhere is starting right where you are.

Bruce Barton

The mild California winter turns to a balmy spring, a transition marked more by calendars than change in weather or foliage. Many pilgrims to California's coast complain about the lack of seasons, wishing there was a little more diversity. I've grown accustomed to it, willing to give up seasonal change for 300 days of sunshine a year and a commanding lack of snow.

The printer kicks out another sheet of business cards just as Brian is pulling apart the last sheet, trying his best to keep up with the printing process. He stops a moment to add another sheet to the printer and start it off on another cycle.

"These are turning out pretty good," Brian says and tosses one to me on the sofa.

The card catches wind and flutters too far right, falling to my feet. I set the laptop computer aside and reach down to inspect the work. It does look good, just as good as if we had had them printed professionally. One more cheer for the beauty of desktop publishing. Across the top of the card is our new logo we just finished designing a few days back. Beneath it, the card reads:

Quest-4
The Pursuit Of Successful Living
Brian Ardinger
Chris Moeller
www.quest-4.com

We decided on the name for our project on my last trip to San Jose to help Brian pack up and move out of his old apartment. We had been tossing names back and forth for days but either the name didn't seem to fit or the URL—or internet address—had already been taken. And since this was to be a real-time web project we needed to be sure the web address fit. Then one night we were driving back from another planning session primed on beer and caffeine and the name hit us.

"Quest, quest, quest…so what are we questing *for*?" I asked, banging on the steering dash.

"We're questing for…questing for…" Brian tried to fill in the blank but stammered over the right words. "It's a quest for…"

"Hey, quest for. Quest four." I say. I then turned to Brian holding up four fingers. "Quest-4. Physical, mental, emotional, and spiritual." As I spoke I lowered each one of my fingers.

"Yes." Brian said raising his own four fingers and lowering one at a time as he read off his thinking, "Career, family, community, spirituality. Quest-4. The quest for…" The decision was made. Our quest had a name.

In looking at the card now, that moment seems so long ago. But it has only been a little over three months. In just three months Brian has left his job, moved out of his apartment and into mine in Los Angeles, and we have made great headway in making our project a reality.

We know in order to share our quest with others we need to make it as professional as possible. Thus we take time now to work on business cards, stationary, and the web site that will be the backbone of our journey.

The decision to use the web to reach out to an audience was an easy one. We are part of the web generation. Yes we can still remember a time before fax machines and knew what the crisp sound of an 8-track tape sounded like, but we are part of the Internet brood all the same. I check and send email on a daily basis, often more than once in a given 24-hour period. In fact, those of my friends and family that have neglected to become part of the email brigade have lost me as a correspondent. Where once I was king of stamps and envelopes, now I replace them with the slick messages of hand-typed email. My morning news comes from a web site, brought to me in a flickering screen of light. So taken with the Internet am I that it has become my chosen profession. Or the profession I have fallen into anyway. The web and I are inseparable. A web geek waiting for the world to catch up to the point where I will be mainstream once again.

Everything seems to click and has been since we've been working full time on the quest. We have already lined up our first interviews and have places to stay most of the way across the northern half of America. The web site is near to completion; our gear has all been collected; we are just about ready.

In collecting gear and planning what we will take we find that Brian's BMW isn't going to cut it for the trip. It would certainly take us there in style, but there is no way it will hold everything we need for the journey. After all, we are taking six months worth of clothes for all weather conditions for two people, computing equipment, camping gear, and piles of junk food, CDs, and audio books. We need a bigger vehicle. What we find is a used Jeep Grand Cherokee, good shape, affordable price, and all the luggage space we could need. Brian, most definitely the financial half of the venture, buys the Jeep and puts his BMW up for sale on a consignment lot. The last vestige of his former life left behind.

We launch our web site on a Monday afternoon with little fanfare. Now all we need is some actual content. But the content will have to wait. In the midst of packing and planning and organizing I have successfully forgotten my rapidly approaching birthday. I have less than a week left in my 20s. Saturday will see me entering the world of my fourth decade here on earth. I don't give it much thought, or at least I try not to. But think about it or not, it is just on the horizon and there is something I need to do first.

FREE FALLING

◆

He who would learn to fly one day
must first learn to stand and walk
and run and climb and dance;
one cannot fly into flying.

Friedrich Nietzsche

We pull into the Terrace Valley Flight School and into a nervously empty parking lot. Sure, there are a few cars but those could all belong to the instructors and staff. Where are the other lunatics? As if on cue another car pulls in behind us and takes a space in the row to the right. So I'm not alone in my madness.

"Ready?" Jeanne asks from the seat next to me.

"Hell yes, let's do it!" I answer.

And ready I am. I have always wanted to hurl myself out of an airplane and see what would happen to me. Of course most of the time these ideas would come to me when jarred awake by turbulence on a passenger flight somewhere over the Pacific or the plains of the Mid-West. I would get up, unclip my seat belt (*"Excuse me sir, but the captain hasn't turned off the 'fasten your seat belt' sign yet"*), push my way to the galley (*"Sorry honey, but I just gotta fly"*), take the food elevator down to the luggage area, and launch myself out of a small hatch somewhere down below. My seat and tray not in their upright position. Just me and clouds and thousands of feet of empty air falling quickly over my head.

But I never did do that, nor will I ever. I will leave that to the stuff of dreams and adventure films. Today I try the more sane way of flying. Little plane, open door, me and a 150 pound tour guide strapped to my back. It was to be the last big event of my twenties, the last big adventure. I planned on making the jump long before deciding to sail out onto the open road. It was a promise to myself I had to keep, even with the pressures and To Do Lists of our pending journey drawing looming over me.

We get out of the Jeep and close the doors. I remember Brian's look when I asked him if we could take the Jeep to Palm Springs for the jump. "Sure," he said. "But you have to be sure and survive the jump so I don't have to find a way out to Palm Springs to pick it up." Ah, the wonders of friendship. More concern for a Jeep than broken limbs and loss of life. His sarcasm brings a smile to my face.

We walk into the school yard and see training mats and fake plane mockups to practice jumping out of, rental shops, a medical center, restaurant, bar, pool, and jump school office. We head for the one at the end. The door waits, the last chance to turn back. With no hesitation I step forward and enter smiling.

"Good morning, are you two here for a jump today?" The receptionist behind the desk greets us.

"He is," Jeanne replies. "We have reservations: Chris Moeller."

The receptionist flips through her book and scans the page marked June 22, locating my name half way down. She hi-lights it with a yellow marker.

"Will there just be one of you today?" She asks.

I look at Jeanne and then back to the receptionist. "Do you have space for two?" I ask.

"I'm sure we can arrange something." She answers with a smile.

"Okay, two." I say and then turn back to Jeanne. "You're coming with me, my treat for *your* birthday. Happy birthday." Her birthday is two months off but I have to get her up there with me. I know she wants to jump too but is just hesitant over the money. And seeing as she is treating for my jump as a birthday present to me I don't blame her. At 200 dollars a leap it can be expensive. But if she doesn't go now, here with me, she may never go. And it would be so much more fun to have her to enjoy it with.

"Okay!" She smiles back, all of a sudden fully wide-eyed and alive. The transition from spectator to participant lights a fire behind her eyes. "But I'm not really dressed for it." She says, pointing out her sun dress and sandals. We both look at the receptionist.

"You have time if you'd like to change." She says.

"Yeah, hop out to the Jeep and change into some pants and a T-shirt." I tell her. She drops the camera off with me and rushes out to prepare for her sky diving experience.

That's Jeanne. Life has a way of bringing important people into your life, people who can give it new meaning and direction. For the past few years that person for me has been Jeanne. We met in Shanghai where I was working and she was studying acupuncture and we immediately took to each other. We fast became the best of friends and then friendship blossomed into love. Our relationship has grown and evolved and we now find ourselves somehow back at friendship. That special kind of friendship, one where each knows the other on such an intimate level it can be wonderfully scary. One where when the boyfriend / girlfriend part fades, and the root 'friend' remains, now more powerful than ever.

Jeanne is back in a flash and we are escorted into a side room to take care of the legal formalities of the jump. I guess when you are having sane people pay you to let them jump out of a perfectly good airplane at 15,000 feet you have to be sure to cover your ass. And that is what they fully intend to do.

Their legal lady hands us each a stack of forms and papers clipped together by a staple straining to make it through the oversize bundle. We are told to read and initial each paragraph, to fill out all the forms, and to sign the back of each page. I stare at the stack in surreal disbelief and start to leaf through the pages when she stops me and says we must first watch a video. She clicks a remote and the tiny screen above us comes alive with a suited gentleman sitting at a mahogany desk in the center of a bookshelf lined room.

"Hello. I am the lawyer for Terrace Valley Parachuting School," the man in the videotape begins. "I am here to discuss the legal aspects of the jump you are about to perform today."

Jeanne and I turn and laugh towards each other, a strange look of apprehension in each of our eyes. We make nervous jokes back and forth as lawyer man tells us how we could go to another school now if we wanted jump insurance. And how there is no way we can ever sue the school for harm, death or negligence. Nor could our family. Nor could our parents. Nor could our dependents. Nor could our first grade teachers, dentists, grocery clerks, dog or cat.

The list goes on and the video with it. We are told of possible problems and how we have no rights to claim fault on the school. We are told of deaths that have occurred in the past and how the families of the deceased had no legal ramifications. All the while Lawyerman sits behind his big lawyer desk and speaks without expression. Occasionally I look around the stark room for relief from Lawyerman's gaze. All that is missing, I think to myself, are graphic photos of jump accidents nicely framed and hung around the room.

The video ends and we are permitted to leaf through the volume of forms, quickly initialing, signing, and waivering. We hand the books back to Legal Lady and start to stand but she asks us to wait a moment longer. From nowhere she produces a video camera and holds up a card beneath it, the camera lens trained on Jeanne.

"Please read this into the camera, just say your name where it's blank." She instructs to Jeanne. Dazed and confused, Jeanne stares into the red record light of the camera and reads.

"I Jeanne Cheng hereby waive all rights for myself, my family, and my dependents to make any claims against Terrace Valley Parachuting School in the event of injury or death."

Jeanne reads it nervously. We both feel as if we were being held up at gun point. *Please Mr. President, pay them the ransom. They're serious about the nuclear threat.* I take my turn reading from the card. As I read I visualize being up in the plane, door open, and Lawyerman pushing me out the door without a chute. *Thanks for your money Mr. Moeller, Hahahahahaha.*

I finish reading and the video camera is put away. Do I get a copy of that with my jump video? I want to ask in jest but Lawyer Lady's stern expression suppresses the thought. She thanks us and instructs us to exit to our left down the hallway and enter the last room on the right.

Outside the law offices of We-Could-Kill-You-And-There-Is-Nothing-You-Can-Do-About-It the mood is completely different. Whatever foul air floated around the videos and forms were kept inside that room by air lock. As we walk down the hall with photos of smiling jumpers the excitement comes back to us again. The sense of invulnerability rises from the depths of our guts and we know we could never die. We are the chosen ones, the riders of the clouds. And we are ready to fly.

We enter the small room and see a couple of chairs and a box full of what appears to be jumping equipment. Before we have time to sit down a man in his late thirties enters the room. He is dressed in full flight gear, hair trussed, wildly managed mustache covering his upper lip. He extends a hand and I take it to shake.

"Hi, I'm Gary and I'll be jumping with you today. Chris, right?" He asks offering a firm grip.

"That's right. So you're jumping with me or Jeanne?" I ask.

"You. Jeanne's partner will meet us shortly in the chute area. But first I need to explain some things to you." He says and motions for us to take a seat.

From the box he pulls out a parachute harness. "You're each going to have a harness something like this one. Now what you're going to want to do is step into it like this then…"

As he explains the process I drift a bit. I'm sure we will go through this several times in flight school, he just wants to introduce it to us here. And besides, my mind is racing with thoughts of open skies and cloud rushing by my face.

"…right at 5,000 feet. Okay?" He has finished talking and is now holding an altimeter. He was saying something about it being strapped to our chests, 5,000 feet, and a ripcord. I'm sure I'll catch it the next time around.

"Okay." Jeanne and I confirm.

"Great. Let's get you two suited up and on a plane." He says and motions us to the door.

In the parachute area we are introduced to Jeanne's jump partner Buzz. When we signed up for the jump they asked our height and weight so they could evenly match us with instructors and chutes. At five foot ten and around one fifty Gary seemed evenly matched for me, though a little on the light side. But when they matched up Jeanne and Buzz I don't know what they were thinking. Buzz stands at least a head taller than Jeanne and must have her out weighed by over one hundred pounds. If he falls forward onto her during a landing she will be crushed for sure. Of course, there is nothing we could do about it. Not legally.

We are offered matching jump suits and pull them on over our street clothes. The laces of our shoes are covered with duct tape, just one more use for the most versatile tool in the world. It seems you can pretty much use duct tape, or "duck tape" as I referred to it as a small child— usually in conjunction with taping up my sisters hands and legs and telling them to try to get out of it, a Harry Houdini game only I enjoyed—for anything. It can fix flats, hold planes together, and seal holes. So many things that we would be crazy to go on our journey without any. We bought two rolls just in case. I'm glad we did. Now I know it can be used to hold down stray shoelaces as well.

Gary finishes taping up my shoes and hands me a harness. I step into it and strap it on as he instructs each step of the way. He then hands me an altimeter and threads it onto the strap at my chest.

"Five thousand feet, remember?" He asks with a smile.

"Uh, sure." I say back. I look over at Jeanne and wonder if I look as silly in my get up as she does in hers. I can't help but remember the parachute pants of the 80s and try to remember how any of us could have thought they looked so cool.

Suited up and rearing to go. The excitement bubbles over in me and I begin to make girlish giggles with excitement. I give Jeanne a hug as we walk past the doors to offices and medical clinics and rental shops and bars and head into the training area. Then as we keep walking past the airplane door mockup and training mats I begin to feel a little nervous. When we exit the gate and approach a plane taxiing on the runway I am confused. What happened to the rest of the training?

"Ready?" Buzz asks us, barely audible over the roar of the plane engines. We both give him a thumbs up sign.

"Hey," I lean over to Jeanne. "Don't we get any more training?"

"Guess not." She says nonplused. She is only concerned with one thing at this point: touching the ground again in a few minutes.

We climb onto the plane and slide down long benches until we are seated right behind the pilot. Behind us a group of six jumpers board the plane and fill up the cargo area we are in. The two closest to us on the bench smile and give us a thumbs up. We return the gesture and off we go.

Buzz and Jeanne sit across from me chatting above the roar of the engines. I can barely hear a word they are saying. Gary tries to engage me in conversation as well, but the effort seems too great for both of us and we sit back and enjoy the ride. Out the window the earth drops below us, rapidly falling away as we climb higher and higher. *Wow. This is it. I am finally going to fly. I'm going to see what it's like to be suspended in air.*

On my chest the altimeter reads 12,000 feet. Gary tells me to turn around and put my back to his chest. I do as instructed and feel him tugging my harness into his, slowly fastening the two together and pulling them tight.

At 15,000 feet the door of the plane slides open and air whips by. The arid plains of Palm Dessert lie below in the distance. One by one and without hesitation our passengers slide to the door and leap out of the plane. Immediately I think of the doomed plane that is being evacuated. Only there aren't enough chutes for everyone. Someone draws the short stick and must go without. The short stick rests in my hands as I watch the others jump to safety.

Another hard tug from Gary pulls me back into the plane and the moment at hand. Our turn. We slide down to the end of the bench, stopping just before we get to the door to let Jeanne and Buzz go first. I watch as they move to the door, Buzz towering over Jeanne's small figure. She looks like a child being carried on Buzz's chest in a baby harness. Both are all smiles as they reach the door. And then they are gone.

The plane's cargo bay is empty save for us as we push the final few feet to the door. We kneel at the threshold, the emptiness before us so palpable, so real. Excitement boils over in me, not believing that I am really doing this, and as we leap from the plane I begin to laugh.

I'm falling. The air roars around me and tugs at my flesh. I can feel my cheeks buckle and ripple in its wake. My stomach does a quick turn, wanting to flop up into my chest like it does on roller coasters, but it doesn't. The motion this time is constant and it has nowhere to fall back to. It just hovers in weightless space.

And I am flying. Flying! The rush comes over me and I scream with delight. Never have I been so fully in a moment. So totally here. There is nowhere else, no other time. There is only me and the sky and the earth climbing closer and closer. We spin and tumble and right ourselves, all part of the thrill ride. I extend my arms and test the wind resistance, falling faster and slower alternatively. I am Superman. I am flying. I am invincible.

A tap on my shoulder and I remember that I have a man strapped to my back. A man that is responsible for my safety and my life. He knows I can't make legal claims but then if I go down he goes with me. So I'm pretty sure he'll do his job right. He taps me on the shoulder again and yells over the screaming winds.

"How's your altimeter?" He yells.

For a moment I have no idea what he's saying. Then I do but I have no idea what he means. And then it comes to me, something about 5,000 feet and a ripcord. I look down at my chest and see the red needle of the altimeter hovering at the 5,000 feet marking. I nod a thanks to Gary that he probably can't see from his perch on my back. I remember telling him I wanted to pull my own cord after he said he would pull it at 5,000 feet if I didn't. Part of the training that seeped in without me noticing.

I reach across my body and grip the bright orange handle in my left hand. With a yank it pulls free of the chute and we are launched upwards with a jolt.

"Aaaaiiiiieeeee!" I scream as the chute opens above us. Our rapid descent is slowed and we begin to drift toward the earth again, this time in a slow graceful float. The desert landscape spreads out all around us. Barren mountains surrounded by barren plains. From up here it seems so beautiful, an intricate weaving of brown, terra cotta, and burnt umber. It reminds me of finger painting, colors just bleeding together in a comfortable mix of joy and discovery.

Gary points out some landmarks as we drift down toward them: a mountain, a farm, and a flock of sheep. I am slowly falling into a make believe world, a toy train set model display that will soon become my reality.

Below us is the landing strip where Jeanne and Buzz are now rapidly approaching. I know from the video of the landing that I see later that Jeanne is already running hundreds of feet before they land. Her little legs seem frantic next to Buzz's long pillars beneath them. As they approach the ground Jeanne gets a few running steps in before Buzz hits ground stooping over her. Then in full command of his legs he simply picks her up and runs to a full and graceful stop, the chute trailing behind them.

I don't think of running. I don't even think of moving. All I think about is that I don't want this to end. I want to go back up, not down. I want to soar with the eagles, to fly above the clouds. This was just a tease, way too short. Up, up, dammit, how do you make this thing go up?

"Okay, here we come. Get ready." Gary says from behind my ears. It's easier to hear now; the air is light and fluffy once again.

I look down at the ground racing for us. Shit, I didn't know we would be going so fast! Now what was it he said in the training room that I thought wasn't really the training but just an introduction. What did he say? Something about jumping off a chair. Yes, that's it. It's like jumping off a chair. You just bend your legs and

THUMP. I actually hear a loud thump as my right leg hits the ground first and I crumple over it. I guess Gary gets a step in before hitting my lumping form before him and falls into me. We collapse onto the ground in a pile of humanity and parachute. No legs a runnin', no grace, no finesse. Just one big, ugly, embarrassing wipe out.

And I don't care. I leap to my feet and howl with excitement. I did it. I had flown and had landed (albeit sloppily) and had lived (just barely) to tell about it. Jeanne rushes over as Gary stumbles to get us unstrapped. Now free of the tether I throw my arms around Jeanne and squeeze tight.

"You did it!" I congratulate her.

"YOU did it!" She says. "Happy birthday!" She hugs me back and then with a smirk, "Oh, and nice landing."

I turn to thank Gary and see him gently rubbing his chin. Apparently his jaw took most of the impact of the landing when it struck my shoulder.

"Gary, thank you so much. That was incredible, simply incredible. Sorry about the landing though." I shake his hand excitedly.

"It's okay. You'll do better next time." He smiles and pats me on the shoulder, either in friendly gesture or to see exactly what bony extrusion rammed into his jaw.

I go to Jeanne again and we jabber about our experiences, reveling in our euphoria. All that anticipation and all those expectations and I was in no way prepared for the experience of free falling. I could never have known without taking the leap. I could never imagine without the experience. Good, bad, incredible. There was no way of knowing until I stepped out into the unknown and took it head on. Now I was ready to leap out of the door of my twenties and free fall into my thirties and all the experiences they had to offer. I think of all the expectations and anticipation I have over turning thirty and heading out onto the open road and I wonder if they too will be useless when the actual experience comes. Isn't following my dreams and what feels right just another leap of faith?

CONTACT

◆

Even if you're on the right track,
You'll get run over if you just sit there.

Will Rogers

Our first interview comes to us via the Internet. As we search the web for information on US travel and further research routes for our trip we stumble across a website called *RoadTrip America* that intrigues us immediately. The site tells about Mark and Megan, a couple in their 40s, who together with their road dog Marvin have been traveling across America for the past four years in a custom built recreational vehicle. As we surf the site one thing in particular strikes us immediately: their current location. They were presently in Pasadena, California, just twenty minutes away. Brian and I think this more than coincidence, having seen how things have recently been clicking into place all too smoothly. We quickly compose an email and send it out to the RTA team, telling them of our project and asking if they'd be up for meeting us and sharing some road advice.

We are given a quick lesson in the power of the World Wide Web. Within an hour they come back to us and say they will be happy to meet us. We volley a few more emails back and forth and a time and place is set. We will meet them tomorrow afternoon in a Starbucks coffee shop just up the road from my apartment in Culver City.

During the afternoon we also finalize arrangements to meet with independent film director Mark Tapio Kines. I met Mark once or twice through mutual friends, each time he was in various stages of production on a film he was making. The first time we met he was a film student / web designer with a screenplay and a dream. The next time he was writer / director / producer of an independent film in progress. When I talk with him today he is in the finishing stages of the movie, still seeking funding for final editing and sound. When our quest was being developed I immediately thought of interviewing him. In the little time we had spent together in the last year he seemed like someone with both an interesting story and a good outlook on life.

With the first interviews set things just seems to be clicking together and I find myself still riding on the clouds. It's incredible, yesterday I flew through the air and in six days our quest begins. My head is still reeling, it is all happening so quickly.

Six days. It's been over four months since we came up with our crazy idea and now we are on the verge of departure. My mind starts to race with all the things I have yet to do. People to call, things to pack—both for the trip and to put into storage while I am gone—stuff yet to buy for the journey, web site amendments still to be made. As usual my mind is way ahead of the rest of me, making plans and schedules and lists. I try to sit back in my seat and relax, letting the rising stress level drain away.

ROAD TRIP

◆

Only those who will risk going too far
can possibly find out how far one can go.

T.S. Eliot

We show up at the Starbucks intentionally a little ahead of schedule. It is our first meeting with the "public," and we want to be sure it was going to work. We walk from the front of the coffee shop to the rear, trying to find an area where the music and noise aren't so loud. Sarah McLachlan is crooning over the sound system and echoing throughout the shop. We stop at a table near the back.

"Well this is as good as it gets." Brian says plopping the laptop onto the table. "The music's a little softer and from here we can see them and they can see us when they come in."

I nod in agreement and put down the bag of recording equipment I am carrying. I take a seat on the outside of the table so the RoadTrip America team could see me from the door. We had told them to look for two guys, one with red hair. It now seemed kind of silly in light of all the computing and recording equipment we had strewn across the table. *Just look for the techno-geeks*, we should have said.

Brian sets up the computer to display our web site in case they are interested in checking it out. We want to be sure they know we are genuine and not some psycho web stalkers. Meanwhile, I take out one of our little Sony micro-recorders and cue up a fresh tape. I'm still fidgeting with it when the door opens and we see a couple enter looking a little lost. They wear matching shirts, both with the words Road Trip America emblazoned across the chest.

Brian sees them and jumps up to greet them at the door, business school etiquette coming into play. I am right behind him.

"Hi, Mark and Megan?" Brian extends a hand. "I'm Brian Ardinger and this is Chris Moeller."

We exchange hellos and handshakes. Brian steers Mark to the counter where he offers them coffee or tea while I escort Megan to the table. We're both offering up our own introductions to the project and ourselves so by the time we all arrive back at the table everyone is equally informed on our quest and the reason for the meeting today.

"Thanks again for meeting with us." Brian starts up the conversation, now including all four of us.

"Our pleasure," Mark says. "Your project sounds very interesting."

"Thanks. But I'm sure you can give us lots of tips and advice on how to make it work. I mean you two have been on the road for what, four years now?" Brian asks.

"Four years and counting." Megan replies.

"How did that all come about?" Brian asks. We had read a little about their background from their website but wanted a more first hand account of what took place to send them out onto the road.

"We got started doing this because our home burned in a wildfire in '93." Mark tells the story as if he has recounted it many times before, which during four years driving the country we are sure he has. "We went from two yuppies with a home in the hills, two cars, and professional careers to having nothing overnight. Our view at that time was: How many times as an adult do we get to start from ground zero? That gave us a sense of strength and peace in a way that we felt there was almost nothing that could happen that we could not really handle. Sometimes the best things come when things are looking grim."

For Mark and Megan the best thing to come out of the fire was the birth of Road Trip America. Having lost everything in the fire, the two decided to set off on an adventure in search of their fame and fortune on the open roads of America. They bought a custom vehicle (aptly called the *Phoenix 1*), set up a web magazine, and set out to explore the country.

"What made you guys decide to take to the road?" I ask. "Was it something you always wanted to do or…"

"I don't know where that came from, but it came fast." Megan says laughing.

"The day after the fire, maybe it was a little longer." Mark adds.

"I always traveled a lot, so it wasn't like I had no idea about travel." Megan continues. "But I certainly never traveled like that in a motor home. I don't think I'd ever even been inside one. In fact I scorned them!" She smiles and looks over at Mark.

"We left town with less money than you are taking with you on your trip," Mark says. "And without any prospects of money. We just decided to do it. We also thought we would be on the road for some sort of sabbatical and it might be 6 months to a year. It was totally open ended, it had no end date at all, nor did it have a purpose other than go out and seek our fortune."

"But how did you feel about that? Didn't that scare you?" I ask intrigued.

"A little," Megan answers. "But the most important thing is to decide you are going to do it—to follow your dreams—like you two have. You're going to do it, no matter what, and nothing is going to dissuade you at this point. And it's not really about money. Yes, you have to make money because you have to buy gas and things but it's not really about making money, it's about making a difference." She starts to continue but Mark is already speaking over her.

"Money more than anything else holds people back from doing what they ought to do," Mark says. "The question we ask ourselves when we are facing a decision is: would I do this if money was not a consideration? And if we wouldn't do it if money wasn't a consideration we'd turn it down."

Megan nods in agreement as Mark continues. "It would be nice to have an extra amount of cash, well even a normal amount would be nice about now." They both laugh and we join them. I secretly wonder what a *normal amount of cash* really is. "But last year we turned down some very potentially lucrative contracts because if we were doing it it wouldn't make us feel good."

"You have to just ask yourself: How does it make you feel." Megan chimes in. "And if it makes you feel like some kind of whore you just have to turn it down."

"The stomach is really an effective tool in figuring things out," Mark adds. "If you're going to do something and you get a funny feeling— and there's good anticipation butterflies and there's 'oh my god, let's not do this'—then think about it. When I'm in those positions I listen to what my stomach says and if I get a bad feeling about it then I just don't do it."

Brian and I nod. We both know very well what they are talking about. Our current venture had nothing to do with making money. It was all about making a difference, a difference in our lives and hopefully in the lives of others. Or perhaps at least one other person somewhere somehow. And though it showed no potential of financial gain it felt right. I remember the *light-bulb moment* at Gumba's the night we thought of the quest. We felt so alive and the decision felt so right. Our gut was screaming at us to do this thing.

"It sounds like you both are very positive about your situation." Brian says as our guests enjoy a sip of their iced coffees.

"Most definitely," Mark says in reply. "One of the things that we find helpful is to ask what's the worst that can happen, and I can't imagine what could happen that would be so bad. If we went back to where our truck was parked and it was blown up in the middle of the night or our computers weren't there any more, we could always go and do something else."

"Right now I want to write a book," Megan picks up from Mark. "And the challenge is in myself, it's not whether or not I have a computer or something for lunch. If I wanted to use all my energy to worry about whether I can pay my cellular phone bills I couldn't write. You just have to think: Can I do what I want to do? Then go and do it."

Over the loud speaker Roy Orbison sings a melody as a blender behind the counter spins an icy concoction of coffee and chocolate. *Are they turning up the stereo?* I think to myself as it seems to be even louder than before. I have to lean in to hear Mark speak as he answers Brian's latest question.

"Did you have a rough adjustment to your new lives on the road?" Brian asks.

"Not really rough, but there were some adjustments to be made." Mark answers. "Before starting RoadTrip America, we had different careers, we saw each other occasionally, we had a really different life. And all of a sudden we're living 24 hours a day in 200 square feet and it was a stressful period. We had to reinvent our own relationship. And we also had to get to the point where we just decided that no matter how much grief there was from some of that, that it was something we wanted to do and we were going to be happy about it. And that decision that you are going to enjoy what you are doing makes all the difference."

"What about careers and such," I say thinking back to my vision of the Suit and his maniacal laugh as he presses the button and banishes me from the corporate world. "Do you ever feel like you should be doing something more mainstream?"

Megan starts to say something in reply but Mark is already talking. "A lot of what our culture teaches us is that there are certain jobs that are good and certain jobs that are not. But life is too short to do something that is not fun. And if fun for you is being a garbage collector or being a tax attorney or whatever, then if you're really doing what you love then all the other obstacles in your life will switch around to where they're not so important. Or you will find new things opening up to you. But if you're constantly doing stuff because you think you should or if you have some fixed notion of what success is, ultimately that doesn't work. We know so many people who have accepted other people's view of what success is and their lives are hell."

There's the word again. *Success.* Word of the day. The end all, beat all goal of existence. I wonder if we are any closer to discovering its role in *successful living.*

"Has the Internet site really helped you in your travels?" Brian asks, changing the direction of the conversation.

"Yes, most definitely," Megan says. "First of all, when we first started out I wanted to be able to continue writing and file my stories by electronic means. And that wasn't very common then in '94, newspapers weren't really wired then. But I really wanted to do that, to write. I liked the idea of being in Montana or somewhere and writing and sending a story, I just really liked the idea. Once a week, every week, I would upload a story. As the Internet grew it became easier and easier to do that."

"With the Internet and through our web site the sense of a larger community is very real." Mark adds. "The first couple of years out traveling we talked about going back to California, back to Pasadena. Our families are there and it's nice to see them. But we now feel no more at home in Pasadena then we do in Texas, or Manhattan, or Seattle. Home is on arrival there. And that's a nice comfortable feeling. Home is everywhere."

"And the web has made a huge difference in that." Megan says putting down her drink. "The community was the original holy grail for email and joining the web world."

We continue to talk about the Internet and compare web site notes. Brian flips open the laptop and begins to show them our site, maneuvering the mouse to show them the various sections of the site. Overhead a Spanish love song plays out through the sound system. *Just what the hell kind of radio station is this anyway?*

We listen as Mark and Megan share more road stories with us. And with each one we grow more and more excited to hit the road and gather our own experiences and stories. They offer a lot of sound advice, hints on places to go and road safety, things to pack that we may not have thought of, and the need for a launch party. We had thought of having an official launch at one point but put it out of mind, deciding it would be better to approach the media once we have some stories, interviews, and insights to share. Mark and Megan convince us otherwise, telling us of the psychological and symbolic need for an official launch—an epic beginning to the Hero's journey. So it is decided, on Sunday we will crash champagne or alternate beverage of choice against the Jeep and they will be there to cover it for their web site. They and any other media we manage to attract in the next few days. With this new item on our To Do List we thank the RTA team for their time and bid them farewell until Sunday.

IN THE DIRECTOR'S CHAIR

◆

Every time I start a picture...
I feel the same fear, the same self-doubts...
and I have only one source on which I can draw,
because it comes from within me.

Federico Fellini

Mark Tapio Kines lets us into his apartment after the first knock, commenting on our perfect timing. I refrain from telling him we actually arrived at his place over forty five minutes earlier and then left to explore the neighborhood. Brian and I both tend to run on the early side, especially for appointments. To insure this his watch is set five minutes fast, mine ten. Between the two of us we somehow ended at Mark's forty-five before seven p.m.. But then with the unpredictable L.A. traffic you never know.

Mark shows us into his kitchen where he has a few mini-pizzas on the stove. "Sorry, I haven't eaten yet and am starving. Can I get you anything?" He asks.

"No thanks, we already ate." Brian says.

He continues to re-heat his pizza and asks us about our quest. "I checked out your web site, looks good. How's the project coming along."

Project. It's how our quest is usually referred to, often by ourselves as well. It's difficult to know how to describe it. "Quest", while the most appropriate, tends to invoke such grandiose images in the minds of others and leads to obscure questions and long explanations. And though we are working on it full time, "job" didn't seem right. After all, we aren't getting paid for it and don't have a pension, W2's, or a health plan. "Project" on the other hand is a safe word. It can be said with little bewilderment. It is a word used often at work and school and can lend itself to either nicely, giving the listener something to grasp onto, something real and tangible. A project has a goal, some analysis, and an ending. Much more easily defined than the emotional, free-flowing, self-feeding quest we are undertaking.

"It's going well," I say as Mark sits down at the kitchen table with his pizzas. "In fact, we are now having an official launch party this Sunday before we head out of town. We just emailed out press releases this afternoon. Sunday at noon in Culver City if you're bored and not doing anything."

It took some doing but we managed to get the press releases finished the night before following our meeting with RoadTrip America. Writing them proved much easier than finding people to send them to. That had taken most of this morning and would have taken longer had we not found a friend with a list of local Los Angeles press contacts through her work. We ended up sending out a couple dozen or so emails and faxes to local TV, radio, and newspapers offices. The title read:

Journey Across America in Search of Successful Living
A Cross-country Tour and New Web Site Tackles the Questions Of Success,
Happiness, and Personal Greatness

"But enough about the quest," I say as Mark finishes up the first of his pizzas. "Tell us about your movie. How's that coming along?"

"Good," he says. "We've finished filming and doing pre-edits, now we have to do final cuts and sound. Of course, we have to get funds for all that first."

"What's it called?" Brian asks.

"'*Foreign Correspondents*'. It's a story idea I've had for a while but didn't have the means to make it. But I've been working and saving for a few years and have had some private investors as well: friends, family, and strangers who found my site on the Internet. Now we're getting very close to completion."

Listening to Mark it isn't difficult to be impressed. He knew his passion was in film making, but instead of taking the usual Hollywood ladder approach, he has forged his own way. Working as a web designer to earn and save up money to write, direct, and create an independent film in his spare time.

"How did you get into film making? Is it something you always wanted to do?" I ask intrigued.

"I was very lucky in that at a very early age I had an idea of what I wanted to do," Mark finishes a bite of pizza and brushes his hands with a napkin. "When I was seven I saw *Star Wars* and I basically wanted to be a film director from that point on. I didn't really know it, but I'd run around my house not necessarily pretending I was Luke Skywalker, but pretending that I was Mark Hamill portraying Luke Skywalker; seeing the best way to stage this action scene." He holds up his hands and forms a make-shift picture frame with them, peering through it at Brian and me.

"So basically since I was seven I wanted to direct films," he continues, dropping his hands back to the table. "And everything seemed to be plotted pretty much along a straight line. I forced myself to do that by telling everybody: Okay. This is what I'm going to pursue. Now I'm 28, have directed my first film, and I have no idea what I'll be next year. I'd love to be doing another film. If somebody said 'Do you want to start working on one tomorrow?' I'd say 'Yeah! I'd love to.' It's extremely hard work and it's taxing. The blood, sweat and mostly the tears that go into it, and at the end of the day you wonder if it's ever going to get done."

"But it looks like it is going to get done. What about when the film's finished? What then?" Brian asks.

"It's hard to see what the future's going to bring. Five years from now I could be world famous or five years from now I could be back behind a computer doing artwork. But I don't think that will happen. I've worked so hard that I can't take a step back. Again, it felt so natural to do this thing. I was in my element. I was organized. I had fun." Mark says with a smile. "This is a real project and it actually means something to me, I just don't want to get rich. I don't really want to get rich. Success for me would be just selling the film and getting the money to make another film."

Mark gets up from the table and walks over to put his empty plate in the sink. "Sure I can't offer you guys something?" He asks pulling a glass out of the cupboard.

"Okay, I'll take some water if you have it." I say.

"Water. I think I may have some lying around here somewhere," he says taking down another glass. "Brian?"

"Sure, thanks." Brian says as Mark begins filling glasses with bottled water. Nobody in L.A. drinks from the tap. "So do you have your next moves all planned out?"

"I pretty much have to take things as they come, because you plan for something and you break your leg. You want to do something and you expect this to happen and it's silly because you'll close yourself off to all the possibilities that life has to offer. I used to be a little more closed minded about things like this. I was like: 'No, No, I have to do this. I'm not going to even bother looking in another direction.' But sometimes, you look that way and it leads you someplace else. And who knows, maybe I'll end up being a doctor." Mark laughs and hands us each a glass of water and sits back down at the table.

"I have a plan in the sense that I know what I want to do," he continues, "and that I can do it eventually and that I can do it tomorrow if I wanted to. Of course there are the certain restrictions of money and stuff like that. I don't really have a firm plan. Everything just sort of gets thrown at you so randomly that they will always affect what you plan on doing. Some for better, some for worse. And sometimes things happen for no reason at all. That was the hardest thing to accept, that not everything happens to you needs to be significant. I used to think that everything happens for a reason, now I think that everything just happens. It's up to the individual to give it reason, to decide whether or not the thing that happens should have a reason to it."

"You mentioned 'success' a moment ago. What does that word mean to you?" I ask.

"Success for me would simply be that at the end of my life I've left all these films behind, that I left all these stories behind, that some stranger somewhere was affected by something that I had thought about. And it isn't so much ego as it's a need to share the way I feel about the world, or share my ideas, or share my emotions with people. And I think that's the great thing about films. After all these decades and all the cynicism and all the really trashy films that get made, people still go to these films because they really hope that two hours later they will be immensely moved by something; whether they laughed their head off or cried their eyes out, or just saw the most intense spectacle. I think that because of that emotional response film is a wonderful thing." Mark leans forward, obviously excited about the subject at hand.

"Film is one of the few outlets that people really have these days to let themselves become emotional about something. It's a romantic notion, but I like it. I'll be a bit disappointed in myself if I never make another film. Provided I live another 60 years—which is my plan—I will have made something else, because 60 years is a pretty long time. Going that long without making another film is not even really an option. I can't think of living a life where I just give all this up and I wind up being a clerk somewhere. It doesn't even seem like a possibility. Not to sound conceited, it just doesn't. There's no reason why I shouldn't make another film."

"Do you feel like you'll live up to your definition of success?" Brian asks.

"I think my life will be pretty successful," Mark says without hesitation. "I don't know along what front. It's a little terrifying, but it's also a little exhilarating too to be able to say 'God knows what I'll be doing next year.' Because there's always possibility out there. That's what keeps you going."

"A lot of people have problems with that ambiguity of life, how do you stay positive and focused given the flexibility you need in life in general?" Brian asks.

"I've found out that the only real way to get through the day is to sort of keep an eye on the very little things in life and the little accomplishments. You can't really count on people. You can't really count on the future. You can't count on education, a job, a house, Mother Nature, a car, on a relationship, on anything. You can try to count on yourself. It sounds kinda new-agey and cheesy, but I think it's a major step to be able to depend on yourself, to know that at any given time, I can do this."

"In the meantime," Mark continues, "I just enjoy the little things that are always going to be there, like grapes, or very pretty clouds or a little ant crawling around on the sidewalk that's doing something so fascinating that you just have to watch. And that's the stuff that makes life interesting. So I need to focus on those little things. It's ironic. You think the world revolves around you and sometimes, for me anyway, when I'm the happiest is when I realize there is something going on that doesn't matter if I'm there or not. It's just happening. It's just part of the joy. I just get to observe this beautiful thing, or this fascinating thing, or this bizarre thing, and that takes me to the next day."

His comment sinks in for a moment, and we all sit as if enjoying the moment. Then I continue what feels to me more like a chat with an old friend than an interview. "We hear people talk about 'success' all the time. When you're out and about, Mark, how do you judge if someone else is a success or not?"

"Unfortunately living in L.A. people tend to wear their success on their sleeves in terms of fancy clothes or designer sunglasses or a fancy car parked out front. To me that doesn't fairly denote success, it just denotes money. And the money can come from family, or luck, or they could be successful but not happy." He thinks for a moment. "Usually I consider someone successful if they just seem to be cool about who they are. At this point I can pretty much tell if someone is saying a comment that is self-serving or self-conscience, or they don't feel comfortable with saying it. When someone comes across as being fearless, I think that is a sign of success. When they can say whatever they want, where they can act like a jackass or have a goofy laugh and don't care and laugh until their sides ache, and if everybody is staring at them in the room, it doesn't matter because they are happy with who they are."

"Well I know quite a few people with goofy laughs that would agree with you!" I say with a chuckle, suddenly self-conscious about my own laugh. "As far as achieving your goals is concerned, are there any key elements you have found that have proved crucial?"

"The one thing that I think everybody who's been successful in some way or another—some that had money, some that won money, some that worked hard to gain money, whatever that was (substitute any word for money—love, power, respect)—is that they persisted. It's funny. You hear all these clichés when you grow up and they're such tired clichés, but as you grow older you think: 'Oh my gosh, they really are right.' This whole idea of never ever giving up is something that is very easy to forget. People hear it and say, 'Yeah, yeah, yeah, yeah, yeah, it's not as easy as that.' Well it is. If you just keep at it, eventually you're going to do something. It especially helps if you have the talent to back it up, but I've seen a lot of untalented people make successes of themselves because they never give up. I've seen a lot of really talented people never get anywhere because they didn't have the courage or ambition to go wherever they wanted to go. That's a shame. It's a real shame. I've seen people, just wonderful writers and artists, that just didn't have the energy. And you ask, 'Well, why didn't you do this?' and they reply 'Eh, I couldn't do this because of…' Geez it's so easy!"

"But you have to be persistent and you have to be brave," Mark continues. "The one thing I found out about being brave is that it really is an easy step to take. The greatest difficulties people have with doing a courageous act are that they are very afraid of what other people will say. I think that the one thing, if there's anything I can share, is that everybody, unless they have problems, really does respect someone who does what they want to do. If somebody does claim to lose respect for somebody because they went ahead and did what they said they were going to do then obviously you know who the problem is with."

Brian and I both nod in agreement. "Good point. And speaking of speaking your mind openly, we really appreciate you talking with us tonight." Brian says. Some internal clock of his must have just gone off and told him we have reached the respectable length of time for a friendly discussion, and any further questions would enter the realm of interrogation.

"Mark it has been a pleasure seeing you again," I add, acting on Brian's lead. "I can't wait to see the movie when it is released. Any ideas on when the premiere will be?" I think of the bright lights of the premiere and Mark standing before a mass of reporters, cameras and microphone. Entering the theater behind him is a crowd of L.A. beautiful people, each with a fancy car parked out front and wearing the finest jewelry, clothes, and successes on their sleeves.

"Not for a while," Mark says. He is probably asked this question all the time. "Perhaps sometime next year. First we need to raise some more funds and then get the final stages taken care of. But I'll keep you guys posted."

"Please do." I say. We collect our things and walk with Mark to the door.

"Best of luck on the journey," he says. "I'll be following along with you guys via the Internet."

"Excellent. Then we have our first viewer!" Brian says.

"Best of luck on the movie too Mark. We'll be watching for you on *Entertainment Tonight*." I say. We thank Mark again, exchange hand-shakes, and leave him to his evening.

Outside Mark's apartment Brian and I are alive with chatter. We walk with light footsteps around the house that Mark's apartment sits behind and continue across the street to where the Quest-Mobile is parked.

"Great interview eh?" I say.

"I think it went really well. You know, this just might work." Brian says.

"I know what you mean. Many of the things he said made me stop and think. A lot of it I agreed with, some was similar to my philosophies as well. I could even relate to some of his artistic endeavors, and the ones I couldn't I found very interesting." I ramble on as we reach the Jeep.

"We give it: two thumbs up." Brian says holding up a thumb. I instinctively do the same as he completes his scoring. "He was extremely easy to talk to. I wonder if all our meetings will go so fluidly and every-one will be so forthcoming with answers."

"Probably not. I think we just got really lucky for a first time out. But hey, I'll take it. Maybe it's just reinforcing that we are doing the right thing. Just meeting up with him and talking has made me feel high, like I'm on the right track." I say.

"I know what you mean." Brian says from the driver's seat. He starts up the Jeep and we head out of Hollywood.

"It must be nice to have known since age seven what you want to be doing with your life. As many things as I've tried and as much as I've done, I still haven't a clue." I say staring out the window.

"That's not entirely true," Brian counters me. "You know something about what you *don't* want to do. That's headway right there."

"You're right. But still, to know with certainty that you are on the right path, to know that 'this is what I want to do.' It must be a liberating feeling. Think we'll find many people like that out there?" I ask Brian as I motion for him to turn right at the next light.

"Don't know," he says. "Judging from the friends we've talked to I highly doubt it. It seems that for most people even if they did know from childhood what they 'wanted to be when they grew up,' events and people and obstacles have tended to throw them off course. But who knows, maybe we're completely wrong. Maybe everyone's like Mark, while we...we're the strange ones."

Yeah, we're the strange ones. We're the ones who have left our worlds behind and are about to head off on a 25,000-mile journey in search of answers that may not exist.

I gaze out the side window at the city street racing past: car washes, fast food, filling stations, restaurants, shops, homes, stores, auto-repair, apartment buildings. The crowds of L.A. lives calling it a day. The end to a very good day. I smile at my reflection in the window.

SIX. TWENTY-SEVEN

◆

At thirty a man should know himself
like the palm of his hand,
know the exact number of his defects
and qualities…
And, above all, accept these things.

Albert Camus

I remember my 21st birthday. Brian was there for that one too. I was staying out in Nebraska with him for the summer and as the day I turned "legal" approached I grew more and more excited. After all, I would now be legally permitted to go out drinking in bars and go to nightclubs and do all the things adults could do.

We celebrated that evening on the streets of Omaha's Old Market in true 21-year-old fashion. I stumbled from bar to bar, screamed it was my birthday, and produced my ID demanding a free drink. In most places this worked and by the end of the evening I had lost my ability to walk or say anything above the most rudimentary English phrases, all due to friendly bartenders contributions of free alcohol. Lucky for us Brian's younger brother Nick was a kind soul who volunteered (or did we volunteer him?) to drive us around for the evening, sitting in cafes reading as we went on our drink-fest.

That was my last big birthday. There have been others after that, a few cakes, some candles, even a surprise party that included a Christmas tree. But none have been as momentous as my twenty-first. None of the other years held any significance. No free stuff, no new abilities. Nothing.

But now I was turning again. Not the happy-go-lucky times of entering the age of adult inebriation. That had come and gone and frankly had worn itself out long ago. Now I was on the threshold of a new form of adulthood. It was finally time to turn the big THREE-OH.

This was the age that was always used as a benchmark. It was "by the time I'm thirty I'll…" Usually the statements concluded with material accomplishments, such as owning a big house, or a boat, or a place by a lake. Sometimes it was having this career or that, or achieving a certain level of corporate respectability. For the familial inclined it could be being married or having kids. All to be reached by age thirty.

But as my day approached I found I didn't have any of these things, nor was I even close to getting them. The only thing my turning thirty had to offer was the ability to check a new box on information forms: 19-24; 25-29; 30-34…check, that's me! I was in a new age bracket now, one that came with much more urgency and responsibility.

I had spoken to my older brother Frank once about the upcoming transition into my boring thirties and he offered a bit of wisdom from someone who had been there just two years earlier. "It's just some arbitrary date western society has come up with, Chris," he told me. "You don't see anyone celebrating or fearing turning 10,000 days old do you? Well why not? That sure seems like a much more logical point of celebration than thirty years." Spoken like the true engineer.

        *   *   *

My birthday arrives cloaked in a To Do List. I wake up thinking of all the things that still need to be done before our departure the next day. Last minute packing and shopping, things that couldn't be done until now. I climb out of bed ready to begin checking off the list and walk into the living room to find Brian already awake. He has already folded up his sleeping bag and sat it and his new Therma-Rest inflatable sleeping mat in the corner, trying his best not to fill the room with the clutter that so annoys me. He sits at the desk with the computer and seeing I was awake clicks the mouse to start the modem dialing. The irritating *click-chong-ring-buzzzzzzz-pling-plong-ting* of the modem connecting to the server fills the small apartment.

"Morning." I say entering the living room and sinking down into the sofa.

"Good morning," Brian chimes in good humor, his perky morning attitude a sharp contrast to my grumpy one. "And might I add, happy birthday!"

The words fall over me. *Birthday? Oh yeah. I'm thirty now.* I sit and let it sink in, mentally feeling my bones and joints for any new aches or pains. Nothing. The event had taken place while I was asleep. I had passed from my twenties into my thirties without recourse. My body didn't change. My mind didn't become feeble over night. I was just the same 'ole Chris, one day older.

"Thanks." I say humbly.

I look at the front door for a few minutes. *Are they coming?* I wonder. *Is someone going to show up at my door with a long list of failed achievements? Is the day of reckoning upon me?*

A loud pounding at the door. Outside a group of men in black stand waiting.

"It says here, Mr. Moeller," the Birthday Police will say, "that by today you are supposed to have a beautiful wife, two kids—one boy, one girl—a big house with two cars, a motorcycle, and a boat. Oh, and according to

your childhood plans you are now a famous writer, artist, musician, and corporate mogul."

"But I don't have any of that." I exclaim.

"No? Well then, we'll just have to add you to our LOSER list won't we?" The Birthday Policeman screams as he tears up the list and throws it in my face, confetti raining down on my pity parade. "Come on boys, we have a lot of posters to print up and hang around town, not to mention the news stations to notify." He says as he and his fellow Policemen stomp away. "Chris Moeller, failure at age thirty."

"Well do you?" Brian says.

"Huh, excuse me?" I say, shaking myself back into the living room.

"I said, do you want on the computer to send out any email." Brian said, apparently for the second time.

"No, thanks. I'll do it later." I reply. I guess he hadn't seen the Police.

"You okay?" He asks.

"Sure, just not all the way awake I guess. I'm going to go take a shower." I say getting up from the sofa and heading for the bathroom.

The To Do List gets checked off quickly into the day. We shop for last minute items, buy snack foods and soft drinks, and deliver more of my things into storage. It's amazing to see all you own consolidated into boxes and stacked on top of each other in a five by eight metal room. Thirty years of living in forty-seven boxes.

We return to the apartment in the late afternoon, now living entirely out of our road provisions: packed clothes, road towel, economy sized toiletries. The apartment seems lonely without my belongings, it is missing me already. We take turns in the bathroom cleaning up and washing the dust from the moving boxes off. We each choose some clothes from our respective bags to wear for the evening. It is our last night in Los Angeles and we have celebrating to do.

*   *   *

Birthday gatherings are odd events. Your friends are all there just like any other time you all go out together, but only this time you are the center of attention. No matter how the conversations stray along their usual course, they always somehow have to come back to you and your birthday. It's just one of those facts of life. At the birthday gathering someone, the birthday person, has to take on the responsibility of being the main attraction. Many people take to this responsibility easily, but I always find the sudden attention a bit unnerving. I am much more comfortable having someone else the center of attention and then making a game out of trying to steal all the glory for myself. More of a sideshow act than the headliner.

But as the carrot cup cake with one burning candle is set down in front of me I know I can't escape the spotlight. Everyone in the little Indian restaurant is staring at me over their curries, tandooris, and vindaloos now. As my friends sing and I blush by candlelight I sit and wait for a chance to blow out the candle, thank everyone, and volley the attention onto someone else.

"...happy birthday to you!" They finish singing in much better unison than when they started out.

"Yeah! Make a wish." Jeanne says from beside me.

A wish. What do you wish for on the night of your thirtieth birthday and the eve of departure on a grand and adventurous quest? I think for a moment, surprised nothing comes to mind. *Clarity*. The word pops into my head all of a sudden. *I wish for clarity*. Not really sure what the Voice Inside means by that, I stick with it and blow out the candle wishing for clarity. I am thankful they could only fit one on the cup cake.

A round of applause and I notice the other diners have gone back to their biryani, korma, and rasmali.

"Thank you, thank you. I thank you all for coming this evening from the bottom of my heart," I say in my best Cary Grant impersonation. Perhaps he would do better at birthday parties.

Then I think perhaps it isn't the light of the birthday spotlight that is causing me such uneasiness. Maybe instead it is the clouds of confusion over my impending departure tomorrow morning and leaving these friends behind.

I look around the table at the faces of my friends. Many I didn't even know two years back. The few I did know longer, save Brian, I hadn't known more than five years. And yet in the little time I've had with them they've already become part of my world. My entire L.A. social life seated at one table in the corner.

"So, are you all excited about the trip tomorrow?" Vivian asks from across the table.

"I sure am. I think the trip's going to be great, just what I need. Of course, I'm also still a little apprehensive about just upping and going. I hope you guys will still remember me when I get back!" I say, only half jokingly.

"So what's the plan? You leave tomorrow and then…" James asks from the end of the table.

"We leave tomorrow at noon," Brian begins.

"Yeah, we're launching from Media Park in Culver at noon if anybody wants to come and see us off." I butt in.

"And then we should hit San Jose by tomorrow night," Brian again.

"Unless we break down in the first hundred miles or so," I say and we both knock on the table. Knock on wood.

"Then it's up the coast—Sacramento, Portland, Seattle—before heading inland and across the northern half of the country to Boston." Brian says.

"At which point if we're still speaking to each other we will head south and continue back across to L.A." I say with a grin.

This comment brings a laugh from everyone at the table. "If we're still speaking" was often the subject of debate when we told people about the journey, including several of the people seated at the table. "You guys are going to drive each other crazy," people would say. But we never pay it any attention. We know what we are doing. Or we think we do.

"Well, we all wish you the best of luck on the trip, many happy times, an educational experience, and a safe return to us some months from now." Jeanne says raising a glass in toast. "Cheers!"

Everyone raises a glass and clinks them together before taking a swallow. The glasses return to the table and for a moment the spotlight is off and everyone engages in their own personal conversation. I pick at the cup cake in front of me.

"And if you find out any secrets to happiness and finding the right career be sure and give them to me!" Vivian says with a smile. She was one of the many people I talked to before the decision to take the quest was made. One of the army of people that seemed to be missing something.

"I will do that. But you should follow along with us via the web site and see if there is anything you find useful. Just don't let your boss see what site you are exploring; we're not sure if it will be mistaken for an employment search site." I say.

Conversations flow and soon we find ourselves no longer at Nawab's but at the Santa Monica pier standing in line for the Ferris wheel. When asked "what next" this was the first thing that dropped into my head. I have done the bar scene several times already this week as my birthday approached, and I thought something different for this evening was in order.

The view from atop the Ferris wheel is incredible. On one side the Pacific Ocean stretches all the way to China, pausing briefly to crash on the shores of Hawaii, Fiji, and Japan. On the other lie the cliffs of Santa Monica and the long spans of flat lands leading to downtown Los Angeles and the San Gabriel mountains way in the distance. Now in the falling darkness the city lights shine and sparkle, casting a glowing haze of light into the air. There never really is darkness in a city of this size, just a duller brightness.

On each rotation of the wheel Jeanne and I can see the others in the cars above and below us, jeering and shouting at each other just like kids. I lean over the side and fake vomit on Brian, Vivian, and Chantal in the car beneath us. They just look back and laugh. Leaning over the edge I think back to our sky dive. The Ferris wheel doesn't seem as exciting when I think of it in comparison to the jump.

How will the skydiving seem, I wonder, in comparison to the jump I am about to make in the morning?

THE LAUNCH

◆

It does not matter how slowly you go,
so long as you do not stop.

Confucius

We're up at eight and launch into a fury of activity. We pack and move last minute things into storage before beginning the long process of loading up the Jeep. Boxes and books and bags are meticulously loaded with scientific precision. Every bit of useable space is occupied, filled with something carefully chosen for strategic reasons, everything in its own special place. And somehow through it all we manage to keep a viewable space through the rear window. Once the doors are shut, this is what we have inside:

Two black duffels of clothes:
    Jeans
    Khaki dress pants
    Shorts
    Hiking Pants
    T-shirts
    Polo shirts

Button down shirts
Sweatshirts
Sweaters
Swimsuit
Socks
Underwear
Thermal Underwear
Polartek jacket
Goretex jacket (blue Eddie Bauer for Brian, eggplant Northface for me)
Hats (for me mainly, Brian looks incredibly goofy in hats)
Running shoes
Hiking boots
Sandals
Water shoes
Toiletries
Sunscreen (spf 30+)

Garment Bag
Dress suit, shirt, and tie (x2)
Dress Shoes (x2,...well 4. Okay, 2 pair)

Camping Equipment
Tent
Sleeping bags (x2)
Inflatable sleeping mats (x2)
Kerosene stove
Freeze-dried meals (x5)
Flashlights (x2)
Folding camp chairs (x2)
Pillows (x2)

Computer Equipment
Apple Powerbook G3 laptop computer
HP Deskjet 870 printer
Apple QuickTake 2000 Digital Camera

35mm Cameras (x2)
Sony Micro Recorders (x2)
Micro cassettes
Cooler
Bag of road snacks
Box of food
Box of books
Jump-rope
Dumbbells (x2, and I don't mean the passenger)
Frisbee
CDs
Music audio cassettes
Books on tape

By the time we finish loading the Jeep and take one last walk through the apartment to make sure we didn't forget anything it is already close to noon. We want to be sure to be at Media Park early so we can set up before the reporters and camera crews arrive. We stroll around the apartment, I say my good-bye to the ghosts I leave behind, and we hop in the Jeep bound for the launch site.

We arrive at Media Park after a short stop to pick up some helium balloons to tie to the Jeep. We thought since we don't have any signs on the Jeep yet we could use the balloons to draw attention to where we were parked. Not that it would be hard to spot us. Media Park is a small triangle of grass and trees lying right in the middle of Culver City, surrounded by major thoroughfares. While quite beautiful with its rose bushes, shade trees, walkways, and Southern gazebo, it is hardly big enough to get lost in.

We pull into the park and choose a strategic location just off the road, positioning the Quest-Mobile for the best shots. Brian and I both grab a bunch of the balloons we somehow managed to cram into the back of the Jeep and then tie them to each side of the roof top rack. The wind pummels the balloons as we do so, providing a bit of challenge to the task.

Then we sit and wait.

We didn't really expect anyone to show up. It was a Sunday and we had given the media little more than a 48 hour notice. Not only that but the people we did send the press releases to may not have been the right people for the task of covering such a momentous event. Hell, they may not even work there any more, such was our level of research into the matter. But we show up early and patiently wait anyway.

A familiar lime green car pulls in to the parking space next to us and Vivian climbs out. We have one person to see us off and that's a start.

"Good morning Viv, thanks for coming." I say walking around the Jeep to greet her.

"Am I it?" She asks.

"So far." I tell her. But then over her shoulder I see a huge motor home pulling up with the words RoadTrip America splashed across its side in bold letters. Our media coverage is here.

I had already briefed the group about RTA the night before at the party, so when we walk up to greet Mark and Megan now Vivian already knew who they were.

"Howdy!" I say as M & M step down from their home on wheels. Megan holds Marvin the road dog in her arms and he seems very excited to meet us. Or one of the park's trees.

"Good morning," Mark says back. Everyone exchanges handshakes and greetings and I introduce Vivian to the RTA team.

"Glad to meet you Vivian," Mark says. "So, would you guys like a tour of the Phoenix 1?" He asks extending an open door.

"Sure, that would be great." Brian says and steps into the rig.

Inside we are all impressed with the comfort and sophistication of the vehicle. Bedroom, bathroom, kitchen, computer work station / office, CB, satellite, the works. Immediately Brian and I feel inadequate with our little Jeep overstuffed with stuff we don't know if we'll ever use. Oh to be crossing the country in a vehicle such as this one.

Once outside again Brian and I resign ourselves to the fact that we weren't getting any press for the launch. We write it off to poor planning. But then we never did plan on trying to promote the venture until we had some content up on the website. And then it would only be to let people know about the site in hopes of reaching an audience who would find what we were doing useful somehow. Press at this point, while it would be nice, was not entirely necessary.

"I guess we'll get started," Megan says, the obvious writer of the RTA team. "So Brian…"

She begins interviewing Brian as I talk to Mark. Vivian spots Louise and James walking up to where the Jeep is parked and excuses herself to go meet them. More friends to see us off. After a few minutes Megan turns her questions to me and I recount the tale of how the idea hit us, how it developed, and what I hoped to find and accomplish on the journey. It sounds weird telling it now, minutes before we head out of town. It's as if all the planning and time leading up to this moment were a dream and I have just awakened to reality.

The interview over, we all stroll back to where the Jeep is parked and greet the new arrivals. I introduce Louise and James to Mark and Megan and thank them for coming.

"Hey, we couldn't miss out on seeing you off," Louise says.

"Yeah, so when are you leaving?" James asks.

"That eager to get rid of us are you" I ask.

"No, it's…" He stutters, becoming aware I am joking.

"I think we're about ready to head out now," I say. "I don't think anyone else is coming. But first let's take a few shots for the web site."

I climb back into the Jeep and pry out the digital and 35mm cameras. They prove not as accessible as we thought. We snap shots of everyone and everything, the moment in time captured forever by Kodak. Brian then pulls a chilled Mountain Dew from our cooler, shakes it up, and unleashes it across the hood of the Jeep. A poor man's christening but a hearty send off just the same.

"Well my friends this is it," I announce after putting the cameras back in the Jeep and drying some soda from my hands. "Thanks for everything," I say, first to Mark and Megan, with an exchange of good-byes and well wishes. I then turn to my friends and hug them each in turn, Brian following behind me.

"We'll keep in touch via email and hope you do the same. It will be nice getting mail every once in a while on the road." I say finishing up a hug with Vivian.

"Be careful driving." James says.

"We will." I stand and look at them for a moment, not sure what to do or say.

"Ready?" Brian asks breaking my indecision.

"Ready!" My enthusiasm spills out into the air. "Let's do it."

Brian climbs into the driver's seat and I walk around to the passenger's side and climb in. One light-bulb moment, one crazy idea, two life decisions, and four months of planning has come down to this moment.

We pull out of Media Park and head down Washington Boulevard, turn left on Sepulveda and right onto the 405 highway. The 405 carries us to the 10, the 10 to the 5, the 5 out of Los Angeles and into the great unknown.

PART II

◆

THE OPEN ROAD

You must be careful each time you step out of your door,
Because your front walk is really a road
And a road leads ever onward,
And if you aren't careful you're apt to find yourself simply swept away,
A stranger in a strange land with no clue as to how you got there

JRR Tolkien

A DAY IN THE SUN

———————◆———————

There is only one thing about which
I am certain, and this is that there is
very little about which one can be certain.

W. Somerset Maugham

I hear splashing and the echo of laughter: kids playing in a pool. I continue drifting as the sounds ebb and flow with the ripples of dream. Not a pool, the water is flowing. A river. Not laughter, it's the call of birds. The confusion over the new scene snaps me out of my dreamlike trance and I swim back to the surface of consciousness. I wake up and open my eyes to a strange and confusing world.

The sky overhead is clean and clear, still hugging the indigo remains of the night before. Looking down at my feet I see the sun climbing over the mountains to the east, yawning and stretching its beams across my hill. I lay my head back down for a moment and try to let it clear out the fuzziness of sleep. Deep breaths bring lungfulls of sage and firewood.

I gather up some strength and sit up in my sleeping bag, memory of purpose and location slowly drifting back to me. I have awakened in some unfamiliar places over the last few weeks, but none as strange as this: lying in the dirt, surrounded by a circle of stones, atop a hill over-looking a wilderness valley on the outskirts of Sheridan, Wyoming.

Rubbing my eyes, I hear the call of birds overhead again, and as if on cue it is followed by the splash of water. I can see the river below from where I sit but not the bend where the sound is coming from. For this I need to stand. I unzip my bag and pull myself out of it and to my feet. There in the valley below me two deer play together in the water. They drink and bathe and kick and splash, taking turns chasing each other. I watch them in amazement. Never have I had a more incredible alarm clock. I watch them for a few minutes until something in the woods behind them sends them scurrying off in the other direction, up the river bank, and into the woods on the other side.

And then I am alone again.

I stroke the fire and throw another log on, not really needing the light or warmth but thinking the flames would be good company. Then sitting back down my mind drifts to thoughts of coffee, donuts, cereals. My stomach is ready for breakfast. Pancakes, waffles, hashbrowns; all things sautéed, steamed, baked, boiled, and microwaved. I try to kick the thoughts out of my head. There will be no food today. No food, no water. Not today, not tomorrow. Get used to the hunger.

So instead I focus on the rising sun and try to decide what time it is. The sun was just rising so I guess it to be around 6:30am. I could just check my watch except for the fact that I left it in Sheridan with Brian. I decided it would be best not to have it. Otherwise I would be checking it constantly and drive myself crazy.

So in light of the lack of a watch I turn to the sun and a handful of rocks. Not really sure I know what I am doing but trying my best to convince myself I do, I dig a tall stick into the ground next to me but outside my circle. With it sticking securely straight up from the earth I then strategically place a few stones in a circle around it, making a makeshift sundial. I figure I can check it today by trial and error and then by tomorrow when I am really delirious it should be in full working order. This done and feeling smug and proud I sit back in the circle and work to clear my thoughts and begin my day.

The whole morning drags by in a slow progression of thought attacks. I have already learned two things about being isolated. The first is that time takes on new meaning when left to yourself and your own mind. It drags and speeds up with no apparent logical order or system. One moment taking forever, the next hardly an eye blink.

The other thing I learned is that when left alone with your thoughts they can be amazingly loud and excited.

I sit and I sit and I try to clear my thoughts but the resistance is incredible. Trying to think of nothing is like taming a tornado with a hair comb. My mind constantly sends out images and memories and ideas in a steady bombardment, just looking for something to pique my curiosity or catch my attention and pull me into a long stream of thinking, planning, or remembering. I think of my high school prom just after thoughts of a college spring break. A trip to Indonesia is juxtaposed with my brother riding his Green Machine in the backyard when we were kids. Ludicrous, incredulous, meaningless thoughts bounce around me. Someone has hit the "scan" button on my brain and it just won't stop.

Noon-ish.

By the time the hot Wyoming sun has flown up and perched itself at the crest of the sky my mind is a bit fatigued. I look over at my sundial and see the shadow is directly under the stick. High noon. With a grumble from my stomach, immediately the silly thoughts are gone and more pertinent thoughts of food and water come into mind. Burritos, pizza, Indian food, Chinese food, and bowls and bowls of ice cream. I shake my head trying to loosen the mind games. *Just let them go*, I tell myself.

I stand up and stretch and look around at the large boulder positioned on the edge of the clearing and the side of the cliff down to the river. A few of them cast shadows and could offer some much needed sun relief. Marcus had told me it was okay to leave the circle. Toilet activities aside, he said I could also go out whenever I felt it necessary. "There are no strict rules," he told me. "At least not this time."

Four times, he said. I had to commit to do this no fewer than four times during my lifetime. This time, and three more. It seemed doable. My cousin Craig lived here and I was bound to visit many more times as the years went by, so why not just make this part of each trip. Visit cousin, go on Vision Quest. Visit cousin, starve myself for days on a hill in the wilderness. It was perfect.

I step out of the circle, but first take a moment to center myself and thank the spirits for allowing me the opportunity. I wanted to make sure, above all else, that I didn't offend the tradition in any way.

Once outside the circle I feel a strange sense of liberation. All of a sudden the hillside, the cliffs, and the clearing were a huge landscape of excitement. I walk around the side of the cliff, hopping from boulder to boulder. As I walk the grounds of my new world I notice several areas where dry dead wood is lying around and I decide to be productive and collect some more firewood. I make several trips carrying logs and branches back to the clearing and soon have a huge pile of wood just next to the circle. I would be surprised if I managed to get through it all. But if not, it can be used by the next person.

This done and feeling like I have accomplished something for the day I pick out a smooth, comfortable boulder slightly shaded by a dead, battered tree and take a seat. Sitting there with a breeze blowing over me from the valley below I realize how lucky I am. It has been near 100 degrees over the past few days and yet today the weather is quite mild. Not only that but there seems to be a steady and constant breeze from the valley and if there were any mosquitoes around they seemed to be avoiding the hillside. The only real obstacle I had to contend with was the relentless sunshine. I needed to be very careful of this or I would end up a very burned man.

The minutes drag, the hours race, the dance of time continues. Still the inane thoughts of everything worthless come to mind. This is what it's like when you remove the TV, radio, mouse clicks, and constant chatter of society. It takes the mind a while to adjust to the silence and it fights the transition the whole way through.

A strange looking bug alights from a branch in the tree beside me and flies down over my head. I watch it as it crosses a chasm between the boulder I sit on and one just in front of me and lands on the side of the rock. Once there it shakes its wings and bobs its head downward as if doing some dance of significance. I am still watching when all of sudden it is gone, flying away and leaving me looking at nothing but the bare side of a rock. Instinctively my eyes drop to the ground and I notice a little cave under the boulder. There in the shade of the overhanging rock is a ball of fur and an eye staring back at me. I squint out the afternoon sun and focus on the shadowy figure. Rabbit!

"Hello there Rabbit! How long have you been there watching me?" I'm first surprised by the sound of my own voice, weak and airy out of a bone dry throat. Then it's the fact that I'm speaking aloud to a rabbit that comes across as shocking. *Perhaps this is the beginning of The Big Crack-Up*, I think to myself. Even more so when I imagine Rabbit talking back to me.

Good afternoon Chris. I see you survived your first night okay.

"Yes, so far so good. I didn't exactly sleep very well but it was a good night. I didn't see anything though." I say, my voice a little bit better now.

You have to be patient. It comes when you are ready.

"I know. It's just that patience was never one of my strong points. So tell me, what will it be when it comes? Do you know? Are you part of it?" I ask the stoic Rabbit.

Patience.

It's all he says. Or all I think he says. At this point the difference between the voices inside and out is just a thin line of imagination. I smile down at him and watch his nose twitch and his eyes stare.

"Okay Rabbit. Let's just wait and see."

The rest of the afternoon flies by. It takes forever. It floats, it races. Time's little game. The shadow of my sundial tells me it is late afternoon or early evening. Soon the shadow will be lost in the growing darkness.

Inside the circle again I stroke and build the fire until it is ablaze once more. I add a bit of sage brush and wave its smoke over me and the circle. The sunset is spectacular, bathing the plains in a wash of grape, strawberry, tangerine, and banana. At once I am reminded of a box of crayons melting on a hot afternoon in July and the bowl of fruit I am trying to draw with it. The clouds are flavored cotton candy or a snow-cone or a tutti-frutti sundae. I watch as the colors bleed from the sky and the darkness comes. *I see a rainbow and I want it painted black*, Mick Jagger sings to me inside my head, his brush successfully stealing my color and light.

I face east and my fire again and settle into my contemplative posture, sitting cross-legged ("Indian style") on my sleeping bag and staring into the flames. It had been one of the longest-shortest days I could remember. As I sit in silence I notice just that. Silence. My mind had slowed, emptied. Not completely yet. Still thoughts of TV shows (Space Giants vs. Ultraman, who would win…), forgotten faces (that girl in second grade, the one who sat next to me, just what was her name?), and useless home appliances (the sandwich maker by Ronco) creep into my head. But they are less frequent now and with less ferocity. It is getting easier to push them aside and dwell on the nothingness.

The fire fades and more logs are added. It fails once more and more logs are thrown into the hearth. The process of burning, sitting, thinking carries me into the complete darkness of full night. Here in the wilderness, now this is dark. Not the half darks of cities or the almost full darks of towns. Here is an inky blackness that flows over the world like a sea of nothingness. A bubble of blackness pierced only by the bright watching stars in the far distance. The stars and my fire.

The fire begins to die again and I add one more log, this time knowing I will be asleep before the process needs repeating again. I will let the fire die out as I sleep if it comes to that.

I lie back on my sleeping bag and stare up at the mosaic of stars. *Will it be tonight*, I wonder to myself. And then aloud, "Will it be tonight Rabbit? Tell me, will it be tonight?"

Patience.

The word echoes out to me. I close my eyes and wonder what visions will come. But it isn't visions that visit me in my sleep, only dreams of days gone by on the open road…

CREED

◆

Each friend represents a world in us,
a world possibly not born until they
arrive, and it is only by this meeting
that a new world is born.

Anais Nin

Northern California slides by outside, a landscape painted in all the colors of summer framed in the gray box of the windshield. Coming around a bend in the highway we pass the sign for a scenic overlook. When I see San Luis Reservoir in the distance I turn to Brian to ask him to stop off at the overlook but don't have the chance. He is already putting the blinker light on.

"Way ahead of you." He says as we take the turn into the overlook parking area.

We pull to the front of the parking area, and park the Jeep teetering onto the exit ramp back onto route 152 bound for Gilroy. In the distance the cool waters of the reservoir glisten beneath a sputtering of white clouds.

"Cool." I murmur, looking out at the view. "I'm going to take a shot for the web site!"

I climb out from the passenger seat and circle the Jeep to the other side, digital camera in hand. We had decided to add a photo album section to our web site so our friends and family could see where we've been and what we were doing. Of course, we also thought it would be a nice way to remember the adventure once it was all said and done.

"Lean out the window." I call to Brian. He lowers the window and leans out and I take the shot. Brian, the Jeep, the curving road, and a mountain peak in the distance. Visual poetry. "Great shot." I say as I get back into the Jeep.

We pull back onto the highway and continue heading west and north toward our first stop in San Jose. Brian hits the scan button on the car stereo, and it begins to race around the dial looking for stations, stopping occasionally to give us the choice of music it has found. It dances from reggae to rap to country to salsa before landing on a station that makes both of us reach for the stop button. My hand gets there a little faster than Brian's and soon the sounds of ELO are filling the Jeep.

The city streets are empty now, the lights don't shine no more...

Brian and I jump in at exactly the same moment, singing along with the lyrics and occasionally making up our own. Electric Light Orchestra, one of the first LPs Brian got shortly after getting his first record player in grade school. We each got our record players the same Christmas. He received ELO's *Greatest Hits*, and Queen's *The Game* with his. Santa gave me Supertramp's *Breakfast in America* and Styx's *Paradise Theater* with mine. I played my records over and over again in constant rotation on my new JC Penny one unit stereo. My state-of-the-art stereo not only had a turn-table but also had a radio, cassette player, and an 8-track player. All built into one slick faux-wood-panel covered unit. It was one of the most rockin' Christmas seasons in history.

Music has always offered a great way of adding to the quality of life. With the proper tune even the most mundane event can become enjoyable and entertaining. All you need is the right soundtrack. I have taken many songs and symphonies over the years and made them my own.

Songs from childhood conjure up fresh images, smells, and special memories. The Cars' *Magic* brings me back to the summer I learned to drive. *Purple Rain* transports me to high school, and when I listen to Led Zeppelin's *Hey, Hey What Can I Do* I am sitting in Kilroy's bar at Indiana University, the smell of beer and cigarettes and stale corn chips filling my senses. These songs no longer belong to their creators, they are forever mine and a part of my memories.

These songs began inside the head of a stranger where lyrics and tunes bounced around until the author finally felt compelled to spill them onto paper. They then were recorded and played and soon people like me were singing along with them in the shower, or at work, or on a cross-country road trip. The songs taken to heart and added to our own personal soundtracks. Here the soundtrack for our current adventure is just being written.

At one point during the song we both add lyrics where there are none, singing the same thing at the same time seemingly out of the blue. Things like that happen all the time with us. It's as if we have some telepathic connection or are momentarily sharing the same brain. It could arguably be that we are remembering the same thing from the past. Or perhaps it's that we know each other so well we just tend to think alike. I'm not sure how it works, I only know that since we were kids we would have this mental connection occur time and again. We would pick up the phone to call the other only to find him already on the line without the phone ever having rung. Sometimes we would begin to talk about something without warning and learn the other had been thinking about the same subject just at that moment. We can never know when it will happen or why it does. But with the eerie frequency in which it happens and the uncanny way we know at times what the other is thinking I tend to think it is something besides coincidence. Some crazy mystic bond that was forged in the fires of friendship. Wonder twin powers activating.

When taking a long road trip it is important to choose the right travel partner. You are going to be with the person for a very long time, under all sorts of circumstances, both good and bad. You will need to be able to converse on all manner of subjects to keep each other interested. And you will need to know when it is time to shut up and just sit in silence. Finding such a person is not easy. Finding someone who is wanting to travel in the same way to the same places at the same time as you is next to impossible.

The fact that Brian and I wanted to make the trip at the same time was a stroke of good fortune. The choice to travel together was an easy one. We shared common interests as well as had our different likes and dislikes. We have known each other for a long time and knew each other's quirks enough to know we would survive the trip. In fact, we have known each other so long that Brian often jokes to people we meet along the journey: "Chris and I have been friends for so long we thought the only way we could end our friendship and get rid of each other is to live in a car together for six months." But each time he says it across the country we get a little more curious as to if he may actually be right.

Brian and I met the first day of first grade back when we were six years old. I was sitting in the corner of Mrs. Toney's classroom amazing a group of fellow students with a picture I was drawing. Little boys in little chairs drawing with huge oversized fat pencils and crayons. Brian and his mother entered the room unannounced and waited by the door for Mrs. Toney to come and greet them, which she promptly did. As Brian's mom and Mrs. Toney chatted about the Ardingers' recent move from Pittsburgh, Brian broke free to see what the chatter was about in the corner of the room. He walked up to where I sat, looked at the drawing, and said, "Hey, cool picture of Captain America!" And we have been best friends ever since.

Of course, there were times our friendship was tested. There were squabbles on the playground in second grade, jealousies over grades and girls, and the Spider-man incident in fifth grade that threatened to end the friendship forever. But we managed to survive them all. We even remained friends when he moved to Nebraska for high school, sending letters back and forth, making the occasional phone call, and visiting with each other over summer breaks. We knew by then we had a friendship that could not easily be broken.

But then we never spent any real time together either. There were a few weeks here and there in Nebraska. There was the sophomore year at Indiana University when he decided to give my college of choice a try before heading back to the University of Nebraska for the advantages of in-state tuition. And there was the summer of my twenty-first birthday that I spent in Nebraska living with his family and working at a local telemarketing firm. But for the most part we were usually on opposite ends of the country if not the world.

But now here we were, cooped up in a cockpit just three feet from each other for the next six months. But as we sit and share the sunny drive, lost in the lyrics of Jeff Lynne and the Electric Light Orchestra, our friendship remains strong and we haven't a care in the world.

"You know what we need?" I ask Brian, then answer before he has a chance to reply. "We need to have a Creed."

"Okay." Brian says, not sure at all what I mean but sure that I will explain myself in due course.

"Think about it," I begin. "Six months. We're going to be on the road for six months. Right now everything is fresh and new and exciting. But down the road there will be times when we have driven all day and we're tired and we're hungry. We'll come to decisions where we choose poorly based on fatigue and thus miss out on the essence of our quest. If we have a Creed we can always defer to it and thus make the right decisions."

"Okay…" Brian says still unsure about what I am driving at.

"We both have things we want to accomplish on the journey, right? So we'll incorporate them into the Creed and thus insure they get done." I explain further.

"For example…" Brian eggs me on.

"For example, we will pass up no opportunity to learn from someone. Or we will take advantage of every chance to have fun!" I say and then think for a moment.

"We will meet and talk with everyone who wants to meet us." Brian suggests, getting the hang of it. "We will try to be a positive influence on the lives of everyone we encounter, no matter how small of an impact we have."

"Good, I like that. Here," I say reaching in the back seat and pulling a yellow legal pad out of the computer bag. "Let me write these down and then we'll keep the Creed in the glove compartment where it will be easily accessible."

I open the notebook and write as we continue to bounce ideas back and forth, shaping and reshaping the Creed over the next few hundred miles. I feel like we're kids again making up the secret sign and handshake for a super secret private club. By the time we reach the outskirts of San Jose I have a paper that reads:

The Quest-4 Creed

Listen not just to hear but to understand

Have a positive impact on the lives of everyone we meet

Learn and live with passion

Welcome every chance to meet new people

Embrace each opportunity to have fun on the journey,
enjoying the entire trip rather than just the destinations

Relax, smile, laugh

Above all else: friendship

I tear the page out, fold it, and place it in the glove box, intending to type it, print it, and laminate it at some point. I never do, but the wrinkled, tattered piece of paper comes in handy more times than we ever expected.

SAN JOSE

◆

Any path is only a path,
And there is no affront, to oneself or to others,
In dropping it if that is what your heart tells you.

Carlos Castaneda

Silicon Valley is such a weird place. Millionaires are made on a weekly basis as the insanity over all things Internet and computer related continues. You go to the grocery store and wonder if the unshaven, disheveled slob next to you is really some multi-million dollar start-up guru. It's highly possible he is. Here over-qualified staff take menial jobs for unknown companies just for the stock options. A career gamble, throwing the dice and banking they're going to land on your number. The company product will hit, the company will be bought out, and overnight secretaries and clerks join their programmer colleagues in instant wealth and retirement. It is an area where "success" in society's terms is sought and found.

Our time in San Jose is under Brian's control. It is his former domain and I know he has people to see and things to do, so I just sit back and go along for the ride. We end up spending three nights in the city, each night with a different of Brian's friends. He says it is in order to not burden any one person too much, but I think it's just because he wants to spend a little extra time with each of our hosts. The first night we crash with Neal and play a game of catch up over dinner. The next we do the same with PJ and then it's Jennifer's turn. Everyone is happy to see us. Even though it's only been a couple months, they seem to miss Brian already.

Our first full day in the city is spent working: uploading photos onto our web site, writing journal entries, and designing and ordering large door magnets for the Jeep. We thought in order to do this right we had to make our vehicle noticeable by the public. We wanted to open up opportunities to meet complete strangers on the road through questions about our quest. So we order two large magnets, one for each side of the Jeep. Each has our logo in bright colors and read: Quest-4, www.quest-4.com. This should draw some attention to the Jeep and offer a web site of explanation to anyone curious enough to look.

But we don't stop there. Across the rear window in three inch high white letters our web site URL greets cars behind us. Anyone staring at us in front of them during long highway miles would know where to find us. One step up from the "If you don't like my driving, call 1-800-…" To add a bit of flavor we fashion signs out of poster boards and stick on letters, putting one in each of the rear side windows. One reads "Crossing America in search of success" and the other "Los Angeles to Boston and back again." In one afternoon the Jeep has been transformed from just a vehicle into the one and only Quest-Mobile, the official transportation of our adventure.

The next day we keep busy with an interview. We made contact earlier with Brendan Kehoe, author of several books on the Internet, and set up an interview for the afternoon. Here was someone, we thought, that has watched the craziness of the Internet from the beginning. Being a guru on the subject he must have firsthand experience with the Silicon Valley phenomenon. He may even prove to be one of the overnight sensations himself.

As usual, we arrive at Brendan's way ahead of schedule and decide to go grab a bite of lunch first. We back track from his apartment and find a Taco Bell Grill several blocks away. Passing it we are immediately intrigued. We have been to countless Taco Bells, this fast food haven being one of the mainstays of road food. But this was a "Grill". Wow, fast food gone chic. Though I prefer seeing more of the local flavor of a place we're visiting and dining in non-chain restaurants, this one is hard to pass up.

We pull our newly decorated Quest-Mobile into the parking lot and head inside. The Grill offers up fancy architecture and gourmet foods, taking the usual Taco Bell menu and altering it slightly, giving each item a new delectable name. We order, sit and eat. Fast food in fancy clothing. We are not impressed.

As we eat I notice a man sitting alone at a table nearby. He is in turn scribbling into a notebook, tapping his forehead with the pen, looking completely around the room, then scribbling again. He then rustles through a stack of photocopied pages and begins the process all over. He seems nervous about something. Agitated. I watch him for a few more minutes until he gets up and leaves the restaurant, leaving his stack of notes and scribbles behind.

"Ready?" Brian asks ready to go.

"Sure. Did you see…" I start to ask about the madman at the table nearby but then think better of it. We stand, dump our trays and head out the door.

We leave the Grill, full of burritos and ready to roll on to our next interview. As we cross the parking lot I notice the man from the restaurant standing by the entrance to the parking lot. He's dressed in a charcoal gray suit with a cigar in his hand. He spots us and immediately calls out to us.

"What is Quest-4?" He asks from behind a puff of cheap cigar smoke. It throws me for a moment and then I remember that we were wearing

T-shirts with our logos on them. Something we had made up ourselves before we left L.A.

We walk over to where he is standing and offer a forty second version of our project explanation, thinking of the interview we need to be getting to.

"Yep, I knew it must be computer related," he says with a grin. From up close he looks weathered and worn, like an old pair of jeans that are ready to rip but too familiar to throw away. He has the odd look of someone too young or too old for the face he has, lingering there with pepper hair and silver stubble yet a tight face of a 20-something-year-old. His suit is clean but severely wrinkled and when he speaks he does so from behind gray teeth and the stench of cigar. I begin to wonder if he is one of the Valley's hidden millionaires.

"So do you guys use Macs or what?" He asks not offering his name or self-introduction. *His name must be Mac,* I think to myself, *because if he could choose his name this would surely be it.*

The question doesn't come as too much of a surprise. We were only miles from the Apple corporate headquarters. Brian, a true Apple Computer aficionado, is quick to point out our affinity to the Macintosh world and rattles off the array of Apple products that are making the journey with us. This delights Mac and he perks up. He begins to sing the praises of Apple and his great disdain for all things Microsoft. He congratulates us on our choice and I can tell immediately that we had somehow unknowingly been admitted into this man's inner circle.

Mac explains to us that he had just been analyzing an article he was reading about the new Apple operating system (OS) and that we should wait where we stood as he rushed back into the Taco Bell Grill to collect his notes and share his findings with us. Before Brian or I can respond he sets his cigar down on the pavement and runs back into the restaurant. Brian and I stand in bewilderment. I look at my watch and point out that we need to leave within ten minutes in order to get to our interview on time.

Mac comes running back out of the building with a notebook and several sheets of loose paper. As the door swings behind him a sheet blows away and he stops quickly to snatch it from the ground. When he reaches us he is already explaining his findings, his excitement kicking off his speech well before he was clear of the doorway.

He tells us he has deconstructed an article from some computer magazine and has made notes about the history and future of the Apple OS. He has drawn charts and tables in his notebook, as he shows us while he speaks, and has made comparisons and cross analysis. He speaks with such zest and enthusiasm he begins to draw us in.

He reads from his notes and hands Brian each sheet as he finishes reporting on its contents. The work and detail he puts into this dissection of a two page magazine article is equally amazing and frightening. The intensity with which he shares it is just a tad bit freaky. His eyes glow from some backlit fire and stare at us, as if looking for any bit of incomprehension. Or perhaps to see if we are really spies from Microsoft looking to squelch his Mac OS dreams.

His gaze makes me feel a little uneasy and I casually look around the area for possible hidden cameras.

Brian tries to politely interrupt him and tell him we have to go for an appointment, but Mac will have nothing of it. He has two interested listeners and he is only beginning his ministry of sharing the Apple gospel. He speaks with such delightful force that there is no way to wedge a word in and break his steady flow. If we are going to get out of here anytime soon, we will have to blow a hole into his conversation and jump through it screaming.

Then our opportunity strikes. Mac notices his still lit and nearly forgotten cigar lying on the pavement at his feet. When he bends down to pick it up Brian jumps in with our regrets of departure, and we angle for the Jeep across the lot. Mac catches up to us and thrusts the remaining notes into Brian's hands.

"Here take these. I've made myself another copy already. Maybe these can be useful to you." He says looking deep into Brian's eyes. Brian takes the handful of scribbles on notebook paper and we both thank him.

As we open the doors to the Quest-Mobile Mac throws out an invitation to visit him again. He tells us he can be found right there at Taco Bell Grill. He is a cashier there he explains, working to save up enough money to buy the Apple computer he has been dreaming of, one of his own construction based on the complex analysis he had just completed. The computer and a trip to Europe he has always wanted to take.

Mac had his dreams and wanted to share them with us. We pause for a moment and consider this, wondering if we are not giving Mac the time his story deserves. Here is a man with a passion, and a dream, and a way and means to get there. An odd fellow with a strange dream, but then who were we to judge that? We sit in silence for a moment and think about this. But our time is slipping away and someone is waiting for us in his living room, so we bid Mac farewell and quietly drive away.

"Thanks for the notes," Brian yells back to Mac. He has made the executive decision for us.

"Bye." I say in turn.

We bid farewell to Mac and wish him the best in his ventures. Then we climb into the Jeep and head out in search of other stories.

INTERNET GURU

◆

All men have happiness as their objective;
There are no exceptions. However different
the means they employ, they aim at the same
end.

Blaise Pascal

Brendan Kehoe is waiting for us on the sidewalk in front of his apartment complex as we walk up from the parking lot beneath it. At well over six feet with full ruddy beard and Hawaiian shirt he is hard to miss. He smiles at us as we approach and I find myself liking him immediately, he seems to radiate a friendly energy all about him.

"Hi, glad you guys could find me all right," he says as we reach where he is standing. "I'm Brendan."

"Hi Brendan, I'm Chris," I say taking his hand for the required shake.

"Brian," Brian says in turn.

"Come on in. Can I help you with anything?" He asks, noticing the backpack slung over my shoulder and the computer bag over Brian's.

"No thanks, we got it." Brian answers.

We walk down a path through the heart of the apartment complex to Brendan's apartment. If he is one of the gazillionaires from the Internet boom, he hides it well. The complex, his attire, his apartment all lack any hint of pretension. Inside the apartment I first notice a stark lack of hi-technology. I have been in the apartments of computer engineers before and they always had computer circuits, wires, and gadgetry lying around everywhere. Any order in their lives never translated into their living space, their apartments always a wreck. But Brendan's was spotless and organized. Books in shelves, pictures on walls. Everything as you would expect from any non-computer engineer's home. And if there was any computer equipment around, it was well hidden.

"Can I get you two anything?" Brendan asks.

"No, we're fine. Actually we just ate." Brian looks at me and I can see he's suppressing a smile, obviously thinking about our friend Mac and if he should be mentioned. My lack of action tells Brian all he needs to know. "So, should we tell you a bit about ourselves to begin?"

While Brian brings Brendan up to speed on who we are and why we are in his living room, I fiddle with recorders and tapes, taking on the role of sound man for this interview. Brian finishes up our tale and it's Brendan's turn. He takes a few minutes and tells us a bit about himself and where he's coming from.

Born in Dublin, Ireland, Brendan Kehoe moved to the United States at age four. He grew up in Maine and after graduation from high school left for college where he majored in Computer Science, spending most of his time hacking on software. After completing his first year he realized he couldn't afford to go back without finding a way to support himself financially. So he decided to take a year off to work both in the computer department on campus and as a computer programmer at a local software company. During this time, his university had just been wired to the Internet. Both students and staff constantly bombarded Brendan with tech support questions about this new technology, looking to him for a variety of answers. Brendan acted on the situation. Every time someone came to him with a question he wrote it down and answered it, working to have something to hand out so he wouldn't have to answer the same questions repeatedly. In February of 1992 he put the first edition of his tome out on the Internet, thinking there must be others out there who were going through the same difficulty of answering questions as he had been.

A few weeks later he received calls about his manual, calls asking him if he were interested in publishing. After talking with several people further about it, he published *Zen And The Art Of The Internet* in July 1992, making it the first book ever published about the Internet.

While Brendan was being published, he was in the midst of making life decisions to move out to California, start a new job with a computer software company, and begin a new path. A little over a year into his new life in California, Brendan was in a car accident and was admitted to the hospital where he underwent brain surgery. The doctors expected Brendan to suffer a loss of long term memory, but when he woke up a few weeks after surgery he surprised everyone with a near full recovery.

The accident couldn't keep Brendan down. Since then he has continued working and currently manages two teams of programmers. But his accident brought out hidden passions in the education field that he is now just beginning to explore.

"How did your interest in education come about as result of your accident?" Brian asks after hearing Brendan's background.

"At the time, after the car accident," Brendan begins, "a friend of mine, Mary Ellen Miner, took me around to visit some schools for gifted and talented children. Once there I would sit down and talk with the kids. Doing this I always left with such a great feeling. It was so cool to see the kids perceiving things and understanding what you're talking about. This made me more interested in getting involved in education. It made me start thinking, while I still enjoy a lot of the stuff I'm currently doing I want to go back to school and get my credentials to teach elementary school, 2nd to 4th grade. That's what prompted the writing of my second book: *Children and the Internet.* I wanted to go and sit down and try to address all the concerns that parents have and that teachers have."

"Has that affected your opinions on success and what you're striving for? What does 'success' mean to you?" I ask.

"I think success is reaching a point where day to day you feel you've accomplished what you want to accomplish. You're making some difference in the world that you wanted to make. I don't think financial or material goods necessarily mean success. Getting to grow is important too. You should never reach a point where you no longer have anything to seek or anything to aspire to. As long as you have a set of goals and you think what you are doing is helping you grow as a person, you are successful."

"It seems you have done a lot and accomplished a lot. Do you consider yourself a success?" Brian asks.

Brendan thinks for a moment then answers, "I don't know if I would ever rate myself as successful because that is like limiting yourself, like saying that this is as far as you can get. The fact that these books are there is cool, it still blows my mind that they even exist, and that other people are reading them is really nice. The fact that I have a job that I enjoy, and it pays well enough that we don't freak out when the bills show up. The fact that I'm very happily married is nice. So I would say I have succeeded in many of the things I wanted to achieve, and now I can only hope that I will succeed in the other ones as well."

"What do you do to make sure you continue on a path that makes you happy? Is there anything in particular?" Brian asks.

"I try to learn more about things as they present themselves. For instance I'm now learning cooking. Keeping things diverse is really key. If you keep things at a good enough rate of change you don't get stuck down in the mire. If you feel you have a nice broad range of things in your life, a little bit of many different things, you don't feel you are going to miss out on things or feel less by your own measurements because you didn't take advantage of something."

Brendan answers our questions so directly and comfortably and it hits me all of a sudden as utterly amazing. Here we are, complete strangers, sitting in his living room talking about life. To even be in someone's home is one thing, to listen as they speak openly about things so personal to them is incredible.

"What are some of the important things you try to remind yourself or others about tackling life's challenges and forging out a path." I ask.

"It's important to set very high limits on what you would accept in terms of changing your life. There are folks who know that something is the *one* thing they want to do, or that some place is the *one* place where they want to get to—something or somewhere completely different than what they are doing now. But they set these really high bounds on what it would take to get them to the point where they would really be willing to make that kind of a change. But you can go and say you are going to do it, and you just have to make sure that you feel driven enough so that you follow it through. As long as you try and as long as you realize that things are going to work out in the end, you have a way of doing it." Brendan stops for a moment as if collecting his thoughts. Then continues with a look to us as if we are in on a little secret.

"If you want to be a teacher for instance," he says with a smile, "it's just a matter of deciding at some point that regardless of the impact on a lifestyle we're trying to maintain, or the connections you made in some other field, you come up with the decision 'this is what I really want to do' and then just do it. Don't hold back just because it doesn't have this, that, and the other thing."

I think about pointing out his jump from "you" to "we" in his last statement and ask about his own plans for teaching, but let it slide. Brian is already moving on to another question.

"What would you tell a friend of yours who is struggling over their life's direction, Brendan?" Brian asks.

"I'd tell them to concentrate on yourself to some degree. Try not to live your life for other people too much. It's always good if you do to some degree, but at the same time don't forget that you are the one who is going to have to finish this game so you're going to have to make sure you end up in a place where you feel…not confident, not necessarily happy. You just feel good about where you are and what you're doing," he stops and then adds, "try to find a route for your life so you can explore the things you want to do at some point. It's never an immediate thing, you can hope to do it and then 20 years later you achieve it. Just always remember, maybe in the back of your mind, what it is you are really trying to get."

"Good advice," Brian says and then looks over to see if I have anything to add. I don't, I am still thinking about what Brendan had just said. "Thanks for meeting with us Brendan, it was great having this opportunity to talk with you.

"My pleasure and I wish you both the best of luck in your travels. I think what you're doing is very interesting."

"Thanks. We wish you the best of luck too. Let us know if you have any more books on the way." I say packing up our recorder.

Brendan takes the opportunity to once again ask if there is anything he could get us. We decline again and he walks us to the door where we say our good-byes.

Back at the Jeep I climb in on the driver's side and take the helm. Brian stows the equipment in the back seat and then gets in from the passenger side.

"Interesting fellow," Brian says as I pull out of the parking lot and head for Brian's friend Jennifer's house, our home for the evening.

"He was," I agree. "His comments about setting high limits on what it would take to change your life were especially interesting. I think that is very true. So many people want to make changes in their life but feel they have to reach some critical mass or breaking point before they will do so. They say they'll stick it out for X more years and see what happens, knowing good and well that they should just make the change now."

"In careers *and* relationships." Brian adds.

"I'm sure I've been in that position before," I say.

"It is very easy to get into a rut," Brian says. " You get stuck with that feeling of comfort or familiarity. You get used to the situation, even if it's one you might dislike."

"The devil you know versus the devil you don't sort of thing." I add.

"I wonder how different his outlook would be if he hadn't had a near death experience. The impact of illness or the death of someone near you must really create a shift in the way a person views the world and their priorities." Brian says as we turn onto the highway and head toward the southern end of San Jose.

"Yeah. But it's terrible if that's what it takes to make you see the light. It would be so much nicer to come to the conclusion to take action and make a change without the impact of tragedy."

We both think about this in silence for the rest of the drive to our home for the evening.

SACRAMENTO

◆

The question for each man is not
what he would do if he had
the means, time, influence and
educational advantages, but what
he will do with the things he has.

Frank Hamilton

I can't help myself. I continue to pace back and forth, throwing questions at Brian as he responds with more questions thrown back my way. I pause and look at Brian sunk into the cushions of the sofa then over at Davis the wonderdog in the corner. Davis' big brown eyes stare up at us in silly wonder as he is undoubtedly trying to figure out what the two crazy humans could be so anxious about. I begin to wonder the same thing.

"I think we have it," Brian says, breaking my train of thought. A train that has, as usual, veered severely from the course we had laid before it.

"What?" I ask, turning away from Davis and back to the sofa.

"We know the material," Brian continues. "We know our questions. We know the format, or at least how we think it will go. We are ready."

I think about it a moment, my pacing brought to a sudden halt before Davis. We have only been on the road for a few days, that is true, but we have thought about the project for several months now. Whatever challenge lies before us is only the next step. But a crucial step it is. This is where we find out if the project will really fly, if others are really thinking about the same issues we have been. Today we will meet a group of strangers—a group of our peers—and present them with our questions and see if what we are doing will make any difference in the lives of others. And Brian is right. All our planning and all our past efforts has led us to this point, and for what it is worth we are ready.

"You're right," I answer back slowly. "I guess we are." And with that I plop down next to Davis and give him a friendly pat on the back, sending a clump of yellow hair flying into the sunbeams falling through the window from yet another beautiful California July afternoon.

It feels good to sit down. Ever since arriving in Sacramento earlier in the day I have been pacing around, walking back and forth, and busying myself with preparations for the evenings activities. Sacramento is our first unplanned stop, the first location added onto our journey due to the input of others. Before we left Los Angeles we sent emails to friends and family telling them about our quest. Brian received a reply from one of his brother's high school friends he hadn't seen or heard from in years, Jennifer Fearing.

Jennifer was living in Sacramento and found that our quest struck a chord with her. She was struggling with some life issues of her own and said she would love to see Brian and I and discuss it with us if we were willing to add a stop in Sacramento. She went on to say if we were interested she could get a group of people together and we could have a group discussion. The idea immediately intrigued us. We thought it must be a completely different dynamic to talk with a group than with individuals, especially a group of complete strangers. We readily accepted Jennifer's invitation and added Sacramento to our itinerary. Soon after we received another email telling us not only that the group discussion was a go, but that a reporter from the local paper would be attending to cover it. All of a sudden we were on stage.

*   *   *

There is a knock at the door and the first of our guests has arrived. Jenny welcomes them, acting in impeccable hostess fashion. In the living room Brian and I are introduced and exchange handshakes and salutations with the new arrivals. We get no further than the next room when another knock at the door brings another guest. Soon the dining room is filling up with people gathered around a table full of pizza and snacks, exchanging job stories and casual introductions.

As we mix and mingle, meeting our friendly guests, Brian and I listen to the conversations being carried out around us. People offer up their names and job titles and tell about where they work and what they do to earn money. Brian and I glance at each other from other sides of the room and in an instant we know what the other is thinking. That funny telepathic link again. The words and sentences and grammar don't come through the mental wire, we just simply feel and understand the subject of each other's thoughts.

We let the telepathic connection pass for the moment, but will catch up to it later. We will discuss how we would like to change the way people interact socially. How it would be so much more meaningful and insightful if questions about work and livelihood were suppressed in conversations until later. If the question "what do you do" would be taken more as "what do you do in life that you enjoy" or "what is your passion" rather than "where do you work." We decide to never answer the question as is expected by societal norms, but instead to break out of the mold and run with our answer along a different path. What do I do? I like to travel, and meet people, and write, and read, and paint, and draw, and see foreign movies, and…

The pizza slowly migrates from table to plates and the crowd that has formed is guided onto the back deck. Outside the air is warm and smells of fresh cut grass and flowers. We gather around a small table, sitting in a circle facing one another. There are eleven of us in all: Brian and I, our hostess Jenny, a reporter from the Sacramento Bee newspaper, and seven of Sacramento's rising stars of the business world; men and women from all different backgrounds and occupations. We go around the circle and introductions are made once again. Next to me and going around the circle sit: Alison apRoberts, newspaper journalist; Nicole Kimmel (25), entrepreneur; our host Jenny Fearing (27), economist; Steve Johns (30), attorney; Sailaja Cherukuri (30), senior consultant for the California government; Greg Hayes (28), public relations executive; Laura Mahoney (32), journalist; Seth Merewitz (28), attorney; and Joel Schwartz (32), research director.

Then we are back to Brian at my left. "Great. Well my name is Brian Ardinger and this is Chris Moeller and we are what makes up Quest-4. We'd like to thank you all for coming this evening, it's great of you to participate in our project." Brian begins.

I feel the ball bounced over to me without gesture or action and I pick up from Brian. "Yes, thank you for coming out to meet with us. What we will be doing this evening is having a casual discussion on the meaning of success and successful living. We hope you will speak freely and openly, as this is just a friendly forum and there are no right or wrong answers."

"But first," Brian continues without missing a beat, "I guess we should tell you a bit about our project and what has brought us here to you today. Well in the way of background, the Quest-4 project came about around six months ago when Chris and I were both living else-where in California…"

I look around the room as Brian recounts how the idea for the quest came about, what we were doing at the time, and what steps we have taken to get us to Sacramento today. Everyone listens attentively and with genuine interest. It seems like the story is reaching some of them on a personal basis. Our quest is all of a sudden not ours any more.

The conversation jumps and runs as Brian finishes our story and I turn the attention on our guests, throwing out questions to start the discussion. The crowd needs little push and soon the discussion is full force and self-feeding. Subjects are thrown into the pot, questions brought up and tossed back and forth. Brian and I are now merely observers, watchers from the outside looking in on a council determined to find answers to the questions plaguing society. We hear:

"A lot of people our age are on the right path, but not necessarily the right career. As long as you keep learning, you're probably going to be on the right path. As long as you try something. If you find you don't like it, you can move on."

"I think everyone does have their own path and for me at least, a big portion of success is being happy and knowing yourself and then pursuing with vigor whatever it is that continually makes you happy. "

"Maybe success requires that you have to be willing to take a step off your path. Probably most of us growing up were going to go to college and we had some interests we were going to pursue, and then the job you were supposed to take became clear based on what you studied. And then when you realize that it might not be the right path it feels risky to step off the path. But sometimes you have to be willing to do that."

"I think one of the reasons our generation changes jobs is that our goals aren't as tied to a single career. My goals are beyond my career. My career is part of those goals, but I'm on the exact same path that I've always wanted to be on. I've had multiple jobs, but my path hasn't changed."

"People shouldn't define themselves solely by their jobs. It has to be a complete picture. My job serves a particular role, but what I do outside of my job can fulfill me as well. Sometimes I sit down and feel so overpowered by my career and job that I'm trying to find *everything* in my job. I'm trying to find money, job satisfaction, and doing good. No job is going to do all of that. So you have to draw a line at some point and say: My job stops now, and my life begins here."

The conversation progresses and its focus grows more and more narrow and soon the group is concentrating on the Sacramento scene. They discuss the city's advantages and disadvantages for struggling to find the right path and what they can do to improve local problems. Brian and I sit back and let the conversation play itself out, not really wanting to interrupt. We are more interested at this point in seeing the momentum of what has been born and watch the direction of its growth. But soon it is obvious to us that the conversation is wearing itself out. With a few quick injections into the conversation we pull in on the reins and bring it back to a broader picture. Then slowly, we steer the discussion to an end.

As the discussion breaks up so does the crowd; people pair off or form little groups to discuss their own issues and ask their own questions of one another. I walk over to where Brian is talking with Jenny.

"So Jenny, what did you think?" Brian is saying as I approach.

"I thought the evening went very well, I got a lot out of it. How about you? Did you enjoy it?" Jenny asks.

"I thought it was great, thanks so much for arranging everything," I say.

"My pleasure. There were a few things that I wanted to bring up and discuss but..." She is interrupted by a series of good-byes that were being thrown at her as people got ready to leave. "Excuse me." She says as she hurries over to see her friends and new acquaintances off. We'd be there all evening and had plenty of time to talk later.

"This really is going to work, isn't it?" Brian asks as we watch the crowd mingle and disperse.

"I think so. Everyone was so receptive it was amazing."

The evening was a success by all accounts. We can tell by the animated conversations swirling around us, both during the discussion and now, that the quest clicked with the group. They understand, empathize, relate. The issues at hand were not ours, were not limited to our circle of friends. There is something more to it, some underlying current pulsing through our generation that we have tapped into. We weren't crazy after all. Or if we are, we're setting sail on a crowded ship of fools.

But the question remains: why? Why is it that so many of us seem almost lost, sailing without a rudder. Is it the enormous pool of options? The constant change and "upgrades" we see in society around us? Or is there something happening out there that we just don't see.

And if this is prevalent among us, this confusion, then why aren't we talking about it? Why aren't we sharing and supporting one another in our quests? So many questions yet to answer out there on the roads of America.

NIKE TOWN

◆

Take things as they are.
Punch when you have to punch.
Kick when you have to kick.

Bruce Lee

I throw another punch and try to break off his attack but he just keeps coming. A left and a right and I'm falling down again. I fight the invading darkness and roll out of the way just before his massive form comes crashing down on where I had just lay a second earlier. On my feet again I circle around behind him and let loose my attack. A kick to the back staggers him. I follow with an artillery of punches: left, right, uppercut, hook. For a second, for the briefest moment in time, I think I have him. I think I will walk away from this and live to tell about it.

But it only takes a second to turn it all around. He spins on his heels right into my right hook and takes it without flinching, so huge and powerful is he. Then with one well timed and directly placed jab I am down and out. My head reels from the impact as I'm lifted off my feet and thrown backwards from the brute force of the blow. I hit the ground in a motionless pile of hurt, and there I stay defeated.

And dead.

"Man! What a fight!" The gloats come as if from some other plane of existence.

The laughs come from right beside me, guttural chuckles of amusement. Funny ha ha's from my travel companion. Brian laughing and enjoying my painful death.

"Man, he slaughtered you!" Brian yells and slaps me on my lifeless shoulder sending me a jolt to jump back into animation.

"Hey," I say, "it was close. I'll get him next time. No way Spidey will go down twice in a row. Here big shot, you try." I toss the game controller over to Brian and melt back into the huge white cushions of the sofa next to Morgan. "Kick his ass buddy." I whisper over to Morgan as I shake the tension of the video fight out of my tired thumbs.

With a few clicks the game starts again. Morgan chooses the Juggernaut again while Brian opts for Iron Man. The battle of the Marvel Heroes starts anew.

That's Morgan. My one time partner in crime on the streets of Shanghai, *Punisher* fan, sports fanatic, Chinese scholar, and rising star in the Nike empire.

"You boys still at it?" Bindi says turning the corner of the sofa. She says it more as a comment than a question. Being the soon-to-be-wife of my old friend Morgan Keldsen, she is used to such juvenile behavior from him and his friends when they visit. And she's so understanding of it that she has even taken it upon herself to bring more beer and chips and salsa to us. "Why aren't you playing Chris?"

"Killed him," Morgan says without looking away from the game or showing any emotion. He has his determined video face on now.

"Yeah well, I'm in the next round and you won't be so lucky." I say spraying tortilla crumbs.

"Were you guys warm enough last night, or do you need another doona?" Bindi asks. At first I'm not sure what she means and then I remember my lesson in Aussie speak from the night before: *doona* means comforter or thick blanket.

"I was just fine," I say trying to mimic her accent and failing miserably, "If I get too cold I'll just throw on my jumpah." I remember *jumper* meant sweater.

This morning I woke up from under a *doona* and went into the kitchen for *brekky*. Then after a quick bite of vegimite *toasty*, I went upstairs to get dressed for the cool, cloudy Portland weather. Unfortunately I didn't pack any *skivies*, so I relied on my *wind cheata* for warmth. I was living in the land of Oz.

"All right then. I'm going to leave you boys to your games. I'm off to bed. See you for lunch tomorrow right?" Bindi asks as she stands, gives Morgan a slight kiss on the cheek, and heads for the stairs.

"Sure will. G'night." I say for all of us, knowing the other two are too far into their death throws to have noticed any of the conversation that has just passed. Bindi nods and heads up stairs.

"Oohhhhh!" A mutual yell from the players. Brian managed to beat Morgan while I wasn't watching. Now it would be him and me, our childhood rivalry revisited.

"Night hon, I'll be up in a bit." Morgan yells back at Bindi as he passes his controller my way. "Sure you guys don't want to stay another day or two?"

"Wish we could, but we have to get to our next stop for interviews." I say. I have thought about staying longer many times during our three day stay in Portland. Though they both headed off to the Nike Empire every day for work we could see them in the evenings and we had such a great time hanging out over the weekend. But we have to get to Seattle and then further on in our itinerary in order to keep appointments we have already made. As much fun as seeing Morgan has been, we must be moving on.

"Pick." Brian says from the other sofa. I look up to see he has stuck with Ironman. I toggle with my thumbs over to Spiderman.

"But we'll stop in to the Nike offices tomorrow for lunch for sure." I say as if offering some consolation prize.

"Ready?" Brian asks, drawing my attention back to the screen again. "Let's do it."

And with that I punch Brian and begin the battle to the death.

*   *   *

We notice the Nike Campus long before we reach its front gate. It's difficult to miss with its grassy hillside wall with a large "swoosh" on the side. As we pass under the running track at the front gate I notice a couple of runners circling the track at a brisk pace. Nike employees taking their usual lunch time exercise.

We continue down the flag-lined entrance and pull off to the side and into one of the guest lots. Morgan told us again this morning where to park though it wasn't really necessary as we were just here a couple of days back. We stopped in to see Morgan and find out if there was any chance we could meet with Nike's CEO Phil Knight. Unfortunately, due to severe poor planning on our part and a business trip on Phil Knight's, we were unable to.

As we enter the campus arboretum we pass buildings called Prefontaine Hall, McEnroe Building, Bo Jackson Sports Complex, all on the way to the Michael Jordan center where we will find Morgan and Bindi's offices. The area is spotless. The buildings, the grounds, even the air seems to conform to a Nike decreed cleanliness. I imagine several teams of custodians wearing Nike shoes and different colored smocks running around the campus picking up trash and slam dunking it into the trash receptacles. Each day the cleanliness score for their area would be posted in a never ending Nike Janitorial Tournament.

We enter the shiny Jordan Hall and are greeted by massive photos of the man hovering above glass encased relics of his illustrious career: an autographed ball and jersey from his days at UNC, the first pair of Air

Jordan's he ever wore, and Chicago Bulls uniforms. An ample shrine to the living legend of the game.

We make a call up to Morgan's office, and in a few minutes he and Bindi join us in the lobby. They greet us as if they hadn't seen us in years, smiles and handshakes and hugs for everyone.

We decide on the cafeteria out of Nike's four restaurants to choose from. We enter and go our separate ways, each heading to the a la carte area of preference. I bump into Brian at the salad bar and can't resist an under-my-breath comment.

"Jeez, are we in some youth utopia or what?" I say as I shovel greenery onto my plate.

"I know," Brian concurs, "I haven't seen anyone here much past thirty years old."

We both look up from the salad bar and around the room. The place is packed with hungry lunchers. But it looks more like a yuppie university dining hall than the cafeteria of corporate America. Khakis and polos and running shorts and sports shoes and pullovers. No ties, no glossy shoes.

"Maybe it's like in the movie *Logan's Run*," I say back in the direction of Brian, "Once you turn thirty it's time to 'renew'. They either kill you, retire you, or ship you off to the sweat shops."

I turn to see Brian's chuckle over this and instead see a young blonde woman standing next to me with a bowl full of beets and cabbage. She is looking at me perplexed and obviously not amused.

"Hi." I say out of nervous reaction, then offer a feeble smile and scamper away to hide behind the sandwich bar. Brian has disappeared into the check-out lines.

As I collect the last of my things and head for the check out stand I hear a roar from the crowd of employees (*renew, renew*) packed into the central dining room. Once I pay and break out of the check-out line I can see what is causing the commotion and emotion. On a big screen TV at the end of the room the World Cup is being played out live via satellite. Meanwhile the boys and girls of the Nike Empire cheer on their team in frat-like manner as they chew macrobiotic meals and sip herbal teas.

Renew, renew!

I go outside to clear my head.

I intentionally walk very slowly as I look around for the others, listening in on others' conversations as I pass by each table. One group is talking about a game they had just seen. Another hosts a group of young men comparing torn ligament stories. At the next table a young woman shows her male colleague proper rowing technique.

I find the others sitting at a table in the sunshine next to Lake Nike. Of the collection of multi-colored Nike umbrellas they chose one of the red ones.

"Quite a spread you got in there guys. And you sure can't beat the view or the dress code. Think there's any openings?" I ask in jest as I sit down. Not that I hadn't thought about it before, working in such a beautiful environment with beautiful people cheering on beautiful events.

"Could be. I've been telling you that ever since Shanghai." Morgan says across the table.

He was right. Ever since joining the Nike team Morgan has been talking it up to me and saying how I should go out for a job. Having secured his dream job, Morgan's next step was to try to align all his friends around him. He has already succeeded in one of our mutual friends, getting him on board a year earlier. But he was still working on me and has been ever since joining the team himself.

Morgan is one of my "China Friends." I find I tend to group my friends into sets based on time and geography. I have my "High School Friends" that consist of anyone I knew in or before high school. Brian is included in this group. Then there are my "College Friends" that I met and shared my life with during my college years. After that I traveled to Hong Kong for a year of study abroad and made my "Hong Kong

Friends." When I then decided Asia was too interesting for just one year of exploring I landed a job that would keep me in the area working across the border in China. That's where I made my "China Friends," my last group prior to my handful of "L.A. Friends."

Morgan and my China Friends were part of the new breed of young workers in the global economy. Asia is crawling with them. A young generation of executives and entrepreneurs that traveled overseas to play and ended up staying on, getting employed, and becoming pillars of their expatriate communities. There they are given great responsibilities that are passed on to more senior personnel in the corporations' domestic counterparts. In China it wasn't uncommon to see twenty-something general managers, marketing managers, and senior consultants who were fresh out of college or off one of the many Asian trekker trails. It is always amazing what a clean cut, good suit, and a ton of corporate faith can do for these fresh young men and women, all trailblazers on the path of new global enterprises.

I guess I could be counted among their ranks. I went from student of Chinese language and literature to office manager to branch manager of an international shipping company in just three easy steps: apply, get accepted, get promoted. Not bad for an art student without an hour of business training.

Maybe that's where Nike fills its ranks. The young faces walking these halls and panting on the running paths are pulled from the pool of international seekers, from my peers who braved foreign lands in search of something that eluded them at home. I wonder if they too are still wondering what exactly that is.

It's something I've wondered from time to time, if there is a side effect that goes along with international experience that we don't realize at the time. When exposed to more of the options and choices the world has to offer, does it lead someone to become more restless and less decisive? In short, is my experience overseas a result of my confusion over life and the desire to explore all options, or the cause of it?

"Did you find anything to eat?" Morgan asks eyeing my heaping plate of food.

He snaps me back into the scene. Without knowing it I drifted into looking around the courtyard and trying to imagine everyone's background and life history. How many of them went over *there* and ended up *here*?

"Yeah," I answer looking down at my plate. "Maybe I went a little overboard. But whatever I don't eat I'll save for later. We have a cooler in the car." I reach down and take a bite out of my sandwich.

Whatever the cause and effects of my previous travels, they will have to wait. For now I have a new quest to discover and a new journey ahead.

SEATTLE

─────────◆─────────

If you want to see the sun shine,
You have to weather the storm

Frank Lane

We arrive in Seattle by late afternoon and immediately try to find my brother Randy's place. I had visited him in Seattle before, but he has moved since then and all I had to guide us to his new apartment was an address and my memories of the city. Each proves to work quite well.

We continue north of the highway five—or as we like to say in the South: I-5, pronounced "eeeeeeeeye-fiiiiiiiive"—past the city center. When we reach an exit for U-Dub (localese for the University of Washington) it looks familiar and I exit off the highway. Acting purely on instincts now, I hang lefts and rights with my gut navigating us. I continue past where I think a GAP might have once been, turn left off the street where that Irish bar was, go past a grocery store where I might have shopped once, turn right at the Futon Store that I always wanted to go in. And then we successfully find ourselves in Fremont, home of Seattle's art community, trendsetters, and my brother.

We turn right onto Fremont Avenue at the bridge leading back into the city and climb the long hill away from Lake Union. Now we have

just to find the right address. Toward the top of the hill we find a number match and pull the Quest-Mobile into a spot across the street.

Bzzzzzzz-click. The intercom at the front door of the apartment complex rings into nothingness. *Bzzzzzzz-click.*

"Maybe they're not home yet." Brian says.

"Hello-*snap crackly pop*," the faint voice comes over the intercom. I
can tell it's Tamblyn, Randy's wife but can hardly hear what she is
saying.

"Hi! Hey, can you speak up I can't hear a word." I yell into the little
box. The line goes dead again.

Bzzzzzzz-click. I ring again, not sure if I'm being rude or logical.

"Hi," It's Randy and much clearer this time.

"Hi, we made it!" I say covering both the trip and our new found
communication.

"How was the trip?" Randy asks through a relay of wires and gizmos.

"Good. But couldn't we talk about that inside?" I ask.

"Sure. I'm going to buzz you in. Go all the way to the roof, up all the
stairs. There's a roof-top garden there with a great view and we'll meet
you up there." *Cla-chink.* And the line is dead and the door buzzes open.

Randy was right, the view from the top of his building is amazing.
From its perch high on the hill you can see all the way down to Lake
Union and beyond. Were Seattle's Mt. Rainier not so elusive we would
be able to see it as well. But today the clouds keep it from view. We enjoy
the warm breeze and glassy view a few minutes longer when my sibling
and sibling-in-law finally show up.

"Quite the view, eh?" Randy calls over to us as he enters the roof area
from his apartment building.

"Very nice." I say. We haven't seen each other in over two years, but it
always takes a while for our conversations to get past short comments
and quirky statements. So instead of asking how each other has been or
bringing the other up to speed on the latest challenges, life events, and

triumphs we instead banter about old TV shows, soft drinks, and fresh ideas for movie screenplays. Brian and Tamblyn play right along.

Soon we turn the conversation more to the moment at hand and decide to hit the streets to see a few sights before Brian and I move on to where we will be staying for the night. Brian had a friend living in town and we thought staying with his single friend would be more comfortable than with my married family members. Kristina, our host for the evening, would not be home until later however. So the rest of the afternoon was ours.

We walk down the street and begin a rushed tour of Fremont. We seek out the Fremont Troll, a huge concrete sculpted creature that sits underneath a bridge clutching a discarded concrete VW Beetle. From here we head south to the Freemont Library where Tamblyn checks on some books on order and Randy sketches out a makeshift map of Joel Garreau's theory on the regionalization of America he thinks might be of use to us.

Outside the library we head back into Fremont, stopping momentarily at *Still Life in Fremont* for a cup of real Seattle coffee. Not Seattle's own Starbucks or other mass produced chain java, but real beatnik blend served in a unique coffee house with original art and weekly poetry readings.

With hot coffee in hand we stroll back past *Waiting for the Interurban*, a statue of four people waiting ever patiently for the bus to arrive at the corner bus stop and whisk them away to Ballard or Green Lake. As is the norm for the statue, it is decorated for some local event, this time with balloons and streamers and a sign wishing Debbie a wonderful birthday.

Further up our tour guides show us the Freemont Rocket and the Red Hook Brewery, pointing out the statue of Lenin on the loop back into town. The tour ends back on the corner of Freemont Avenue where we ponder what to do next.

"I need to call up Kristina and see about meeting up with her later," Brian suggests.

"Okay. Why don't you see if she would like to meet the four of us out somewhere for dinner. Then we can just follow her back to her place." I suggest. Brian takes the suggestion to the pay phone across the street while we lean against a wall outside a bookstore and wait.

"So what are your plans while in town?" Randy asks. "Who are you going to talk to?"

"Let's see, we're meeting with two ladies tomorrow. One's an entrepreneur and the other is an accountant. No wait, that's Tuesday, not tomorrow. Tomorrow we're meeting with Steve Roberts."

"Oh, you did get a hold of him. Good."

"Yep. Do you want to go with us?"

"I would but I have to work."

I first heard about Steve Roberts when I called Randy about the idea for our quest. Randy was immediately supportive of the idea as he usually is of all my creative ventures and was quick to make suggestions. One of which was to try to contact Steve Roberts.

"Have you ever read the book *Computing Across America*?" Randy asked me.

"No. What's it about?" I confessed I never heard of it. Randy, on the other hand, seems to have read, or heard of, everything.

"It's written by this guy named Steve Roberts—who incidentally lives somewhere up here near Seattle—who quit his job and traveled around the country on a bike fitted with computer equipment and wrote about all his adventures. He sounds like a really cool guy. I even emailed him once and got a reply back. You should email him and see if he'll talk to you."

I did and he would. I did some research on Steve after talking with Randy that day. I found a copy of his book in the local library and read through it. I learned of how he is now taking his computerized bike travel idea and transferring it to the open seas through his new dream:

the Microship. This is to be a computer fitted catamaran that he will use to sail around writing about his continued "technomadic" ways. Steve definitely seemed to me to be the sort of person who followed his own set of rules and would have some interesting insights into the topics of successful living. I was looking forward to our meeting tomorrow morning.

Brian appears from around a group of shoppers and walks over to us.

"She said she could meet us at seven. She suggested meeting at the Red Table, but said if that didn't work to just pick the place and leave a message telling her where we will be on her machine at home." He says.

"No that sounds fine. That gives us about another hour of touring. Randy?" I say looking back at our tour guides.

"Right this way…"

We continue exploring Seattle while Randy and I talk more about our quest and our pending meeting with Steve Roberts. As Brian and I are currently living somewhat nomadic lives of our own, I am very anxious to hear what the technomad has to say in the morning.

THE TECH NOMAD

◆

Keep away from the people who try to
belittle your ambitions, small people
always do that. But the really great
make you feel that you, too, can become
great.

Mark Twain

I walk out of the mini-mart and climb back into the Jeep.

"Yep, we've gone too far," I say to Brian. "It was supposedly back there somewhere. The lady said about a mile."

"Okay," he says simply as he backs the Jeep out of the parking space, wheels it around, and is back on the road heading the other direction.

We travel backwards a mile and see nothing but trees and green. A mile and a half, two miles.

"You know, I hate to say it, but I think…" I begin.

"No. We're not." He cuts me short.

"But we've been…" I start again.

"No! We are not!" He says a bit more forcefully. *Had I been driving…I* think to myself.

When we reach three miles past where the kind lady at the mini-mart said we need only go a mile to find the road we were looking for Brian turns into a gravel driveway and reverses our direction again.

"Okay, maybe." He grumbles under his breath.

We drive a mile or so back in the direction we had just come from when we see someone walking a dog on the side of the road. Brian slows down and pulls the Jeep over just across the street from where an elderly woman is waiting for her Irish setter to sniff and plod around the grass and leaves.

"Excuse me," Brian yells over to her from out the window. "Could you tell us where to find Dunster Street?"

The woman looks up from her dog and tugs at its leash to follow her a bit closer to the roadside. At first we think she didn't hear us, but then she begins to look up and down the street slowly and scratch her head.

"Yes, yes," She says softly. "You go up about a mile further and it's on your right. You'll have to look hard though. As I seem to recall the sign is easy to miss."

"Thank you very much. Have a great day." Brian says with usual early morning enthusiasm. "Ha! The sign is hard to see."

"Yep. But then again we did have to stop and ask for directions. Twice. And we did have to turn around several times." I look over at Brian. "I think we have to count it."

Brian sighs and gives in. "Okay, okay. We got lost."

I hate admitting it too, but it seems hard to cover this one up. Our first lost trail of the trip. It wouldn't be so bad that we are keeping track of the number of times we got lost if it wasn't for the fact that we are posting it on the web site for all to see. It is part of our *Trip Statistics*. It is right up there with number of visits to Taco Bell, cans of Mountain Dew consumed, rolls of film used, and number of times "do you want to drive" is said. All vital road trip statistics.

We reach a sneaky bend in the road and see a sign partly covered by tree limbs on the right hand side. A little closer and we can deduce that it is the street we are looking for.

"Ah ha!" I say as Brian makes the turn. "Now we're getting close."

We continue to wind along country roads, over small bridges, and through little towns as I read off the directions from Brian's Newton palm computer. We are now just a few turns from Steve Roberts' house in the woods.

We reach the last turn off on the list of directions and pull into Steve's drive way at last. Brian maneuvers the Jeep up the dirt and gravel approach and brings it to a halt under a huge oak tree. Off to our right sits Steve's house teetering on the edge of a thick forest behind. We hop out of the Jeep and start sorting through our things to get the recording equipment when we see Steve Roberts walk out of his house to greet us. Wearing a T-shirt and pair of shorts draped over his six foot six inch frame, Steve carries a cup of steaming coffee in one hand and has the chaotic hair of someone who just woke up. With the way he stands to greet us it seems as if we are old friends just out for the weekend.

"Good morning!" Steve calls out to us.

"Hi!" I call back. I secure the bag of recording equipment on my shoulder and walk over to meet the man of the hour. "I'm Chris." A handshake.

"Brian." Another.

"Welcome to my world." Steve says with a grin. He turns to head back into the house and pauses when he notices his wife kneeling down and tending to some gardening a few feet away. We hadn't seen her on the walk up. "Oh, that is my wife Lisa."

Lisa looks up from her soil and plants and throws us a smile. "Hello."

"Hi," Brian and I say almost in unison. Steve then turns and leads us into the house.

"Thanks for meeting with us." Brian says as we are lead into his living room.

"My pleasure. Did you find my place okay?" He asks.

"No problem," I say, hiding our statistic from him.

"Good. So tell me more about this thing you're doing." Steve says as he leans against a wall in the living room. He looks at us like he's still unsure we're not disguised IRS agents out on assignment.

As always I let Brian recount the tale of the quest and explain why two strangers are now standing in Steve's living room. The further along we get on the road the more we see a natural division of labor begin to form. This task of explaining our past and purpose is one I seem to have handed over to Brian. As he talks I look around the house at electronics equipment, stacks of books and papers, bicycle paraphernalia, and an assortment of plants. It looks as if the house has just awakened as well.

"So what can I do for you?" Steve asks after Brian finishes our story, now more secure in the notion of talking to us.

"We'd just like to talk to you a bit about your thoughts on this whole 'success thing' and how you happened onto your current path and career." I say breaking my silence.

"Oh, okay. Where should we do it? In here?" He asks.

"This is fine," Brian agrees.

"Okay," Steve, noticing we are still standing, motions us to sit. "Where would you like to begin?"

"We usually like to start with some quick bio information so we know where you're coming from, who you are, that sort of thing." I say.

"Okay. Well, my high school guidance counselor looked at my test scores and said I'd never make it in industry so I'd better become a nomad," he says with a chuckle. "No, actually I had a company for about six years called Cybertronics, which was basically an outgrowth of my hobby in microprocessor design. It started to own me instead of the other way around. Somehow I found myself in the early 80's in Columbus, Ohio, in a house in suburbia doing writing and consulting for business, and I just realized I didn't want to be there."

Something connects when Steve says this and we can all tell without it being said that everyone in the room could relate to this realization.

"So the great epiphany," Steve goes on, "if it can be said I had one, was just suddenly realizing that I was doing things I didn't like for things I didn't want. So I looked around at this house, an acre, a riding lawnmower, station wagon and all this stuff and I just hit reset: the control-alt-delete of my life. That's what led to the whole idea of becoming a nomad. Basically the whole nomadic-thing was a very simple outgrowth…the idea was, 'Well if this isn't fun, what would be fun? Maybe I should identify my passions, which seemed to be drifting away.' You start young with a lot of passions and you start doing business and the passions become less and less in the forefront with clients and deadlines and stress. So I started to go back a little bit, identified my passions and found a way to blend them into a lifestyle. My passions were travel, adventure, romance, computers, electronics, communications, change, falling in love, bicycling and things like that. So the obvious solution was to build a computerized bicycle and travel full-time while writing full-time."

"What did you do to identify those passions?" I asked, curious about the process.

"Just thought about it," he tells me. "Nothing formal, really just kind of musing. The nice thing that was going on, and the way the path took the shape that it did, is the fact that the technologies that were emerging at that time—this was 1983—would support this thing really well. I wanted to be nomadic in some form. I just had this urge to travel and get away from suburbia."

"So when you made this decision to take the bike journey, people must have said you were crazy. How did you go about settling those demons?" Brian asks.

"I stopped spending time with naysayers," Steve explains. "I was doing the cross country bike adventure for myself, not for anybody else. I've always felt that that's a mistake a lot of people make. You learn in school along about third or second grade that you don't learn to satisfy your curiosity, you learn to satisfy the teacher. So we go through school and by the time you go through high school and college, you become very good at satisfying other people to the point where your own interests are pushed into the background. And then you get employed and you work to satisfy your employer and you get married and you work to satisfy your spouse and you go through an entire lifetime trying to satisfy other people. I've always thought that that was kind of stupid. So with making a crazy decision to go off and live on a bicycle it didn't really matter to me that the people around me would somehow lose something from it because it's my life not theirs. Not to be crassly selfish, but it is in fact my life." He looks at us a moment checking our reaction, then continues.

"So to stay in Columbus, Ohio, because my girlfriend would be sad if I left would be a really stupid decision. It really wasn't an issue. My parents of course were horrified. The first article that came out about this, in fact before I even left, was in the CompuServe magazine. It was called *Steve Roberts: Computing Across America*. I hadn't mentioned my bicycle journey to them yet so I sent them a copy of the article thinking this was a good way to inform them. It explains it well and they can deal with it. About two or three days later I get a phone call from my Mother saying 'What's the matter Steve? Are you going to be a bum all your life?' Well, it depends on how you define that, Mom."

We all laugh at this. Mothers are always a special issue when making off the beaten track decisions, never quite seeming to *get it*.

"Did you have any struggles with giving up the security of your day to day job?" Brian asks.

"Having technical consulting and writing background—my past occupations—in my bag of tricks, even though I haven't done it for years, gives me a little bit of security," Steve explains. "Security is not what's in your bank account at all. It has nothing to do with it. People who think that security is the dollars they have in their investments, or the relationship they have with their employers are really in for a nasty surprise when their employer goes belly-up or the value of their investments turns around because of some merger or something. Then all of a sudden they're panicking. Well, security is what's in your head, and that's all. Nobody can take it away from you."

"Security is just one of those catch words we hear when talking about life decisions and choosing a path in life. Another is 'success.' What does success mean to you?" Brian says.

"I thought about this for awhile," Steve says without pause, "and I think it was some conversation I was having once with somebody who was about my age and technical bent with about my same technical skills and intelligence and so on who had made completely different choices in life. He was married and had two kids and a secure job with stock options and all of that kind of stuff. He was an old friend and was kind of giving me a hard time in a gentle way for wondering through life in this sort of playfully irresponsible fashion that didn't accumulate 'success.' So that got me thinking. It's not your dollars or relationship with your company that makes success. You put out some combination of things: time and effort and risk and maybe money, and inconvenience. All this stuff you spend: effort, sweat, etc. And you get back a bunch of stuff: money, interesting friends, sex, and interesting places to live, and fun conversations, and new toys. So there's this whole set of transactions that are going on all the time. How do you choose to spend your time and what are you getting in return?" He pauses and looks at us, not really expecting a reply.

"Success is just coming up with a nice ratio of these things," he goes on. "And the silly way to do that is to just figure, 'I'll just make lots of money and then anything I want I can buy,' and some people do that. I have friends who are multimillionaires and have taken that approach that everything else is secondary to accumulating cash. The theory being that if they need a house or computer or bicycle or whatever it is, they can just buy it. But what that often ignores is the quality of life and the environment you end up living in. Would I want to be a millionaire in Los Angeles? No, I'd rather have 10 percent of that and live here on this island."

"How do you go about finding that right ratio or mix of things?" I ask.

"You pay attention to your passions." Steve leans back in his chair and clasps his hands behind his head. "I think a lot of people sort of push their passions into the background because of things they 'should do.' Making decisions based on other people's expectations or paths that are supposedly laid out for you as the right way to do it. You've got to go to school, get your degree, be an employee for a while, work the career path. All of this is sort of defined as the way things are supposed to happen in our culture. I think that's a bad mistake because listening to your passions, especially if they're valid passions and not just fleeting interests, takes a lot to figure this out. I mean that's really all I've done. I don't have any grand plans for life. I just do what's fun. That kind of automatically leads to success. If you're enjoying yourself and being creative presumably you'll be doing something interesting. There's a lot of ways to approach this whole body of potential knowledge in this world."

"Have you always had a 'go-with-the-flow' philosophy in life or has it changed or been molded?" Brian asks Steve.

"Well I've never been very responsible," He answers with a smile. "The Wall Street Journal did a story about me once, and I'll never forget a line they had in there. It was really right on from a Wall Street Journal perspective. It read: 'Roberts, who is cheerfully irresponsible about money...' and it goes on. So yeah, I guess I always figured that stuff would work out. And I don't know, somehow I seem to be getting away with it. I prefer to not examine it too closely, because I'll start to get nervous and won't be able to sleep tonight."

"Are there any words of wisdom and advice you'd give to people trying to find their path in life?" Brian asks.

"Faith! Faith in what you're doing. Because the worst thing is having a great idea and then the world just dumps on you." The statement comes from Steve's wife Lisa who quietly entered the room moments ago and has been sitting at a computer in the corner working.

"Yes," Steve says in agreement. "The world always dumps on new ideas because they are different and people are really afraid of change. Coming up with a new idea that you actually believe in can actually create hostility. A lot of people get jealous and others are skeptical. There are always obstacles. Just like when I started out on the bike trip. The obstacles were financial, social, family. They weren't huge or insurmountable. But basically my attitude was, 'Screw you, I want to do this and don't bother me if you're not going to believe in it, then don't hang around.' Some people probably viewed that as very self-centered, but again whose life is it? And having fun is a key point. A lot of people forget the amount of fun that can be had in life. There's this whole Puritan work ethic that we've been brought up to think that is very important. Work hard with your nose to the grindstone. And that's a component and tool, but the fundamental drive and passion is fun. That's what turns you on and that's what motivates you."

"And that's such an important point," Lisa adds from her corner of the room. "A friend of mine was on the dole in England. He was a sweet guy, but I'd kinda given up on him. And what he really enjoyed doing was going to raves and dances, but he never had enough money to get in. So he started developing ways to get in for free. He started putting this magazine together and Xeroxing it and stapling it. Then he would go to the raves and say, 'Look, I've got this magazine and I'd like to cover the story.' And they'd let him in for free. Also with the magazine he wanted to be a DJ, but again didn't have any money for records. So he put together a record review section in his magazine and record producers would send him copies of albums to review. Then instead of selling the magazine, he distributed it for free at parties and restaurants. Now all the record people knew that to get the underground party audience, who doesn't watch TV or read typical magazines, they could advertise in his magazine. It became this cult-thing. Now it's glossy with color ads and it's a real thing. And he just followed a simple aim: to get into concerts for free. And he managed to make a success of it by pursuing his interests."

"Sounds like a story to learn by." I say as my mind races over ideas of my own, trying to find my passions in the mix of mental images.

"Thank you both so much. It's been great meeting with you." Brian says as he shuts off the tape recorder signaling the official end of the interview.

"Would you like to see the workshop while you're here?" Steve asks leaning forward in his chair.

"That'd be great. Do you have your bike there?" I ask, thinking of the photos of him on his bike I had seen in his book.

"The bike and the ship-in-progress. C'mon I'll take you back." He stands and leads us through the kitchen and out a back door of the house.

We walk along a gravel road surrounded by trees and forest. Steve is explaining about how he found the property and the pleasure of having trees for neighbors. With the cool morning breeze playing with the leaves as the sunlight dances about us it is easy to share his joy. A bit further back along the road and away from the house we see a large metal shed, home to Steve's workshop. Steve explains that the building is still in the finishing stages. Soon it will be fully wired and connected with high speed Internet hook ups, state-of-the-art security systems, and a few other surprises. All modern conveniences of his own design.

Inside we see the "Behemoth," Steve's transport and companion for his long trek across the country. The elaborate recumbent bicycle looks ready for action; it's built in computer consul, keyboard, and solar panels still in good working order and calling out to be used. Looking at what carried him over 17,000 miles of American pavement, dirt, and gravel I feel a bit spoiled by the Quest-Mobile we have parked out front.

If traded in for a couple of bicycles I am confident Brian and I wouldn't have made it out of California, let alone across the continent. But it would be fun to give it a try and see if I could prove myself wrong.

"This is my new baby," Steve says walking us over to where the shell of a two-person catamaran lies in waiting. Still in the infant stages it is hard to imagine what the finished product will be: a sea faring vessel built to surf the waves of both the open sea and the World Wide Web comfortably. A dream realized, given birth by the ideas and passions of someone willing enough to go after them.

Steve locks up the workshop and walks us back to the Jeep. After so brief a visit into his world I already feel a bit of kinship to him. I easily relate to his nomadic nature and wandering soul. What is it that makes some of us so willing to stay put while others like Steve and I feel the urge to keep in constant motion?

At the Jeep we say our good-byes and are wished much luck from our new friends. Steve watches us as we drive backwards out of his driveway and back onto the roads ahead, perhaps thinking of his own journeys and beginnings and wishing for the time when the road will call him back again.

LONG ROAD TO IDAHO

◆

*There are as many ways to live and grow as
there are people. Our own ways are the only
ways that should matter to us.*

Evelyn Mandel

Mt. Rainier appears on our right as Highway 90 carries us out of
Seattle. It hangs in the distance, hovering above the ground on a bed of
clouds. An immense chunk of white against a pale blue morning sky.

I roll down the window and lean out of it with the digital camera to
snap a shot for the web site. I've always had an affinity to mountains
and this one in particular. I made an attempt at summiting it a few years
ago but got turned back a few thousand feet from the top. The wind had
shifted the night before and inclement weather conditions threatened
potential avalanches. I had to turn around and descend with the peak
just in sight. Rainier and I still had unfinished business to attend to.

Securing just the right shot I pull myself back into the Jeep and put
the camera away. I won't know until later that the picture didn't come
out, that the massive mountain is invisible in the bright sunshine.
Instead I'll have only a shot of the blurred road in front of a blank wall
of blue gray.

We have a long haul before us and are lucky to have gotten off to such an early start. If you can call eleven-thirty an early start. Given that we had met with people all morning and paid a visit to REI Adventure Outfitters' super store, an eleven-thirty departure is pretty good.

Both of the people we had the pleasure of meeting this morning came to us indirectly via the internet. One, Linda Steen, was a cousin of a friend who had heard of the quest via email and emailed back the suggestion for a meeting. We met Linda for coffee this morning and had a great chat with her. Linda, a bubbly brunette from Oregon, sells health insurance for the self-employed. But she has dreams of taking her hobby of dancing to a new level. She is working toward a career as a dance therapist, a career she is planning on molding herself.

After our meeting with Linda we traveled downtown to meet up with Cindy Wuu. A friend emailed me from Hong Kong about Cindy, a young woman who had recently set up a bath and beauty shop with her best friend. We met Cindy at her shop and toured the aisles of soaps, cremes, and shampoos while she told us about how she came onto her path and what dreams the future held for her.

Both were strong, independent, interesting young women and we enjoyed meeting both of them. So different but the same in that both were pursuing their hobbies as careers, one in dance the other in making beauty supplies. And through smiles, enthusiasm and laughter it seemed both were off to a great start.

After the two interviews we found ourselves on the verge of leaving town when I remembered the REI store on the edge of town that I had hoped to see while in the city. It took a bit of political pleading on my part, but we managed to squeeze in a visit as we headed to the highway.

If you want to learn something about someone learn their shopping habits, therein lie the secrets to inner personality. Me, I don't care much for shopping. Take me to a mall and let me loose and I will normally gravitate right past clothing stores, shoe stores, and all else head directly to book stores, outdoor outfitters, or a housewares specialty store.

Book stores are understandable. I think almost anyone can find a way to occupy themselves among hundreds of books and magazines. Once I sat in a book store and tried to guess the magazine of choice a person would pick up as they entered the store. That's another shopping element that is quite revealing about someone's personality: what they read. Actually Brian and I made a game out of it once, describing people by magazines, not necessarily what they read, but what describes their personality. Brian, for example, would be *Fast Company, Small Business, Mac Computing, Newsweek* and *Sports Illustrated.* I, on the other hand, would be *Wizard, Movieline, Discover, Outdoors, Internet Weekly,* and *Adventure Travel.*

The housewares thing is something of a new development. But anyone who has walked in one and discovered all the useless gadgets, decorations, and thingamabobs these stores peddle will understand the attraction. So many things to pick up and explore and wonder just what the hell they are used for.

Outfitters or outdoor sporting goods stores work like a black hole on me, pulling me in and keeping me there by some invisible force of gravity. It takes a huge amount of inertia to get me out, to break me free of the irresistible tug. I will walk in circles for hours around ski jackets, climbing ropes, camping stoves, freeze-dried food, mosquito netting, wool socks, rain gear, and kayaks. I read labels and warranties, try out sleeping mats, climb in and out of tents, pull on pull-overs, pose in front of mirrors in goofy hats. Each item reminds me of a past adventure or a journey yet to be taken.

It's a strange dichotomy, I admit. One so insanely domestic and the other a call to action to jump up and leave, to get going and on your way. Luckily I have never had the experience of finding the two in the same place at the same time. The damage to the structural integrity of my mind in such an instance could be too great to handle.

So when we walked into REI's flagship store in Seattle for a "quick stop" this morning, it took all of both our efforts to get me out again.

The inside climbing wall, three floors of equipment, the Rain Room for trying on rain gear in a real wet environment, the hiking hill to test the traction of new boots, the outdoor bike track to take a spin with your mountain bike of choice…all demanded attention and trial. But somehow, in a little under one hour I managed to avoid them all and stroll out of the store empty handed.

We don't make it far out of Seattle when the gas light comes on the dash. Time for another fill up, number four on the trip so far. Add one more to our Statistics. We follow an exit sign off 90 and into the outskirts of North Bend, pulling into *Ken's Gas & Groceries* for a fast and friendly service.

I hop out of the Jeep and walk around to the driver's side as the door to the gas tank pops open. With the fluid precision of someone who is far too accustomed to the process, I yank out the nozzle, place the nose into the tank, swipe a credit card through the quick pay card reader, key in the gas selection, and let it go. Brian steps out of the Jeep and walks toward me to get the squeegee to clean the windows.

"Hey, don't forget to…" I start to say something but am cut off by the sudden appearance of a familiar song.

Road Runner, He's coming after you, Road Runner, If he catches you you're through…

It's faint but clear and coming from somewhere close. I look and see that Brian hears it too. We both look around for the sound, following it back to the pump. When we turn to inspect the pump we see that the tiny screen where I had just selected the gas of my choice has come alive. It has transformed itself from informational kiosk into entertainment center. There on the little display Wyle E. Coyote chased the Road Runner around the desert with all the ACME technology money can buy.

"No way!" Brian says with a smile.

"Cool." I utter in reply.

And for a couple of minutes we forget about the dirty windows. We forget about the gas fumes. Even the road ahead fades from memory. We're just two big kids standing at the gas pump watching Saturday morning cartoons. Watching as the Road Runner uses his cunning to *Chee-kok*.

The nozzle shuts itself off and the screen goes dead. The endless battle between bird and beast lost in a blackness that now flashes THANK YOU FOR SHOPPING KEN'S.

"Shit. Now we'll never know if the Coyote gets the Road Runner!" I say as I replace the nozzle to the pump. "I guess you have to pump your gas slowly if you want the whole show."

"We'll know next time," Brian says as he commences the window cleaning ritual.

"Looks like they have effectively eliminated human interaction from another common activity," I say watching the squeegee go back and forth across the windshield. "Now not only do they have the credit card swipes so you don't have to go inside and talk to the cashier, they have the cartoons to make sure you don't happen to look around and speak to other patrons getting their gas at nearby pumps!"

"Hey," Brian says looking up from the soapy window, "maybe they'll start installing those screens in elevators and then people won't have to feel so uncomfortable in them any more! It'll be get in, hit your floor number, and watch the cartoon until you exit."

We laugh but can't help but thinking how wonderful it would be. No more close proximity jitters or painful silence or annoying musak. Just a steady progression of Road Runner *Beep-Beep*'s and the clang of anvils hitting the Coyote's head bringing smiles and laughter to a metal box full of Homo Sapiens Corporatis in ill-fitted shoes.

Back on the road, Washington state flies by, the pines and hills of Snoqualmie and Wenatchee national forests waving at us in the distance as we pass. We make a brief and failed stop at the Central Washington University in Ellensberg. I had learned of the Center for

Chimpanzee–Human Communication there and their research on primate communication. I hope to interview one of the chimps on their views on life to add a bit of perspective to our quest. ("*Tell me Bongo, how would you define successful living?*" "*Banana-tree-monkey-monkey-banana-tree.*") But we aren't permitted to see the chimps and have to settle for a handshake and a few smiles from the center's director. Whatever secrets the great apes have to teach us will have to remain locked away for now.

On the road again Highway 82 carries us over barren hills and plains back into Oregon where we are handed off to 84 and the long stretch across the corner of the state. We had a long day of driving today and it is beginning to wear on us. But we continue to race away from the setting sun and drive on into the night and into Idaho (*state #4, chalk it up on the board*), getting to Brian's Uncle Rick's place just on the verge of tomorrow.

WILD, WILD, WEST

◆

There is only one success—
To be able to spend your life in your own way

Christopher Morley

The morning light shines through the windows and I swear in my waking-sleeping delirium that I hear roosters. Either in dream or reality, a perky birdy is screaming at me to wake up and start the day. Giving in to its demands I roll over and feel my hand fall on something squishy and furry. Surprisingly my hand doesn't leap back but starts to probe the fur in search of meaning. A cat. If the contours of its body didn't give it away, the sudden appearance of low purring would. I look over and see a big gray fat cat lying on the bed next to me.

I take another minute to let the sleep drain out of me, just lying in bed with the cat. She (or he?) doesn't seem to mind and is in no hurry so why should I be? But the low drum of voices downstairs piques my curiosity enough to make me get up. I sit up and my cat friend quickly leaps from the bed and runs downstairs; so much for long relationships. As the cat hops out the door I hear something else stir and just then a dog's head rises up at my feet. Ahh, Molly. I met her the last night. Guess

I made a good enough impression to warrant her sleeping at my feet all night. But then again, perhaps I am just in the "barn room."

I step over Molly and out the door, seeing Brian's Uncle Rick's house for the first time in the daylight. It's a cozy old farm house that they have remodeled with all the modern conveniences. Its interior is mainly wood, though with the masses of wall hangings it is difficult to tell. As I walk down the stairs I am smiled down upon by what looks no less than twelve thousand and four framed photos. People and events from Rick and Rose's past commemorated in the Wall Of Memories.

At the bottom of the stairs the aroma of freshly brewed coffee greets me. I decide to postpone it a minute longer and check on Brian first in the living room, the latest addition to the house. I walk into the living room, a massive room flooded in the morning light washing in through large open windows circling the room. Brian is already awake, no surprise to me. I am always the late riser, the slow to awake, the reluctant to enter a fresh morning mood. Brian, on the other hand, wakes up chipper. Just another part of the yin yang balance the friendship offers.

"Morning," I say from behind sleepy eyes.

"Good morning! How'd you sleep," Brian asks our traditional morning question. Being in a new bed or home practically every night, it made a lot of sense.

"Good. I had some visitors in the middle of the night." I say.

"Oh yeah? Molly slept down here with me last night." He boasts.

"Well if she did, she woke up with me." I counter and then look back at Molly who has just come down the stairs, greeting her with a smirk and grumpy morning attitude.

"Hey, there's coffee made." Brian says getting up from his hideaway bed and moving toward the kitchen. He says it mostly for my benefit; at this point he's not drinking normal brewed coffee.

"So who's the big gray cat?" I ask. "It was with me this morning too."

"That's Jim," I hear a female voice answer from the kitchen. It's Brian's Aunt Rose, a hearty woman with long pepper hair dressed in an oversized shirt and jeans. She looks the type of woman strong and sturdy enough to tame the wilds of the Idaho frontier. "Did he bother you?" She asks.

"No, I just like to know who I'm sleeping with, that's all," I say. "Where's Rick?"

"On the back porch. Coffee?" Rose asks.

"Please." She gives me an empty cup, and I help myself to some morning perk-me-up.

"What do you guys usually have for breakfast, we have…" Rose begins.

"Don't worry about us," Brian says. "We are totally self-sufficient. We'll find something to fix, and if not we even have our own cereal stash in the car."

"All right then, I'll leave you to it."

She turns to head out the back door and onto what I assume is the porch. Brian and I follow her out.

Outside I see the countryside that was shielded in darkness when we arrived the night before and I am overwhelmed. Rick's back yard stretches fifty yards back to where it suddenly drops off into a deep and wiggly ravine. The ravine was cut from cliffs of rock by the waters of Morse Creek snaking and winding its way through the valley a few hundred feet below. Across the ravine on the other side of the valley low undulating hills break unexpectedly from a large plain in front of them, rolling off into the distance to either side. In the distance the proud peak of Aldape Summit looks down across the plain and valley below. The flats and hillsides are speckled with the occasional house.

On Rick's side of the valley his neighbors are few and far between. To the left a neighbor's house is visible but to the right we see nothing but tall grass and low weeds, God's answer to Western gardening. The whole landscape was lit up by the brightest sun and clearest blue sky I've seen in a long Californian time.

"Wow." I say stepping down off the porch and into the grass. "This is amazing."

"It is isn't it." Rick says. I imagine many who live with such beauty everyday would become accustomed to it and soon overlook it. However, I don't think Rick is such a person. He looks off at his world just as we do as if seeing it for the first time. "We can take a walk down there a little later if you'd like."

"That would be great," Brian says pulling up a chair and sitting down next to his uncle.

It's not easy to see any family resemblance between Rick and nephew Brian. You would have to know Brian's father and brother for that, for they resemble each other in ways Brian missed out. Family resemblance missing, all courtesy of the random selection of genes. Actually when the comparison is made, with his reddish hair and beard, stout face and broader nose, Rick would be more likely guessed my uncle rather than Brian's. It's not until the personality comes out that someone can tell they're both all Ardinger.

"What would you guys like to do today and the rest of the time you're here?" Rick asks, and then before we can answer, he goes on, "I have a few suggestions. I can give you a tour of the city, Idaho City that is. Or Boise. Or we could take the canoe out later down on the river. And if you like there's a Powwow going on some time soon, we can see about going to that."

"It all sounds good to me." I say. It's too early to try to make decisions.

"It sounds great. Why not do a tour first so we know where we are and then we can figure out the rest." Brian suggests.

"Okay. Well you guys just relax for a while and as soon as you're ready we'll head into town." Rick settles back into his chair and sips from his coffee mug. We are on Western time now; everything is done when you are ready.

✲   ✲   ✲

Welcome to Idaho City, pop. 430.

We pass the sign and pull into a parking space on the edge of the city just across from the welcome center. I feel a bit excited, it is my first real visit to the wild, wild west and this seems to be a great place to start.

According to Rick the area was founded by thieves and outlaws. People on the run would head for the hills surrounding the city and get lost in them, never to be found again. He called the surrounding woods and hills the "vortex area", a place that sucked people in and kept them there. He explains a little further as we park.

"Boise County—where we live and where Idaho City is the county seat—is a large county of free thinkers. Always has been. Until just recently, the county has avoided instituting uniform building codes. People here generally hate government intrusion and regulations. People tend to be conservative, independent. Many people move here to get away from cities. Some move here thinking they can hide from previous lives, live simple lives the way people lived many years ago. And they do. A lot of people are still weekend prospectors. The history is palpable. Idaho City was one of the earliest settlements of the Idaho Territory; because of the gold rush of 1862-1864, Idaho City had a larger population than Portland, Oregon."

We step out of the Jeep and immediately I feel like I'm in a spaghetti western dismounting my white steed to face down the forces of evil. We step down onto a dusty dirt road. The city has two paved roads in town, but this, their main thoroughfare, is not one of them. A breeze picks up and spins dirty twisters at our feet as we begin to look around Main Street. A boardwalk runs down our left, the spinal cord to the city's attractions. We step up onto it and can hear the boards creak under each step. We play out a short tune of creaks and then turn in to one of the city's biggest summer time draws, Redding's Homemade Ice Cream.

Inside we know immediately why there is no one on the streets. Everyone is here eating ice cream. The tiny little shop is packed with locals trying to avoid the rising heat of the afternoon. I notice right away that everyone is staring at us as we enter. Everyone is looking to see who the strange faces could be, what purpose could we have invading their inner sanctuary of frozen cream and ice.

I'm here to kill Evil Bart. Any of you'uns knowse wheres I might find him.

Blank stares and licks of ice cream. We belly up to the bar and make our selections: chocolate chip for Rick, double chocolate fudge for Brian, and pralines and cream for me.

Outside we continue along the boardwalk, our ice cream dripping away rapidly in the heat. We stroll past the Calamity Jayne's Restaurant; The Miner's Exchange, The Idaho World building, the Hummer Bar where locals gather and talk about life, and the Merc, the one and only grocery store in the city. Rick gives us a brief run down on what each shop has to offer. As we walk, a few people come and go, offering hellos and greetings to neighbor Rick and vacant stares and smiles to the strangers in town. Not unfriendly, just un-accustomed.

Across the street from the Merc, a large wooden building boasts western wear via a large painted sign. In front, two Harley Davidsons are parked right next to three horses hitched to the pillars of the front deck, and for an instant I'm confused over what time I am living in. A strange rift in the space time continuum swallowing me up then spitting me back out.

"Why don't we go up and see if Greg is at home so you guys can meet him." Rick suggests in present time. Greg was one of the people he thought we should speak to in relation with our quest.

Rick leads us past Rod Serling's Western Wear outlet and up a tiny dirt road climbing a hill in the back of the city.

"This church, St. Joseph's, is the oldest church in Idaho built by Euro-Americans. It dates back to 1867." Rick tells us as we begin to ascend a series of randomly placed wooden steps leading to a small white church on the hill. "The Cataldo Mission in north Idaho near Coeur d'Alene was built in 1853 by Jesuits and Coeur d'Alene Indians. St. Joseph's actually was built in 1865 and was one of the only buildings left standing in Idaho City after an 1865 fire wiped out the town. In a second fire in 1867, it was not so lucky and burned down. The current church was completed in November of 1867."

At the top of the hill we see a white Ford Bronco just pulling into the church's parking lot.

"Morning Mayor," Rick says walking up to the truck. The driver has his window down and waves at Rick through the cloud of dust he just called up.

"Morning Rick. What are you up to today." Idaho City's Mayor says, a plain looking man of fifty with sweaty sun baked face and working man's clothes. I can't decide if the prospect of running into and talking with the city's mayor on such a casual basis is wonderful or frightening.

"We're going over to see if Greg's at home." Rick says.

"He isn't, I just checked. I was going to enlist his help in moving the church's organ. He might be down at the Pon Yan house. Did you check there?" The mayor says, saving us the walk over to Greg's vacant house.

The city is a true marvel to me. The mayor stops by for a visit, everyone knows everyone else and where they would be on a Friday afternoon. Horses and hogs, church organs, homemade ice cream that tastes actually that: home made.

"Mayor, this is my nephew Brian and his friend Chris in for a visit," Rick says presenting us to his honor with a wave of his hand.

"Glad to meet you," the mayor greets us. "Well I guess I'll just wait here until the cavalry arrive. Should be some people up to help here in a few."

It sounds like an invitation to help. And while the thought of moving a monstrous church organ out of the building and onto a truck in the hundred degree sun doesn't sound too pleasing I prepare myself to smile and offer assistance if necessary. It isn't.

"Okay, well we're going to head down and see if we can find Greg. See you later." Rick politely plans our escape for us.

"Have a good time boys," The mayor says and waves as we walk off.

"So you're friendly with the mayor eh?" I joke as we walk back down the stairs into town.

"It's difficult not to know everyone in this town." Rick says.

"It must have an interesting effect living in a small town like this where everyone knows each other. It seems that would play a big part on who you are and what you do." Brian says.

"Think you could live in a place like this Bri?" I ask.

"I don't know. You?" He counters.

"I don't think so. It's a tad bit too small for me. I like knowing neighbors and having some community involvement, but I think I would need a little more contact with the newest and latest. You know, more entertainment options, more diversity, more…unpredictability." I answer.

"More like L.A.?" Brian asks. I see what he's doing. Clever. Ever since moving to Los Angeles a couple years ago I have had complaints about the city and the living environment, objections that were constantly thrown Brian's way. As we talked about and planned this journey of ours we both decided it would be a good chance to see if there was some place other than our current locations we would rather be living. Brian was sure Silicon Valley wasn't for him. I wasn't sure what it was I was looking for, and at the time I still hadn't a clue.

"Perhaps," I say and let it drop. But mentally I draw a scale and place the sprawling city of L.A. on one side and quiet, little Idaho City on the other. Now I have something to work from.

We walk down the hill and one block past Main Street to the other side of the city where a team is busy at the Pon Yan House. One thing that can be said about Idahoians is they love their state's history. Their streets and highways are populated with roadside historical markers and reminders of the great and infamous things that have happened within Idaho's odd shaped boundaries.

The Pon Yan House is just a small part of that past, but a big part of Idaho City's. It once belonged to a Chinese merchant who stayed on in Idaho City after the gold rush and railroads had faded away. The building, long since mistreated and disused is still in amazing condition and speaks buckets of that period of the city's history. And now the Idaho City Historical Society wants a few buckets more.

Walking up to it, it looks like somebody's old, decaying house. A bulldozer patiently waits on the side of the house behind piles and piles of dirt and deep calculated holes in the earth. Work, perhaps on the sewage system, has led to the upheaval of the whole backyard. That's what it would appear to be were it not for the large silk signs hanging solemnly in the windless alley reading: PASSPORT IN TIME.

On closer inspection I see people pulling up buckets of dirt and sifting through it, pulling out tiny nails and pieces of porcelain, calling out and marveling over bits of glass and the occasional spoon fragment. An archeological dig in progress. The house was being excavated before it would be completely renovated and refurbished to its former glory.

We step inside the house and find it has become the central HQ for the excavation. Tables are set up inside, one for cleaning artifacts, one for bagging and labeling. Inside Rick approaches as few of the staff and inquires about Greg. Before anyone can answer him, Greg walks through the door.

"Hi Rick," Greg greets Uncle Rick. Tall and strong with a youthful face, Greg looks more like the carpenter that pays the bills than the weaver that Rick has described him as.

"Hey, just the man I'm looking for. How is the dig going?" Rick asks.

"Great so far. Look," he leads Rick over to a display case and we follow. "These are some of the things we've found so far."

Inside the case are an old bottle completely intact, a Chinese spoon, several rusty nails, the top of an earthenware jar, and two slightly corroded but genuine Chinese coins.

"Heeeeey, that's great," Rick says with enthusiasm. He too is victim to the passions of Idaho history. "Oh, Greg, this is my nephew Brian and his friend Chris." Rick says looking up from the glass box and remembering we haven't been introduced.

We exchange salutations.

Rick throws out a brief explanation of what we are doing and how he thought Greg would be a great person to talk to. I always enjoy hearing others explain our madness and see which part of it they emphasize. I imagine it offers a sneak peak into where their priorities lie.

"Well I don't know if I'll have anything useful to say," Greg says, slightly embarrassed from the request, "but I'd be happy to talk to you. When?"

"Anytime. We're flexible." Brian answers.

"Why don't I just call you later and we can set a time around your schedule?" Rick says.

"Sure that would be great. Look, I gotta run, but give me a call, okay?" Greg says shaking Rick's hand. Then to us, "Nice meeting you, talk to you soon."

Greg leaves us to the room of dirt and rocks. I look around and wonder if Indiana Jones ever had to deal with the mundane tasks of his chosen profession in archeology. Where were the rolling boulders and angry aborigines and poison darts and vats of snakes?

Outside again. Dirt road. Main Street. The Merc. Hummer's. Harleys and horses. The Quest-Mobile.

We pull out of town leaving a wake of dust tornadoes behind us. Back on State Route 21 we wind along to our next destination. As we pass Rick's place and continue westbound I remind Brian we need new batteries, and he pulls into a mini-mart on the side of the road to nowhere. I climb out to get the batteries and immediately something catches my eye. There in front of the store right along side the Pepsi and Coke machines was a large black vending machine of equal size and shape with a brilliantly lit painting of a wide mouth bass. I stop and walk over to have a closer look.

"Brian, you gotta see this!" I yell back at the Jeep. Brian gets out and walks over to where I am standing.

"Check it out, a vending machine for live bait!" I say as we both stand and marvel over the machine. I think of inserting a dollar just to see what would come out, perhaps setting a carton of earthworms free to enjoy their remaining days in the grounds of Idaho. But with no loose one dollar bills available I chose to head in for the batteries instead.

Next stop is Horseshoe Bend and my first Powwow.

I have to admit, I am ignorant of Native American culture. I can speak fluent Chinese. I can describe the ancient civilizations of the Incans and Mayans. I can converse on the deities of ancient Egypt, Norse gods, and the Greeks. But when it comes to our own neighbors, to our country's true forefathers I am as dumb as a rock in Antarctica.

It's not from lack of interest. I find their beliefs as fascinating as any other. It's more from my general desire to escape America and explore outside its boundaries. Maybe the Native Americans just weren't "exotic" enough for me while growing up. Whatever the reason for my lack, now as I traveled across the country I found everything about them completely and totally captivating.

We walk into the Powwow and I am enthralled at the sights and sounds and smells. People chatter and drums pound out a faint rhythm. The scents of fry bread and corn float around the masses of strollers-by, both Indian and white alike. In booths we can shop for jewelry and art and food and dream catchers. All things one would imagine at such a gathering of tribes, plus many more.

I wonder if this is real. Are the Native Americans really gathering for their fun and fraternity or ours?

Walking all around me are Native Americans dressed head to toe in what I can only guess to be traditional tribal garb. The colors of cloth and feather explosive, a moving rainbow sea. At once I curse myself for not learning more about Native American culture and swear to rectify the situation every chance I get in the future.

I ask Rick some questions that he answers the best he can, but what I really need is a guide. Someone to sit and walk with me and explain all I am seeing. I guess that will have to wait for another day.

We separate to go off and gather food and regroup to watch the festivities. Brian heads off for an "Indian Taco," Rick for the fry bread, and I hunt for the corn.

I find the corn stand and behind it a blonde couple that seem vanilla white against the backdrop of all the dark features of the Native Americans. I arrive just as they're out of corn and chat with them as I wait for a fresh batch. Small talk progresses from "where are you from" to "what are you doing in Idaho," and when I tell them of our quest they spill out their own story to me.

They both used to work in corporate America, working all the time and seldom seeing each other. They found their lives moving away from one another so they decided to take action to change all that. They thought about what they liked doing. After many thinking and planning sessions, they decided to chuck in the world of suits and briefcases and buy a mobile corn-on-the-cob stand. They thought this would give them a chance to travel around as well as spend time together in fun-filled environments. This week they're in Idaho for Powwows, next week it would be a state fair. A new world of travel, sun, fun, and new faces.

They finish their story and I hand them one of my name cards with our web site address on it and invite them to follow along with us. They say they will and hand over two steamy ears of corn. I thank them for both their time and the corn and wish them good journeys.

Back at the gathering point we enjoy our food as the Powwow participants prepare for the dances. I relay the story of the corn people to Brian, still amazed at both their story and the fact that they would share it with me so openly. Amazed at how many people are so open to discussing life and it's pursuits. I guess that's the power of the right message, one that everyone can connect with. Or maybe sometimes all you have to do is ask.

An announcement calls all participants to the field for the opening ceremony. The drums pound and groups of Native Americans stomp and dance into the circle of spectators. The Powwow commences as I sit and enjoy the moment.

WEAVING A FUTURE

◆

Ask yourself the secret of your success.
Listen to your answer,
And practice it.

Richard Bach

"This was the building's original stonework that I'm refinishing and using in the new design," Greg says pointing at the upstairs wall. He's giving us a tour of his home. What will be his home rather. Though he is currently living here, it appears more a work in progress than a place someone would want to live.

The old two-story farmhouse is in many stages of incompletion. Walls are being torn down and put up. Saw horses and carpentry equipment lie in a pile in what will be the living room next to a mass of white sheets covering some hidden treasures. Tape and plastic sheets decorate the walls, hung like fine art in a museum for the artistically deranged. It takes some real imagination to picture what the place will someday be.

"And you're doing it all yourself?" Brian asks.

"Pretty much." Greg answers as we reach the first floor again.

As soon as we step down Max is upon us, his large form hurtling up at Brian. Black, and sweaty, and happily licking all over, Max is a full grown retriever that believes he is still a puppy. He is definitely more interested in us than the fine restoration work being done in the house.

"Amazing work. I guess it helps being a professional carpenter." I say.

Professional carpenter. Historical Restoration expert. Weaver. That is Greg Johns.

Greg was born and raised in Nampa, Idaho, and lived a life of constant relocation thereafter, the fate of being born to working and mobile parents. As a result, he went to three different high schools, two in Illinois and one in Connecticut. During his senior year when his parents decided to move back to Idaho, Greg decided he didn't want to go to a fourth high school. So he found a family to live with and stayed in Illinois. Sixteen and living in Illinois, he studied as an apprentice with a professional weaver. This developing interest lead him to Mexico after high school to further his studies of weaving and then back to Wisconsin for another eight months of study. These studies were followed by college at Boise State and six years of living in Chicago. It was during this time Greg started working on houses. He was making good money, living the high life, but soon realized he didn't want to live in the big city. So in 1991 Greg moved back to Idaho, set up his own carpentry business, and started getting into the history of Idaho and historical preservation.

We push through a wall of plastic sheets and move into the kitchen to find somewhere to sit. That it is the kitchen is only discernible from the sink and coffee maker. Tools, equipment, and cans full of nails are spread out everywhere, and without the tell-tale coffee machine it could just as easily be the work shop. We sit down in two straight chairs, and Greg digs out another from amidst stacked boxes in the next room.

"Is this path you're on something you planned Greg?" I ask as I deflect a slobber attack from Max. He has followed us and still remains interested in his visitors.

"No," Greg tells us as he takes his seat. "My career path is not what I originally planned for, especially not the historical preservation work.

I've always enjoyed art and architecture and history and all of those things, but I never knew or planned to be focusing on historical preservation. But I hopefully want to get more back into my weaving and get more of a balance between the two. Make enough money to live on from the one."

"Do you feel your artwork is your passion?" I ask.

"Well I think all of these are my passions, but you need balance. I don't know if I'd be necessarily happy just weaving ten hours a day or working on buildings ten hours a day, especially something where it's physically hard to do that, like the Pon Yan House."

"How would you define success for you personally?" Brian asks.

"I guess success is being happy and satisfied with your lifestyle and the friends that you have. I certainly don't see success as being money or security or any of that kind of stuff. I obviously want to be in an environment that's nice and comfortable, but as far as having IRAs and such, well…I'm not planning my life for my death. I want to enjoy life now instead of working and killing myself. I'm never going to be somebody who has a retirement plan because I don't work for a corporation, but I want to set up a good life for myself and continue to work until the day I die, do my art or preservation consulting or whatever."

Max decides we are no longer interesting or perhaps just tires out from his draining supply of spit. He strolls over and takes his place at the feet of his master.

"Why Idaho and not Chicago?" Brian says as Greg welcomes Max with a strong pat on the back.

"Ultimately it'll be easier in this kind of place to do my art. Obviously to do preservation work is easier out here because I don't have the same kind of expenses I would have in a major city. Preservation work doesn't usually pay as well as regular construction."

"Do you think your environment has influenced your opinions about success?" I ask, curious after my earlier discussion with Brian about choices of living environments.

"I think so, that and the people I know. I think people here are less oriented toward success equals money. I like going to cities and traveling and doing things like that, and I have friends who have computer jobs and lawyer jobs, but all they seem to do is bitch and moan and complain about it all the time. They look at what I'm doing and say 'God, you have it so great.' But then I say, 'Yeah, but I deal with a lot of hillbillies and…' There are tradeoffs."

"How do you accept and deal with those tradeoffs?" Brian asks.

"I basically learned from watching my parents. My Dad climbed the corporate ladder and did that whole thing, but money didn't equal happiness. They were always fighting and having problems. We moved all the time. Eventually they just decided that the simpler life was the better life. I'm not sure if they necessarily found that, because I'm not sure if they're all that happy here, but I think that's more of a personal outlook on life. They kind of blame the world more, where I try to take more responsibility for my own happiness. You are responsible for your life and what happens to it."

"Do you think the definitions of success differ from small town to big towns?" Brian asks.

"Yes, definitely. Almost everybody I knew in the city was, 'You've gotta work. You gotta work.' If you work 80 hours a week, well it's not a problem. They have all the stuff. There are people up here that I wouldn't necessarily call successful. They don't do anything. They hang out in the bars and things. They would tell you they are happy. So there's a difference between those that have the hundred-thousand dollar a year jobs and no time and the people here who have all the time, but…" he just fades off, as if not sure how to finish.

"What do you think are the key elements for these people to find their path to successful living?" I ask.

"I don't know if I've necessarily found my own success. I don't know what that really is. This may be it, but I don't know. I guess I take it as it comes and deal with each situation. Not every experience is a good experience, but learning is important. From a business point of view I've learned that when the red flags go off to watch it. Listen to your heart, and if you see a problem developing in a relationship, business, or whatever, you heed that advice."

As if just remembering the weaving side of Greg's life, Brian asks, "How did you find your passion in weaving?"

"I don't know, I was young. I've always done art. My Mom was always interested in it. She did pottery. She actually took a weaving class and didn't like it, so she had all the stuff and that's how I started."

"Are you trying to get to the point where you can support yourself off your art?" I ask.

"That would be a perfect world, but I don't see it. It's hard to do that in textiles. I don't think I could fully live based on what I weave. I'd love to have a shop to produce fabrics and do rugs and tapestries, but it seems I have too many passions and not enough time."

"How do you go about balancing all those passions?"

"Right now there's not much weaving going on."

We all smile knowing full well what he means. Time and the way it tends to run from us when it comes to doing what you love.

"How do you think your views and opinions are different from your parents' generation?" I ask, noticing how frequent the mention of Greg's parents comes up.

"I think my parents' generation feels guilty and I think they want us to feel guilty, that if you're not out there working a fifty to sixty hour week then you're not paying your dues. I think part of life is having the time to pursue whatever it is you love. I say this, but it hardly ever happens to me. I wake up in the morning and it's one thing after another all day long. I think they would probably say that their happiness is more financially oriented."

"It takes courage to go against this grain, against society or your parents to pursue a dream. Is there anything you've done to make it easier?" Brian asks.

"I don't think it's easy. My being here hasn't been easy. I think dealing with each situation as it comes and thinking it through is important. You just have to follow your heart. Don't spend all your time planning for your death. Live while you're young and do the things you want to do while you can. I say that, but I don't always do it, but as long as that notion is in your brain, you'll be better off."

Max gets up, stretches, and makes for the doggy-door and the sunny patches of grass outside. He obviously is heeding Greg's advice and following his heart to a warm tree and cool shade.

We take this as a cue to do the same. Without the tree and shade part.

We thank Greg for his time and for sharing his thoughts with us. He in turn thanks us for the visit and wishes us well on the remainder of our journey. He walks us outside and shows us around the landscaping of his house. As chaotic as it is inside, the order of his gardens is amazingly meticulous. We take a minute to enjoy it before heading to the Quest-Mobile and back off the hill, descending into Idaho City and the great beyond.

ACROSS IDAHO

◆

To finish the moment,
to find the journey's end in every step of the road,
to live the greatest number of good hours,
is wisdom.

Ralph Waldo Emerson

We manage to make it up and out of Rick's by early morning and are on the road heading east by eight o'clock. We travel northeast on 21 past Idaho City and Lowman, on through the Boise National Forest, and around Benner Summit on the way to our final destination for the day: Stanley.

We pull into Stanley, Idaho (*pop. 69*) and immediately seek out a camping site. This would be our first night outside of a home and fending for ourselves. After securing a choice spot in a clearing by a river and setting up camp (*tent up in eleven minutes, we can do better than that*) we head back into town.

Stanley is one of those towns you would picture being in the middle of nowhere in one of the lonely western states. Its main street is a state route, ending at a "T" at the end of town and turning left or right on to other places and other lives. For two blocks from the T and between it and the great nothingness we just drove through lies Stanley. It has restaurants and a welcome center and a hotel and a few rafting companies, running the Salmon River being a major source of the city's income. A lot of living crammed into a little valley resting in the shadows of the jagged Sawtooths, the mountains watching in the distance like a collection of dirty ice-cycle stalagmites.

We came for the scenery. Rick told us it was the best way out of town and on to where we were going and we would pass sights that would leave us breathless. He was right. I've never quite seen a place like Stanley and her Sawtooths. Idaho has been full of surprises. It's funny, I had never really given much thought to the state. It was just one of those "out there" that I didn't ever have actual plans or reasons for going. I had dismissed it as a barren flatlands, a western version of Iowa perhaps. Boy was I wrong.

Idaho's landscape and scenery has amazed at every turn. The rivers and mountains and valleys all equally dazzling. I wonder if I would have appreciated the area as much had I seen it at an earlier age. Or had I known more of what to expect. I think it's the sheer lack of preparation for what I was going to see that made the impact once I arrived that much greater.

"Ready? Hold it...okay." I say and Brian is free to move again. He rushes over to look at the little LCD screen on the back of the digital camera. On it, slightly hidden in the reflecting light, is a shrunken image of him standing next to the Quest-Mobile with the majestic Sawtooths towering in the back.

"Looks good. She'll be happy with that one." Brian says.

He's referring to our newest *Full Tank Club* member Linda Strohmeyer who just yesterday signed on to sponsor our stretch from Boise to Stanley. The Full Tank Club is something we came up with before we left Los Angeles. We thought it would be a way others could help on our quest should they be so inclined. They could make a financial contribution for a tank of gas and in return get an autographed certificate and photo of the team—Brian and me—in their chosen location. Or as our advertisement on the web site read:

For The Price Of A Cup Of Coffee You Can Make A Difference:
That's right, for just cents a day, less than the cost of a cup of coffee, you can
become a Quest-4 sponsor by joining the Full Tank Club!

We thought it would help out a bit on the gas for the journey, expecting only close friends and family members to pitch in. We were very surprised when virtually everyone responded to the call to action and started making contributions. So far we have managed to cover at least half of our petrol requirements via the Club.

Having secured the photo for Linda's certificate, we head "into town" for some local pizza and then "across town" to the hotel for drinks. Inside the bar we immediately make a line for two stools by the bar. It is part of our unwritten Creed: when out, whenever possible, sit at the bar in order to raise the chances of actually meeting and talking to people. Our trip is about talking to and learning from others, and we find this generally difficult from a booth in the corner.

At the bar the bartender talks us into the local specialty: a wonderfully smooth darkish beer called Moose Drool. One pitcher, four bucks. The bar is pretty quiet, a Monday evening. Apart from us there is a table of men in the center of the room and an older man at the end of the bar concerned with nothing but his rapidly emptying glass. We sit and enjoy our Drool and watch the Miss Fitness America contest reflected in the bar mirror in front of us from a TV on the wall behind.

We make comments on flexibility and acrobatic ability as we gaze at the images on screen of flipping and contorting women. At the same time the bartender rushes around trying to fill the drink orders flying in from the waiters of the adjoining restaurant. She tells us there is an unexpected banquet of fifty people tonight, and she is short handed behind the bar. We want to offer to help but in her fury of activity are a little afraid to. So she continues bouncing from bottle to bottle, balancing glasses and mixing drinks. She draughts. And she Mai-Tais. And she Screwdrivers. And all the while little images flip and spin and pushup and split on screen behind her. A symphony of female strength and stamina all played to the tune of fizzing Moose Drool.

We're up early again the next morning. We make an insane attempt to wash off in the river, forgetting that its source is in the nearby mountains where snow still clings to the peaks, even in the dead center of a harsh summer. Our bone marrow starts to thaw just about the time we hit the Custer ghost town.

We make a short back track to Custer before continuing on our route eastward. Rick told us about the hidden ghost town, and right away we knew we had to make the trip. Heading across the west and not seeing a ghost town was like driving through Minnesota and missing all the lakes. It just isn't done.

Custer isn't the ghost town that Hollywood often takes us to. There is no long row of old rickety wooden buildings acting as the walls to a dirt lined, tumble weed infested corridor. It has a dirt road approach, but greenery has claimed back the area. And while there are a few wooden buildings—an old school house, a church, a home, a barn—the majority of the city is just crumbled stone foundations marked by stand up plaques. They scatter the area like a series of chalk outlines playing out the death throes of doomed architecture and showing where they fell, relics of someone else's quest.

On the road and heading back in the direction of Stanley we are stopped by road construction. A friendly looking lady in a reflective vest with the tan of someone who works the road all summer long is walking along the growing line of cars. She flashes her stop sign and smile, starkly white against her dark tan skin, and exchanges words with whoever is interested. The truck in front of us asks her how long the wait would be. Fifteen minutes or so, she replies. And in an instant driver and passenger are leaping out of their truck, grabbing reel and tackle

and black dog out of the bed, and sprinting down to the river below for
a quick fix of fly fishing. Brian and I watch as they cast and pull their
lines, laughing and smiling all the way. This is real passion. The smiling
road lady calls down at them and they quickly reel in their lines, run up
the embankment, and are in their truck ready to go before anyone has
to wait on them. True professionals who have obviously done this sort
of thing before.

We head past Stanley and continue south on 21 through Sun Valley
and the yuppie ski towns of Ketchum and Hailey. At each town we stop
briefly and look around considering an extended stay. But with no place
to stay and no camping areas around, we decide to keep moving. It is
still early in our journey and we have many miles yet to cover. So we pay
brief respects to Hemingway's grave (empty scotch bottle by the head
stone, someone must have paid more than respects before we got there)
and move on.

We reach the junction with 20 where we turn east again and pull off
the side of the road. On our map, right at the junction, we see a city
called Magic City right next to Magic Reservoir and not too far off our
road. We sit for a moment, map in hand, weighing our options. Keep
going or take the detour.

We pull off onto a dirt road past a sign marked Magic City. The road
carries us through low grass and desert plain and we are happy to be sitting up high in a big car. Brian's little low riding BMW would have been
in question at this point as we bounce over dips and holes in the road.
We turn a bend and then see the reservoir off to the side and down in a
valley. The road leads us down the hill, past several houses, and to a
dead end by the water.

We park at the water and get out of the Jeep. There's a small pier
where kids are jumping off into the water, a golden lab barking at them
as they splash around. Next to the pier on the shore is a mobile home
with several ladies sitting out front in folding lawn chairs. Next is a
small building marked restaurant snack bar, a small house set up on the

hill behind, and a larger house with half of it marked off as bar and restaurant. This was the heart of Magic City.

We pull off our shoes and walk down into the water. Neither the kids or their dog pay us any attention as we wade out to mid thigh depth. The water is cool and my leg muscles contract upon contact. Across the water on the other side of the reservoir I can see what seems to be another city, maybe a little larger than Magic, but still appearing to be lost.

Back on shore we put on our shoes and decide to stop into the bar for a quick beer before hitting the road again, trying to make the most of our Magic City experience. We climb the wooden stairs and cross the deck and step inside the door marked "bar", marked to distinguish it from the door to the private residence just next to it. Inside there is a bar with three men and a woman seated on one side and an old man and a child standing on the other. Behind them is a small room with a pool table, a few cardboard beer advertisement cutouts, and a poster of John Wayne. As we enter everyone looks briefly in our direction but smoothly continue their conversation. We feel like we are stepping into someone's home from the street, a family gathering too important to be interrupted by the sudden arrival of a stranger.

We sit down at the bar and the old man steps out of the conversation briefly to motion to the boy. The boy asks us what we want and requests two Budweisers from Grandpa. Grandpa pulls two from the cooler and hands them down to us then turns back to the crowd and tells them about busted sewer pipes, turning off water mains, plumbing, and digging wells. The little boy jumps in proudly with his contributions to the well process. We just sit and listen and sip our beer, invisible visitors in the land of Magic City.

Back on the road and closer to the day's destination, wherever that may be. We begin to notice a severe change in the area's terrain as the ground begins to be pocketed with jagged stone and shallow crevasses. We know we're approaching the Craters Of The Moon even before looking at the map. Slowly the presence of volcanic rock begins to infiltrate the land on both sides of us. It grows in number and volume and when we bank a turn ahead we see that it has won out. There on the horizon is a sea of twisted stone, devouring and destroying everything in site.

We pull over at the first sign marking the area for a closer look at the oddity of the plains. Even if our own curiosity didn't force us to stop, our Creed would have: *Learn with passion.*

The sign tells us the whole area was created by volcanic activity, the most recent being as little as two thousand years ago. The lava rushed over the land and slowly cooled into the field before us, creating an eerie landscape straight out of the pages of science fiction. *And thus our heroes descend from their craft and onto the barren alien landscape in search of extraterrestrial life.* We hop out and walk out onto the magma carpeting.

Walking on the rock is difficult and painful, especially if you happen to stumble and reach out for support. Which I did. Several times. I kept telling myself it was due to the heightened gravity on this strange planet we've stumbled across, but somehow that didn't make the blow to my ego any better. Each time I place hand on rock to steady myself I was intrigued and fascinated with the stones and wanted to sweep up a collection for further study and display. But the sign had strictly stated: *Do not collect samples from the area.* Though how in a land of six gazillion rocks they would miss one or two I wouldn't begin to fathom.

Brian breaks my thoughts of felony as he calls out to snap a shot for the web site. *Chris searches for answers on the surface of the moon.* Completing the tourist thing, I exchange places with him and take his photo. Then I find a relatively flat rock, position the camera on top of it, and let the auto shoot function capture Brian and me in mid-crouch among the boulders of painful volcanic sculpture. Visiting time is over, the next shuttle for earth leaves in two minutes.

After the wonders of Magic City and the Moon the rest of our day's drive is boring in comparison. We race into the gathering darkness see how far we can make it, how close to Yellowstone before we would have to stop for the night. We want to get as close as we can in order to get up and in early enough to avoid the RV brigade. We make it to a campsite somewhere just past Ashton and within less than an hour's reach from the park. Register, pitch tent, inflate sleeping mats, unroll bags. Twelve and a half minutes. We're in bed asleep in twenty.

*   *   *

Beep beep beep beep. It's coming from my watch, which is, I think, attached to my wrist. So it should be easy to locate and kill. But this morning in the folds of the sleeping bag it proves to be a challenge.

5:30 A.M.

Time to go. Yellowstone awaits.

We pack up (*10 minutes 37 seconds*) and hit the road. We were told when we arrived last night that the camp site would be half price due to the water being shut off. No water, no shower, half price. It was something we could deal with. The final stretch takes no time and we are in West Yellowstone and at the west gate before we know it. Hungry, unclean, and in need of coffee and a tooth brush, we decide to stop into a McDonald's before entering the park.

Inside Brian orders while I shower in the men's room sink. Dunked head, washed face, brushed teeth, a new man. Feeling very McClean and McAwake and ready to hit my McMorning running. I skip outside and join Brian at the table to break fast, noticing a large Amish family sitting at the table across the room from us. They must be here to enjoy the park as well. We finish up our meals and Brian takes his turn in the

McDonald's health spa, opting only to brush his teeth rather than partake in the whole upper body sponge bathing ritual.

Coffee fueled and squeaky clean, we are ready to move on. A chipper attendant greets us at the gate, a high-schooler working Montana's answer to the summer job. We pass her my Eagle Pass (highly recommended for a cross-country journey, entry into all national parks for one low, low price. Order yours today!) and she admits us with a wave and an offer of a pound of guides, maps, and reading materials.

And we have arrived! Yellowstone. It's one of those places you always hear about and always wonder if it's really as good as all their marketing personnel tell you it is. They boast about it being the world's first national park, rave about its immense size, and marvel over the wildlife. They ramble on in barrels of praise, and in the soft morning light reflected through the caffeine haze of a fresh morning, it seems everything is true.

We drive slowly through the park and take in the beauty of it all. It is amazing. Even with all the hype, it is simply amazing. The rivers and trees and mountains all in perfect composition. Even the corpses of trees left over from the 1998 fire that wiped out much of the park add to the spectral wonder of the area. The decayed, dying forms adding sharp contrast to the life around them.

We continue to cruise through the park passing elk and pine. At one point we have to stop for a Yellowstone traffic jam. A buffalo has wandered onto the street and is strolling down the left lane weaving in and out of cars that have stopped to allow him safe passage. The buffalo brushes past one station wagon as its passengers gawk in amazement, then it lumbers right past our open window within reach of Brian. His big eye looks up through the window at us as he walks past and on his way to his next important morning activity. Car engines start again and cars slowly roll back to life. Just another day in the big city of Yellowstone.

Our morning takes us through the west side of the park. We see the Upper Geyser Basin, the Firehole River, the Lower Geyser Basin, and the ever popular Old Faithful. At Old Faithful we sit and watch as a Chinese tour group congregates behind us and prepares for the big event. The steam flickers and blows, erupting finally and tangos to the beat of clicking shutters and oooohs and ahhhs. Then it delicately dies and the show is over.

Back in the Jeep we head east to the other side of the park. As we do we drive through a camping area infested with Winnebegos and other houses on wheels. We are driving through a nest of poisonous predators and can feel ourselves consciously trying to drive quietly. Trying to catch our breath and not wake any of the beasts up. If we can make it through safely we had it made. If we woke even one of them it would start a chain reaction that would set all engines gunning. The swarm would take to the roads, engulfing the whole world around them in constipated bowels of diesel stench and non-motion.

We continued to tip-toe our way through the campsites and further eastward. The deadly swarm of RVs seemingly unaware and resting safely behind us. We made it. Or so we thought. We were fools.

The morning was breaking and we were heading east from the plains of the west. Almost nobody enters from the west. With all the other scenic beauty found across the states to the west of us, Yellowstone was an after thought. Some place you went in off season or drove through on your way east. No, the traffic came from the east. Eastern tourists with dreams of the wild west. Dreams of seeing it through the safe glass box of their windshield.

We pass the halfway point and see it up on the hillside. Its bumper glitters in the sun, its stark white side glowing. Behind it drags a burgundy Toyota, dangling like some sick forgotten creature connected by a steel hitched umbilical cord. An RV. The beginning of the end.

It is just the first. Behind it there are many, many more. Soon we are surrounded by them. They pass on our left heading the opposite direction into the park and crawl slowly up the hills in front of us trying to get out. Dyslexic drivers read the road signs marked 30 as 03 miles per hour and stick to it religiously. We are hyperactive Davids stuck in a world of lethargic Goliaths.

We relax, we enjoy the scenery (what little of it we could see around the monstrous machines that abound). We look at the map and plan out our drive once we exit the park. A stop in Cody and the Wild Bill Museum. An alternate route on 14 to see the Medicine Wheel National Historic Site just past Lovell. And then on into Sheridan and my cousin Craig's place. Simple enough. We could make it, if we ever get out of the park.

We have been debating our next move all morning. Do we stay in the park for a few days or move on? We have been vacillating between choices all morning until the swarm hit. Now our decision is quite clear. Come back and see the park in the off season, not in its peak, most crowded time of the year.

Construction on the far end of the park slows us up even more. A half hour wait to go over the pass gives us a chance to get out and stretch our legs. We walk over to the river and skip rocks, looking around for more fly fishermen. There are none today. I think of the road workers and the park rangers and the high-schoolers at the gate. What a great environment it is they work in. Coming to work each day to clean air, open spaces, and silent mountains. If the working environment played a part on your happiness what must this wilderness' effect be? Does the stress of the job just dissipate in the open air, dying due to lack of people to bounce it onto? Standing roadside and splashing stones, I can't remember anything that happened before breakfast.

The clog clears and the traffic begins to flow. We jump back into the stream and float along with the RVs and happy campers up the pass, around the bend, and are flushed out of the park and on toward Sheridan.

BIG SKY COUNTRY

♦

I go about looking at horses and cattle.
They eat grass, make love,
work when they have to,
bear their young.
I am sick with envy of them.

Sherwood Anderson

We by-pass Sheridan and head further east toward Craig's place in Ucross. In the forty mile stretch between, this is what we see: A flock of wild turkeys in the road. Several skipping bucks that somehow avoided becoming either a hood ornament or a wall decoration and lived to see adulthood. Two dead red fox road rugs. Farms and hills and houses and trees and horses. Four passing cars. And the constant barrage of kamikaze birds. This is probably not their scientific name (*Wyominial Kamikaziti*) but the one that best fits. As we drive the quiet, windy road these little birds keep flying one by one directly toward us only to pull away at the moment just before deadly impact. I think they're trying to fly through the little gap between the top of the Jeep and the roof top carrier we added back in Boise. They must think it to be some sort of portal, some worm hole to the sunny south that will help them avoid the long commute come winter. If only they could make it into that wind tunnel then *whooooosh* they would shoot out like a missile and be on their way South. *See you Tweety, give my love to Aunt Anna!*

I look at the speed-o-meter and then at the written directions and know we're almost there. I hand the directions back to Brian just as we hear a thump on the roof. The luck of one of the kamikaze's just ran out.

We hit the Ucross T junction and hang a right and then shortly thereafter hang another. A gravel driveway marks the end to another long day of travel, the end of one part of our adventure and the beginning of a new one.

The lights are all off in the house so we rightly assume no one is home. This doesn't faze us though; we knew it was a possibility since I called Craig from Cody and told him we were arriving a few days early due to a bad case of the Winnebego. He said fine but he may be off at a dinner party. Just go on in, he told us, the doors are never locked. And they aren't.

An amazing difference between here in the great spans of the West and what I've become accustomed to: people don't lock their doors. I guess there is so much space between people they figure what's the point. No one's going to drive all the way out here to steal anything. And if they do, they could always just break in, there's no one for miles around to hear them if they do. So why not make life easier for everyone. Quite the contrast from the fidgety attitude of the East and the sheer paranoia of Los Angeles. We can't quite get used to the idea yet, even though it was the same at Rick's. No door keys needed, it's always open. It makes me think of the joke about 7-11 stores. *If they are open 24-7, then why are there locks on the doors.*

Brian and I get out of the Jeep and lock the doors behind us. Old habits die hard. We are greeted by the smell of hay and horses and summer sage. I take a few deep lung fulls, appreciating the severe lack of human scent. We climb the stairs to the newly built front porch that I was told was just completed a few weeks ago. The newest addition since the barn was put up a couple months back. All built, along with the house itself, by Craig, his dad—my Uncle Glen—and friends. Seeing the quality and craftsmanship I am impressed. I remember shoddy tree houses Craig helped me and my brothers build as kids, boards and nails haphazardly placed akimbo between trees. He's come a long way.

On the deck we see the glass front door shaking as we draw near to it, and we see why. Behind it and eager for escape stand Craig's two dogs, Max and Jack: the big old yeller shepherd mix and the young slobbering Bernese Mountain Dog pup. Both ready to make our acquaintance. I open the (unlocked) door and steady myself for the onslaught. They rush out and greet us and already Jack is letting go of his excitement all over the porch in a steady yellow stream. Max stands a bit off and glares at us softly, either not sure what to make of us yet—friend or foe—or very apologetic for the actions of his hyper cousin Jack.

We look inside for a few minutes to get a feel for the house and its amenities. It is in the process of additions and remodeling, and it isn't obvious where we are to sleep so we decide to leave our gear in the car for the time being. I suggest we have a look around outside while we wait on our hosts' return.

We head back out of the house and around the back. A couple of horses chew at grass on the other side of the field. They look up momentarily to regard us then go back to their consumption unimpressed. Across the field and over some low hills the sun is setting and the sky is catching fire. We climb the hills and keep walking until we are on the crest of the highest one and have the best seats in the land to stare off at the horizon. The colors bleed out of the sky, a wet-on-wet watercolor of windy reds and oranges soaking into one another. It's the most spectacular sunset of our trip, even beating out the smog-ignited sunsets of southern California.

"I'm a Big Sky guy." Brian says breaking the long silence since our initial oohs and ahhs over the sights.

"Excuse me?"

"There's something about a huge sky that picks me up, and makes me feel complete. I like a sky unobstructed by buildings, mountains, and trees." He speaks and just stares off at the horizon, as if hypnotized by the scenery. I just watch the colors shift and change and listen.

"I think it was the years living in Nebraska watching a million colors wash over the landscape at dusk that fed my present love. I'm reminded of this 'sky-thing' today. Here we are watching a show that no man could ever create. It's dazzling."

"It is. Amazing." I say, still mesmerized by hues.

"I've seen sunsets over the skyscrapers of Hong Kong," Brian talks on, "the pier in Santa Monica, and the mountains of Appalachia, but nothing compares to the sunsets in lands where 360 degree views are commonplace. You know what the trouble with these scenes is?"

He asks me but doesn't look my direction, his eyes still fixed on the horizon. "What?" I ask.

"There is no possible way to describe or replicate the experience," he explains. "No words can do them justice. No photograph can ever match the scale and detail. We could try, and we can get some amazing scenery, but you really must be here to truly experience it."

"Amen brother, amen," I say as the spirits of the sky ebb out of Brian and he's himself once more, the poet on the hilltop lost and the weary traveler returned.

The light is almost completely faded now and we see a new show taking place. The second act. Heat lightning begins to dance across the clouds, lighting them up one by one in electric blue brilliance.

"You're liking this aren't you?" Brian asks. I know he doesn't mean the sky show either. He's referring to the West. He's referring to the trip.

"Yeah, I am. There's a lot to like out here in these wide open spaces. The peace and solitude. The access to nature. And do you feel that?" I slump and raise my shoulders and roll my head and neck. "Lack of stress. It seems to just dissipate out here. I guess you have so much time and space between you and the next person that it leaks out of you and dissolves into the atmosphere. There's no one to bounce it off onto and into. No one to reflect it off. Or maybe it's just the prevalence of nature that makes me see and appreciate the more important things and forget the petty worries. I don't know. I'm just rambling."

"No, I think you have something. It's definitely a different life style, a different pace." Brian says.

"Yeah. I'm not sure it's me though. I can see where many would love to have this simpler life, and maybe I would too at some point. But right now I think I need a bit more excitement. Access to new and different things. You know, desires for things that lead to stress and require a busier environment to get them."

"Well hey, as long as you realize that and accept it. That's a start."

I don't answer. I just watch the lightning and let the moment sink in. I left L.A. wondering if there was someplace I'd rather be. I left with complaints about the city but now I was seeing some of the city's good side by comparison. As much as I loved this area, the scenery, the space, nature's involvement, I'm not sure this is my path. But our road is not yet complete. I watch as the lightning skirts across the sky and wait for a bolt to hit me, zapping me with clarity. With Answers. Shamzara.

"C'mon Big Sky Guy, let's go see if they're home." I turn and lead the way back down the hill.

We get back to the house and get attacked by slobbering Jack before we can make it to the porch. Then a booming voice from inside tells us our hosts have returned.

"Get him, Jack, eat him alive!" The voice commands. It's Craig.

I hop up on the porch and meet Craig at the door and reluctantly exchange hugs. As per the norm, he nearly lifts me off the ground and cracks a few ribs in the process. I in turn, squeeze as hard as I can to see what damage I can inflict. I am less successful. We release each other and Brian gets a simple—but rather firm—handshake.

"Glad you guys could make it. Did you have any trouble finding the place." Craig asks. It's one of our frequently asked questions. At one point we thought of making up T-shirts that have all the answers printed on them so we could just skip past them upon our initial greetings. The T-shirt thus far on our trip would read.

Not too tired from the drive just yet.

It was easy to find your place, thanks to your great directions.

We're self-financed, but contributions are highly appreciated.

"No problem. We got here a while ago. We've been up enjoying the show on the hill." I say.

"Spectacular isn't it. It's like that every night." Craig boasts.

You can see a little family resemblance when the light hits us just right, the kind normal for first cousins, not like those kooky identical cousins on the Patty Duke show. Faint glimpses of each other in the facial features and tints of red still remaining in Craig's hair and beard. But his much larger Johnson frame sets us apart, he six foot two and squarely built, me five-ten and more sleek of muscle. Our similarities stem more from the non-physical side of relativeness.

In truth, Craig is more of a brother than a cousin. We grew up living next door to each other and as a kid I spent as much time at his house as I did mine. It was Craig, eight years my senior, that introduced me to old movies and science fiction and Led Zeppelin and the Doors. It was Craig with whom I'd sit up late at night and share story ideas, both of us trading tales from our imagination with each other. And it was he that went on to put some of those late night tales to paper.

Craig has been nearly everything. A craftsman, a rodeo cowboy, a mountain guide, a ranch herder, a sky-diver, an actor, a teacher, a playwright. While growing up he was always into something new. And usually I was right there along side him, the little kid tagging along after his childhood hero.

Now Craig has found a life that combines many of his interests and a few newly added ones. Playwright, drama teacher, rancher, retail store owner. It's a good thing he has no need for business cards, there wouldn't be space to put everything on them.

"C'mon, I want you to meet Judy." Craig says and leads us into the house.

Judy climbs down a ladder from the loft bedroom above and I meet her at the bottom with a hug. This time much softer and squishier than before, my ribs come away fully intact. It's the first time we've met, though I have already heard much about her. She is just the combination of beauty, spunk, and vivaciousness I expected.

We exchange greetings, how'd doos, and small talk about our trip. Then Craig shows us around and where we'll be sleeping. We gather our things from the Jeep and I notice the third act has just begun above us. The lightning has gone and left a black ocean dotted with sharp white stars. The huge stream of the Milky Way splashed across its middle. The grand finale in the theater of night.

We grab our things and head back inside to settle in for the night.

        *   *   *

"We come bearing bagels," I say hoisting a large bag into the air as we walk into the Bucking Buffalo Western Supply. Judy looks up from behind the counter and smiles around a customer. I reach into the bag and pull out her bagel and hand it to her. She tells us Craig is in the back in the framing department.

We head back into the store, passing two huge bison heads and several stuffed Jackalopes, their little rabbit bodies straining from the weight of the large set of antlers on their heads. The store is filled with a sundry of Western wear and specialty goods. A boutique with western charm and hospitality and unique and interesting products that would be just as at home on Park Avenue as it is here on Main Street in Sheridan, Wyoming. Craig is found in the framing alcove as directed.

We munch on bagels and recount some tales of our journey to Craig. Craig in return makes some suggestions for people we ought to talk with while in town. He suggests Marcus Red Thunder, a Cree Indian and friend of his that works as a counselor at the Thunder Cloud Rehabilitation Center just outside Sheridan. Another person he thinks will be of interest to us is Richard Rhoades, a big game hunter who has worked as a taxidermist, as a hunting guide to Africa and beyond, and now farms herbs for local restaurants. Two very different and interesting people with unique paths and stories. And two representatives of the culture of the West. He finishes up his lunch and makes a few calls for us. We see Marcus this afternoon. Craig can't reach Richard but tells us he'll keep trying.

We chat a bit and make plans for our stay. Craig tells us he and Judy will be heading south to Denver for a few days starting Thursday and we will be on our own then. But when they return we can spend some time seeing the area. Before then, if we'd like, he would show us out to their lake house in Montana.

We sit and shoot the breeze a while longer and then take our leave and tour the city of Sheridan. We stroll up and down the street peeping in windows and reading signs. The downtown area is lively, with Main Street littered with restaurants, clothing stores, curios, and specialty shops. The mainstay of the tourist trade they enjoy during peak seasons.

We pop in the infamous Mint Bar for a look. Ever since heading inland from Seattle everyone has told us we couldn't miss the Mint if we were traveling through Sheridan. No one ever told us why, they just told us to head here at all costs. And stepping inside I can immediately see what they meant.

The place is loaded with dead things. Dead things on the walls, dead things behind the bar, dead things on the ceiling. A mortuary of animals. A taxidermy showcase. A museum of beasts who all had one really bad day. We walk into the dark, smoky bar and are greeted by two massive caribou on the far wall in front of us, guarding the entrance into the billiard room. Along the wall to our left, deer and elk and mountain goat and stone sheep and a menagerie of other stuffed creatures stare back at us with glassy eyes. A bit overwhelmed by it all we stumble into seats at the bar and order a couple tall beers. No Moose Drool this time.

The bartender hands us our beer and asks if this is our first visit to the bar. We try to figure out what gave us away: our clean cut, beardless faces; the pasty white, slightly sunburned skin; or the shorts and sandals, the garb of travelers, NOT the ranch wear of a true Sheridan native. We fess up to being strangers to these here parts, and she produces two guides to the bar and critters adorning the walls. Inside a chart helps to easily identify each one. We entertain ourselves for a bit playing guess that creature and sipping beer. The whole experience surreal and bizarre.

I have a thought. What if while we are sitting here in this bar staring at dead things and enjoying a brew we are really just little creatures in a glass-domed world belonging to some monstrous entity from Beyond. Tiny inhabitants in Its little snow-dome. And in Its farm. I then look at our reflections in the bar mirror and wonder if somewhere in some parallel universe a couple of Elks sit at this bar and enjoy a beer while looking over their shoulder at a stuffed and mounted Chris and Brian hanging on the wall. The plaque underneath would read:

Chris & Brian
These Homo Sapiens were bagged while on the customary human migration in search of greater meaning and purpose. Our best scientific estimate is they began their migration in California heading east when our hunters got them just outside Sheridan. Notice the differences in

their pelts and skins. While poor specimens of the human race, they do represent the ludicrous search for answers the Humans tend to exhibit. They got their answer. Bang.

Brian says something. He points out the proliferation of dead things since we hit Boise. The deeper we head into the West the more dead things we have run into. Everyone seems to have them. The hotel bar in Stanley boasted a black bear and eight point buck. A Walmart offered their own taxidermy department, complete with examples of their work displayed on the walls right next to the automotive department (making me wonder how many of the animals there had actually been hit by cars and not rifle ammo). Every bar and restaurant in Sun Valley had a minimum of one stuffed something on display. But nothing could compete with this. This was the granddaddy of all western stuffed zoos.

We finish up our drinks and turn down the offer of another one. We still had a bit more touring of the city to complete before paying a visit to Mr. Red Thunder...

LESSONS OF THE
MEDICINE WHEEL

◆

What is life?
It is the flash of a firefly in the night.
It is the breath of a buffalo in the wintertime.
It is the little shadow which runs across
the grass and loses itself in the sunset.

Crowfoot

"We're here to see Marcus Red Thunder," I say to the receptionist. She tells us to wait a moment and rings back to an office somewhere in the belly of the building. Brian and I stroll around the room looking at photos on the walls and then finally take a seat just as a man approaches from the west wing.

"Hi, Chris and Brian?" Marcus says as he walks over to us. We stand to greet him and I offer clarification of our identities as we shake hands. Marcus then offers us a tour of the facilities and we follow him into the building.

The Thunder Cloud is a center for healing and rehabilitation, Marcus explains to us. It was established by the Indian Nation and represents not one tribe but many. All are welcome inside its doors. As we stroll around the corridors I ask Marcus how he arrived at the center, and he recounts to us a bit of his personal history. He tells us a tale of a man who has taken the challenges of life and faced them head on, turning adversity into a life's path.

Marcus grew up in Montana, raised by a single mother and never knowing his father. When he was eight, his mother died and he was shifted from aunt to uncle before arriving at an orphanage where he would grow up. At 16 he went to live with a Catholic priest, who eventually adopted Marcus two years later. Marcus showed a natural scholastic aptitude in High School and entered the University of Notre Dame on a full academic scholarship after graduation. But after a promising first semester, Marcus fell victim to substance abuse and ended up dropping out of college when the problem became too difficult to manage. Marcus found help through his adopted father and a treatment clinic and managed to get his life back on track. During this process he became interested in the people who helped him better himself and decided to explore the field for himself. He began working at the Thunder Cloud center in Sheridan as a weekend supervisor on the graveyard shift. This led him to study to be a drug and alcohol counselor, and once certified he worked as a counselor at the center. Marcus worked as a counselor for about two and a half years before moving into his current marketing and PR position, a position that he believes is the path he wants to be on.

We step through the back door and out onto the lawn behind the building. The center sits on a hill overlooking a plush river valley, green and fertile, an oasis in the surrounding barren plains. Marcus points out the area where their sweat lodge sits, but we can't see it through the trees. He tells us a little about the area and we soak in the scenery. Marcus then asks more about our quest and Brian fills him in on the details to date. I notice how he's now able to say it with such grace and precision, like a pianist playing a favorite concerto by heart.

"Have you learned anything yet on the journey?" Marcus asks. I turn away from the scenery I have become lost in and see he is looking at me, almost as if the question is meant for me alone.

"I have. A great deal. Unfortunately, we've been moving at such a quick pace and have been so active I really haven't taken the time to assess what I've learned and internalize it." I confide in him. "But Craig's going to be out of town for a few days this week so I think I'm going to take the time to just sit and figure it all out."

Marcus seems to consider this and me for a moment. I can see understanding in his eyes.

"You should take a vision quest." He suggests.

"A vision quest?" I ask intrigued.

"Yes. If you're truly serious about it, you should go off by yourself for a few days without food or water and just meditate on things. I could assist you if you like. We have a site for it not far from here on that hill." He points to a hill off in the distance on the edge of the river valley.

"That would be great," I say, excited at the suggestion. Not only would it give me a chance to let the wisdom of the road sink in, but it would give me the chance to try something new and explore an area of Native American culture.

"Think about it," Marcus says. "Should we begin?"

Marcus leads us back into the building and to his office where we set up to talk. I'm still lost in the suggestion of the vision quest but manage to pull my mind back into the discussion. Brian starts off asking Marcus a little more about how he discovered his life's work.

"I kind of fell into my path," Marcus says. "But I wanted to be involved in this field. Growing up around drugs and alcohol, that's what I knew. I wanted to better my life and my children's, because with Native Americans there is a real vicious cycle of poverty, a vicious cycle of addiction. So that moved me right into this role. I didn't want to be a counselor, but then I kind of figured that there were a lot of people who have been in the position to help me out in my life...I don't want to make out like I am a martyr or something, but I wanted to give something back. I thought maybe I would do it for two or three years at the most, that's all I wanted to do it, and then I'd start to look for something else. I tried it, this is what I did, and then I wanted to move into more of a business, because that's what I really want to do. Business, marketing, PR, that's what I'm really doing now. So I paid my dues and now I'm doing what I really enjoy doing. Now I do a lot of marketing to tribes, a lot of programs."

"What kind of counseling do you do here at the center?" I ask.

"I don't really preach sobriety, I preach a holistic living, a balanced lifestyle." Marcus explains. "We talk about our Creator or God, but not only just in the spiritual. We separate God and our lives a lot in the modern society. God is just one day out of the week for just one hour where we pay our dues. Where this way it's more of him being with us 24-7. It's not only when you're going to church. Or for Native Americans I tell them it's not only when you're going to a sweat lodge. He's not only there when you're going to a sun dance. He's in every part of your life. It's how you speak to people, how you treat them, how you dress, how you conduct yourself, how you raise your children, it's all of that. It's in everything, not just in one part of our life. That's what I try to promote as a counselor. It's a holistic approach, living a really strong balanced life. Not taking it to an extreme on one side or the other."

Marcus pauses for a moment to find a blank piece of paper under a stack of forms on his desk. He pulls it out and takes a pen from a desk drawer. On the page he draws a circle and two lines running through it, one vertically and one horizontally, the lines intersecting in the circle's center.

"A balanced life is like a Native American medicine wheel," he says as he draws. "It has four spokes going to the center. I was taught that reflected in that is two roads, two positives and their negatives. And if you take a look at it that way, the center is where you want to be, that balance is what you need. The negative is not so bad all the time, we need some of that. But if you get too far into it, it isn't healthy. The same with the positive. You get too far into that and it isn't healthy. If you get to the point where you feel 'holier than thou' that isn't good. You need to try to achieve that balance."

"Where did this philosophy come from?" I ask.

"There is a medicine wheel on top of this mountain on alternate Highway 14, outside of Dayton..."

"Right, we stopped off on the way to Sheridan and saw it." Brian says.

"Great. This is an ancient medicine wheel. There is no tribe that claims it, but they all respect it. When my wife and I first moved here to Sheridan there was a lot of controversy about that medicine wheel. There were two factions, one was primarily non -Native Americans and the others were Native Americans. One faction wanted to commercialize it. They wanted to pave the road up to it and build a visitor center. But the other faction, which was primarily Native Americans, said this is one of our sacred sites. Just leave it the way it is. If you do this, it's just going to get desecrated like the Black Hills, the Great Horn Butte—what many call Devil's Tower—Bear Butte, all our sacred sites. When they build centers like this they just become desecrated. So anyway, there was a lot of controversy when I first got here about the medicine wheel. I'd go to different prayer meetings and there would be talk about it. So I started thinking maybe this is trying to tell me something. So I started reading about it and I read a lot of books about it and I started asking my elders about it and that's where I got the teachings. Simple teachings about the medicine wheel."

"What kind of teachings?" Brian asks.

"The medicine wheel looks at how you live your life and tells you that you are not alone within it," Marcus explains using his drawing as a tool again. "What the medicine wheel represents is the whole world, and those four spokes that go to the center are the four basic nations in the world. They call them the sacred colors, which are Red, White, Black, and Yellow. And from each one of those nations, the road is their paradigm, their perspective, and they are all part of the world. But they are different. For example, the Native Americans do things a lot different from the White people."

"This is the world as I explained it," Marcus points at his medicine wheel drawing representing the world, "and each of these spokes is a nation: red, yellow, black, white. And from here we break it into the nations, for instance here," he draws another wheel to represent the Indian Nation. "Here we have just the red nation, we have our own medicine wheel. The reason for this is because of our tribes, that's what these spokes represent," he says, pointing out the lines in the circle. "And there's not just four, there are many. And in the wheel of the tribe," Marcus says as he draws another wheel, "each spoke represents the individual and their own paradigm. Their own path or life. And then we break it down to the final one," he draws yet another wheel to represent the individual. "That's you. Your own personal medicine wheel. The same element is in the center of all these...the same circle, always."

Marcus looks up to us to see if we are following what he is saying. We both nod along with his explanation and he continues.

"And then you break your wheel down into your own parts of yourself, and you decide that. It can be whatever: your physical, your social, your emotional, intellectual, spiritual, whatever you want in there. But each one of those within itself has its own medicine wheel. And you see the two roads there are positive and negative. And the one that sits in the middle is where we need to strive for, for that balance. And if this is strong and balanced, then that is what you bring into the tribe wheel, because you're part of this. It's one thing to say that, 'I am part of this tribe.' That is only half of it. The other part is to say that, 'This tribe is part of me.' If we can say that second part, then you can't remove yourself, because the tribe is part of you. It's the same with spirituality. So many times people will say 'I'm part of this religion, I'm part of God,' but that's just one part. If you can go the second step and say 'He's part of me' then we can't separate ourselves and say, 'well He's over there.' So you're not alone."

Marcus taps the bottom wheel—the individual wheel—then the one above it and continues in order back to the top wheel. "You're part of this tribe, this tribe's part of this nation, this nation's part of this world. So how you want your world to be is how you want to live your life. The medicine wheel has a lot to be learned from it."

"It seems it's pretty universal in its teachings too." I observe.

"Yes. The medicine wheel teaches that we are different yet we are one and the same. We need to accept those differences with one and another. My ways are different from yours, I'm an Indian and my ways are different; there's no doubt about that. But we see those differences, we accept them, let's move on. That's what this teaches, many roads, one direction. Call it what you want: Jesus, Allah, God. It's the same. This teaching has been around for thousands of years. And when we tap into it as Native Americans, when we tap into it, we have these thousands of years of prayer backing us up. If we can tap into this and get it back into our lives, there is nothing that can stop us. No matter what we do, whatever we set out to do, if we do it in a good way, we're going to succeed. There are times when we've gotten away from this. We've taken something holy out of the center and we've put in money, put in drugs, put in alcohol. Each one of them is powerful, yes, but not as powerful as something spiritual."

"When you talk about succeeding, in what way do you personally define success?" Brian asks.

"My personal success comes from my family, my children...I really value my family, my kids—my three boys. Seeing my boys and they're happy and they're provided for. We're not rich by any means, but we're happy. It's simple. What I get out of my family is peace, happiness, for myself. I also get a lot of guidance, my kids teach me a lot. I've learned a lot about balance and getting things right. If I do something wrong my kids will point it out, those little guys are smart."

"Do you think success and happiness go hand in hand?" I ask.

"If you are Native American and went into the reservation, success would be more happiness, being content with your family and that they were taken care of. Not really rich or anything like that, just that they were taken care of. It's really simple, but yet on the other side of that at times they get complacent with that. Because on the reservation it's really protected; they have their own communities there. Many have their basics provided for and they're happy so they become complacent and they don't strive for more, don't try for continual growth. This is an example but it's not only on Indian reservations that this takes place. It can happen with anyone. This is what my uncle told me: we should try for a balanced journey, balanced life. It's our decision to go in a positive way or a negative way or a balanced way. When you become complacent you become stagnant, in the spiritual part of you or physical or whatever. You can be out of balance. If you get complacent, you lose your drive for balance."

"How do you go about finding this balance?" Brian asks.

"I think what Chris said outside was excellent. Too many times we get caught up in the everyday life that's going by. It's boom, boom, boom. We have to take care of this and take care of that. Things are flying all around. We just need to stop, take a couple days off by yourself, go without water or food and just sit. I don't know if you believe in God, but just sit and take care of yourself and just meditate. Quiet everything down, sort it all out. When you don't eat or drink for a couple of days, you find out what's really important in life. It's pretty simple."

I think about this. No food. No water. The thought of actually doing it is thrilling. And scary.

"Take time," Marcus goes on. "Stop what you're doing. Just stop, take some time out. Even if it's just for an hour, just stop. Stop and reflect on what the hell is going on. Taking that time out is tough. I've been taught that there are two kinds of suffering. There's neurotic suffering and there's existential suffering. And taking time out for yourself, like for fasting, is existential. It's not neurotic. You're doing it for a reason and there's a lot of strength that's going to come out of it. It will teach you. Our elders tell us, they speak in a way that's spiritual, they say if you go out and take time for yourself and pray, that's where you get your protection, for yourself and if you have children, or a spouse, protection for them too. And that's protection from the unseen, or protection for whatever your interactions are in everyday life. There are always struggles that are going on. We're never going to learn everything about it, but try to learn a little bit about it and take care of what we need to take care of and you'll be all right."

"It sounds like great advice Marcus. And if it's okay, I think I will take you up on your offer to assist me on a vision quest." I say.

"Sure. I'll make the preparations. When were you talking about?" Marcus asks.

I tell him that Craig and Judy were heading to Denver for a few days starting on Thursday, so some time around then. He says I would need to come in on Wednesday night just before sunset and stay until sunrise on Saturday. We discuss some of the details. Before further discussion he tells me in order to do the vision quest I will have to commit to doing it at least three other times during my lifetime. Four vision quests is normal in Native American belief. To this I promptly agree. He then explains what I can bring with me, a short list of bedroll and something comfortable to wear. It will be the easiest packing job I've ever done. He then instructs me to meet him back at the center at eight o'clock on Wednesday evening; he will then take me to the site.

We thank Marcus and tell him we'll see him later in the week. He shows us out and sends us on our way.

INTO SOLITUDE

◆

When one's expectations are reduced to zero,
One really appreciates everything one does.

Stephen Hawking

It's still bright out when we make the drive back to the Thunder Cloud Center Wednesday evening. We're used to it by now, Idaho stayed light until ten at night. We drive out in silence on a quiet road, passing only one car between Sheridan the road off to the center. It really is out there.

We pull into the parking lot and wait for Marcus. A basketball game is being played out on the far end of the lot; we sit and watch for a while until a blue van pulls in the space next to us and obstructs our view of the court. Marcus.

"Good evening," he says as he climbs out of his car to meet us.

"Hi," Brian says lowering his window.

"Ready?"

"I sure am!" I say with enthusiasm. What else could I say at this point?

Marcus instructs us to follow close behind him as he gets back into his van. He turns around in the lot and drives off into the grass at the other end of the lot away from the road. We follow his lead. We drive across a large field and then begin to climb a series of small hills, the center and ties to civilization falling further and further behind. After a series of hills we circle around one and then climb up the side of another to park our vehicles. Marcus dismounts and we do the same.

As he begins walking further away from the cars, we follow on foot. Up the hill, around the bend, and into a clearing overlooking the valley. As we enter the clearing I can see that it is the spot. In the center lie two stone circles separated by the remains of a long dead fire. I look from the stones to the hill to the clearing to the valley. I couldn't pick a more beautiful location to spend some time in solitude.

"Brian, help me clear away that circle. Just toss the stones away." Marcus instructs Brian. Brian walks over to the second circle and dismantles it stone by stone, leaving only one circle facing the hearth. I still just stand and stare at my new home.

Marcus walks back into the clearing carrying some wood and promptly drops it next to the hearth. He then asks Brian to assist him in gathering some more. I ask him what I should do and he tells me to set up my bedroll in the circle and put everything else just outside it. I'm busy unrolling my sleeping bag when they return with hands full of dry wood.

Marcus instructs me to make my fire. Suddenly I'm back in the Boy Scouts and can feel the pressure of having fire duty at camp. It seems the fire never lights when someone else is watching. But I'm lucky this time. My fire building skills have grown with age (can I get that merit badge now please), and the wood they offered is bone dry. I stack some pine needles and twigs and set them a flame with one of my recently purchased waterproof matches. The fire flickers and I add more wood, watching it grow into a healthy flame.

Marcus asks if I brought a knife and I tell him I didn't, immediately wondering why I would need one and at the same time creating images and needs in my mind (lions and tigers and bears, oh my). He pulls a sheathed dagger out of his back pocket and hands it to me, telling me to take it just in case. He also produces from nowhere a leather pouch full of tobacco and a zip lock baggy full of pine needles. They are both for blessing, he tells me then proceeds to show me what he means.

He takes some of the pine needles and throws them on the fire where it burns and throws up a cloud of fragrant smoke. Marcus directs me to stand over it and wash the smoke over my body and head. Once I have done this Brian and Marcus both take a turn. A cleansing, he tells us. He then says a blessing for the quest and for the questee. This done, he discusses with me what to expect and gives me a few instructions to settle me in. He tells me the tobacco can be used for blessing and thanking the gods. I should take a clump in my right hand and hold it to my chest while I thank the North, then drop the tobacco to the ground. This would be repeated for the West, South, East in turn, then once for the Sky and once for the Earth. He tells me I should do this once they leave and then again whenever I feel the need or desire to do so.

They sit with me a little while longer before getting up to leave. Marcus tells me he will be back to check on me on the second morning. Otherwise, they would see me at dawn on Saturday. I smile at Brian when Marcus says this wondering how he feels about getting up at 5:00 A.M. to come and pick me up.

I thank Marcus again for being so kind in helping me with my quest, and he humbly accepts my thanks without word or action. And with that they stand and walk out of the clearing and back down to their vehicles. And there I am. Alone in the spreading darkness. Just a fool on a hill.

PART III

◆

VISIONS

I am a part of all that I have met;
Yet all experience is an arch wherethrough
Gleams the untraveled world, whose margin fades
For ever and for ever when I move.
How dull it is to pause, to make an end,
To rust unburnished, not to shine in use!
As though to breathe were life.

Alfred, Lord Tennyson, *Ulysses*

WHAT VISIONS COME

◆

The man who has no imagination has no wings.

Muhammad Ali

My eyes shutter open and I can see it's day break from the light creeping into the blue clouds above me. I raise my head slightly to peer over at the horizon and see the sunrise. Then they shut again and when I open them again it's daylight already. The funny symphony of time again: allegro, adagio. Fast, slow. Here, gone.

I sit up in my circle and let my mind clear a bit from the dreams of the night. Dreams, not visions. Marcus told me the vision quest ended when the visions came. No early departure for me, I was here for the duration.

I lick my lips and wonder if I should be doing that. They are already parched and I wonder if the added moisture of spit would just expedite their chaffing and chapping. Where is Suzy Chapstick when you need her? The fire is pretty much dead, though some embers remain from its last incarnation. I lean out of the circle and throw some twigs and branches onto it in hopes of a quick revival. I luck out and the flames catch quickly. I settle back into the circle and watch it for a while.

Minutes pass. Or hours. Duty calls. I stand and collect myself then step out of the circle and over to my favorite bush. On my walk back to the circle I see something heading my way. At first glance it looks like a wolf and I fear that Coyote, the Trickster, has come to see me and has found me out of my circle. I stop and stare at the beast as it walks over to me and then realize it's not a wolf but a dog. A big shaggy, wolfy-looking dog. A dog that must belong to…

Marcus comes around the bend in the hillside and I remember he told me he would come to check on me this morning. I bend down and pat the dog a few times on the head and walk toward Marcus, meeting him at the clearing. We greet each other in silence for a moment, I'm not sure if I'm suppose to talk to him.

"Good morning. How are you doing?" He says in a soft, slow voice.

I wonder if I should answer. Am I supposed to? Should I break my silence? Will my voice work even if I want it to? Silly thoughts mold in my head. This isn't really Marcus, it's all a trick. I'm still dreaming. Coyote is playing with me.

"I'm doing great," I hear a faint, cracked voice say and realize it's my own. This is reality. "I sure could use a drink of water though." I say with a smile that comes close to splitting a lip.

Marcus doesn't comment. He just walks over and squats by the fire. We're together in silence for a few moments. He then raises a bundle of leafy branches he's been holding in his hand and I notice them for the first time.

"These are for you. You may feel a bit nauseous today. If you do, you can sniff this. It's mint leaves. It's good for upset stomach. You can try chewing it if you wish but it will give you dry mouth."

He hands the bundle to me and I take a whiff. It smells cool and comforting. I take the bundle back down to put aside and realize some of the scent has rubbed off onto my beard stubble. Now the world was filtered through a minty-fresh aroma.

"This is for blessing," Marcus says holding up the other bundle. I've seen it before. It's dried sage. I know this only because I had a run-in with it a few weeks prior to taking this journey. I was at the Third Street Promenade in Santa Monica with Jeanne, and we passed a Native American selling sage. He caught both our eyes and Jeanne went over to buy some. While she did he looked right at me, right through me, and told me how it could be used for blessings and cleansing. He seemed to be explaining this directly to me for some reason. Convinced, Jeanne bought a bundle. And as we thanked him and went to leave, the man clasped my arm in his, a firm grip on my forearm, and wished me well. I can still remember the piercing warmth of his eyes as he bid me well.

Marcus throws the bundle of sage onto the fire, and we repeat the cleansing and blessing ceremony that we did at the start of the vision quest. I wash the smoke over me as does he, and then he says a few words of blessing, inviting the visions to come. This completed, we squat by the fire in silence a while longer. It's strange having another person around again. It's even stranger to have someone there and not be talking. But as strange as it is it seems right for some reason. Fitting.

Marcus stands and says goodbye. He tells me he will see me at daybreak in the morning. I thank him for coming and watch as he and his dog stroll back out of view. The hill and valley were mine once again.

It's an awkward morning. I'm caught in the eddies of time still, being thrown and pulled quickly through the day and then being caught spinning in moments that go on forever. I sit in the circle, I stroll along the cliffs. My body has adjusted to the hunger pangs so that I feel them less and less. Hunger has given away to thirst. Cotton mouth, parched throat, and chaffing lips bring thoughts not of distant memories and lost relationships but of a variety of liquids I plan to splash down upon returning to the world of the living. I think of ice coffee and Mountain Dew, of Vernor's Ginger Ale and Snapple and lemonade and ice tea. I think of gallons of pure, clean water. And then I think of a freezer pop like the ones I used to have as a kid. Those plastic encased sticks of flavored ice, the blue kind that have no real flavor except *blue*. I think of how good they used to be on hot summer afternoons and my mind becomes fixated. It takes way too much effort to drive the craving away.

I keep the fire tended today, considering it a beacon for the visions. It being my last night, I want to be sure they find me. And besides, with all the wood I have collected over the past couple of days I could keep it going for a long time. The fire takes on a different essence sitting and looking at it in the brightness of day. Much of its power and mystery is missing, hidden in the daylight. And yet it has a sense of foreboding, of a power that is building to burst onto the scene at some undetermined point in the not too distant future. It still demands respect.

As I sit and stare into the fire I think of nothing. Nothing. My mind is clear. And then I realize it is clear, and it isn't clear any longer. The tribulations of meditation. I have finally managed to bleed the racing thoughts from my mind, to let go of the satellite transmissions of past TV shows, school assemblies, and Star Trek guest stars. But even with the emptiness of time and deprivation I still remain unfocused. It's a cat and mouse game of finding nothingness, then realizing it and losing it again.

It's afternoon. Morning has blinked by. I try to think back to morning and it seems like ages ago. I'm sitting on my boulder looking down at the valley and hear a shriek from above. In the air above me an osprey circles looking for prey. I nervously look around me, wondering if Rabbit is safe. I hop off of the boulder and look under the shaded overhang of the rock in front of me. There he is, hanging out in his favorite spot. Good 'ole Rabbit, safe and shaded from sun and danger. He seems asleep so I let him be and return to my perch on the boulder to watch the osprey some more. It reminds me of the bald eagle I saw fly overhead earlier (this morning? yesterday?). It flew so low and so close I caught a great look at it. It seemed so regal, so proud, so huge. Its white head lost in the clouds above, it's blue feathers (blue!) sparkled and shined as it flew over reflecting beams of sunshine. It was an amazing creature.

It's later. Not much sunshine to sparkle right now. Clouds have rolled in from the distance and have hung over me for over an hour now. The sun gone, the weather has cooled with shade and stirring breezes. I hear faint thunder and smell moisture in the air. Rain is tempting the skies. I'm not sure how to react to this, to be happy or disappointed. The relief from the sun is wonderful, but the thought of sleeping in the rain is not. And if it does rain would it be "illegal" to turn my head skyward and take a few gulps? Would the gods not be providing the water and wouldn't it be an insult not to accept their gift with gratitude? My skin already feels more moist. It is sucking the wetness from the air like a forgotten sponge suddenly dropped onto a wet counter top. I feel invigorated from the change in weather. I decide with the new environment I should be back in the circle and hop down from my boulder.

On the walk back a stone catches my eye and I bend down to pick it up. It's a burnt sienna with speckles of turquoise and cobalt blue. I clean the dirt off with my fingers and roll it over and over in my hand as I walk back to the circle. Stepping into my circle of stones and taking my usual posture I take the new stone and add it to the circle along side several others I have collected since arriving on the hill. I'm not sure why I am doing this, the rocks just seem to attract my attention and placing them there in the circle just seems to make sense at the time.

I build up the fire a bit more to help it brave the winds and sprinkles that are now falling lightly from the air. I think again of drinking the rain when it comes and again wonder if this was right. Still in debate with myself, I find myself positioning my hiking boots out in the open where they could collect water and serve as cups in the event of a heavy rain. A crazy man's delirium. At least they were relatively new shoes.

I look over at my makeshift sundial and see one of the pitfalls of my new weather. The dial is no longer working. It is solar powered and that power is gone. A blackout on the hill. This cloud cover and disappearing point of reference—the sun—wreaks even more havoc on the element of time. Now there is no passage of time at all. Just one long, drawn out moment.

It constantly looks like night fall, and I wait expectantly only to see an hour or two or three pass. The pseudo nightfalls come and go in constant rotation. I begin to wonder if I'm caught in some time loop, or if I'm dreaming and have missed nightfall altogether. The expectation builds an anxious feeling inside of me that I can't shake. I wonder what visions were in store for me this evening. What forms will the gods take? Lacking true night I decide to create my own visions, dreaming up some possibilities for the evening's festivities:

A beautiful woman walks out of the shadows and into the light of my fire. She gazes at me seductively and beckons me to leave the circle and join her in the night. I refuse. She steps closer into the light and I can see the most gorgeous woman I ever imagined. Amazingly attractive, glowing in the firelight. Eyes so warm and enticing. Lips whispering my name. She sends her invitations but I remain motionless. She begins to sway and dance slowly around the fire. Closer and closer she comes. I can see she is wearing the pelt of some animal on her back, the pelt and nothing else. Her dance is so inviting, almost irresistible. Almost. She calls out to me, almost reaching into the circle, but I remain still. A flash of fire and her eyes ignite. They change from jade green to pale yellow, large and round. She snarls at me and drops to the ground on all fours. The pelt billows in the wind then becomes rigid around her body. Not her body; Its. Coyote. Coyote stares at me from across the circle of stones and bears Its teeth. Coyote has lost and knows it. I have passed his test, resisted the great temptation and remained true to my quest. I have won.

I catch myself smiling at this make believe vision. It had all the elements of a great vision: sex, trickery, temptation, the possibility of violence, and Coyote the Trickster. This must be what my vision will be like.

I look up at the sky again and try to hurry the night along, now even more excited for the visions. Spurred on by the visions of my own making. Seeing that there has been no change in the passing of time, I stir up a few more possible visions. A few more similar ones, this time involving massive grizzly bears threatening my life or zombies or blood thirsty eagles. I try to think up all the animals I remember hearing of in Indian lore and conjure up images of how they would fit into my visions.

And then I catch myself. I am putting too much energy into these fantasies. My imagination has run wild long enough. Time to reel it in and give reality a chance. It's difficult, but I manage to put the business of vision creation aside and concentrate on the fire and my surroundings once again. Almost as if I found some hidden key to time, as soon as I turn my attention back to tending the fire the night begins to creep into action. Someone slowly turns down the lights, dimming them softer and softer in the hazy cloud-covered sky at an almost imperceptible rate. The swelling intensity of the fire is my only real clue to the coming of night. And then it's dark.

Thoughts of visions are long behind me now. As are cravings of food and drink and distant memories and forgotten plans. The rain isn't coming, it was all just a trick. Now that night is here nothing else seems to matter except falling asleep. I thought I would be dead tired and exhausted to the point of dropping off at sunset, but now with the last night on the hill looming at me I find myself insomniatic. I just sit and stare at the flames until slowly sleep over takes me.

I awake with a jolt. I throw my eyes open and try to see where the noise was coming from. I sit up in my sleeping bag and look to my left. I can see in the faint light of early morning two guys, probably in their early twenties, unloading backpacks and camping gear. I look around in bewilderment. Same clearing, fire still burning, the slightest light of morning just kissing the sky. I look back at the new arrivals with anger and frustration.

"Excuse me!" I call out to them. "Hello?! Excuse me! Can't you guys see I'm on a vision quest here?" No reply. "Hey! Could you guys maybe go set up somewhere else? I need to have this clearing to myself."

There's still no reply. I start to yell again when I hear a loud thump from my other side. I turn and see a man and a boy setting down a canoe loaded with camping gear. They too begin to pitch camp.

"Hey!" I yell at the new comers. "You can't camp here…"

But they pay no attention to me. Already their tent is stretched out on the ground. I begin again but am interrupted by sounds from behind me. More people, more campers. I rub my eyes, not believing what I am seeing. People are arriving all around me. Loners, couples, groups. They are over running the clearing and the hillside, taking every available inch of space. Crowding out my solitude.

"Stop!" I find myself yelling into the air. I see my chance for visions slipping away. All that work, all that time spent only to come down to this. Failure at the last moment due to the intrusion of others. I reach for the zipper of my sleeping bag and begin to climb out and try to talk sense into everyone. I go to climb out of the bag and

Darkness. My eyes open on darkness and the cloudy star-dotted sky. I sit up in my bag and look around me. No campers, no disturbances, no one. No one but me. I sit there for a moment and can feel my heart pounding and my body slightly shaking. The dream has really agitated me. That silly, stupid dream. I stir the fire and watch it for a while, trying to get the dream out of my head before attempting sleep again. I try to erase the dream to make way for the visions. With considerable effort I manage to forget and settle back down into my bag and sleep.

Boom. Down go the packs and out come the tents. I open my eyes and can't believe what I am seeing. It's the intruders again. They've come back.

"Look, I told you last time, you can't stay here!" I scream at them.

But they don't listen. They go about their business as do the old man and the boy with the canoe. I look at them as I implore them to move on to somewhere else. They are a little clearer this time, as if I'm more awake and seeing them a little better. "Excuse me!" I yell to no response. "Hey!"

No one listens. They just arrive and set up camp. Slowly encroaching on the space I thought was mine and mine alone.

Awake. I open my eyes again to the dark clearing. Alone again. I'm confused. I thought for sure I'd see the people this time. That this time the dream was the reality and the reality the dream. *Dammit, get the dream out of my head. I'm so busy dreaming I'll never get the visions.* I reprimand myself and force my head back down to sleep.

Eyes open to a growing crowd of newcomers. The dream again. People all around, old man and boy on my right. Screams of frustration and waking up to the stillness of my clearing.

The process continues: dream, wake, dream, wake. I don't know how many times it happens, but I find myself getting angry. It seems the harder I try to get rid of it the more forcefully it comes back.

Sleep. And the coming of the visitors. The guys on one side, the old man and the boy on the other. Others all around me.

"Why do you keep doing this to me?!" I yell at the old man. This time he looks up at me, looks directly at me. He is actually seeing me for the first time. Someone is acknowledging my presence. I notice this and look at him a bit closer. He's clearer now, familiar. It could be the familiarity of seeing him so many times already this evening, but I don't think so. There is something about him that seems to make sense to me.

"Why are you…" I begin to repeat myself then stop.

Not a dream. A vision. This *is* the vision. The realization makes me both elated and embarrassed.

"Yes," The old man says looking directly at me with kind, friendly eyes.

I was so wrapped up in what my vision would be that I didn't realize it when it hit me.

"Yes." He says again as if reading my thoughts.

I feel strange. I feel awake but know that I'm not. And yet I wasn't dreaming either, was I? *No.* The answer floated into my consciousness, from where I don't know. I think it may have been the old man, so I direct my thoughts to him. I find myself speaking.

"So this is it. This is my vision?" I ask him. When I get no reply I go on. "But I don't get it. What does it mean?"

"What do you think?" The old man answers.

"I don't...I have no idea. I..."

"Enough questions. Answers."

"Answers?" I repeat. "Answers."

His face comes into focus and then fades away. The boy behind him is smiling at me in a playful fashion. I almost notice him when he too is gone. I am floating now, riding a tide of ether. Flying back to reality.

I open my eyes and it's just like in the vision. The sunlight peeking in on me, the day slowly arriving. But unlike the vision I am still all alone.

I sit up and look all around me just to be sure. Yes, all alone. My thoughts are muddled and I don't know what to think. Was it a dream or a vision? Why did they keep coming back for me? Why not give up on me after my refusal to accept it as a vision? Was I that stubborn to hold onto my expectations of what my vision would be that I didn't see it when it hit me?

I sit with my thoughts and the lingering sensation of travel. It didn't make any sense. The vision made absolutely no sense whatsoever. I'm confused and disappointed. Then thankful and grateful. The vision could have given me just one try then went away. But it didn't, it stuck with me. Sure, I had no idea what it was but maybe that's what I'm supposed to experience: confusion.

I toss the meaning of the vision back and forth and analyze and dissect it but still come up with nothing. The process tires me out and I decide just to forget it for a while. Marcus and Brian will be here soon, they'll probably want to hear all about it. I can deal with it then. I throw another log on the fire and stoke the coals a bit to fan the flame. I then sit back for the remainder of the sunrise and enjoy my last few moments alone on the hill.

*   *   *

I hear them before I see them. Marcus says something and Brian laughs and I know they are just around the corner. I'm sitting in the circle when they see me. My sleeping bag already rolled up and stashed in its bag, I figure it will smell like smoke from now on. They walk up to me with cheerful good-mornings, far from Marcus' silent approach the morning before. I see Brian is carrying a plastic shopping bag and a gallon jug of water. Water!

I just sit and let them arrive, not really ready yet to jump up and leave the hill. They reach the clearing and ask me how I'm doing. I answer with a good morning that sounds so distant, not my voice at all. I surprised my vocal chords with the attempt at speech.

Brian sets down his cargo and Marcus walks us through a closing ceremony. More cleansing and blessings, sincere thanks and hopes for a safe journey on the roads ahead. It's a subtle ceremony, sublime. A quiet close to a quiet event.

This done, we all sit down to enjoy the fruits of the morning. I watch as Brian produces bananas, grapes, apples, plums, and a baguette of French bread from the bag. I'm shocked that I don't dive for them all. Actually surprised that my reaction to the arrival of food is indifference. Even more surprised when the jug of water is passed to me and I almost feel like not drinking it. Almost. I take a few long gulps and cough almost immediately. Drinking too fast. My shriveled, dry throat just isn't ready yet. I relax for a moment then go at it again. This time slower and with more success. Marcus tears off a piece of bread and passes the loaf to me. The feast begins.

"So, any visions?" Brian asks eager to hear if my time alone was worth it.

"Yes. I think so. I'm not sure what it means though," I say and I recount the events from the previous evening. I tell them of the recurring dream and the waking up and how the dream turned out to be the vision. I tell them about everything but the old man and the boy. This detail slips my mind in the sucrose induced utopia of my fruity feast.

I ask Marcus if he knows what it means. He tells me the meaning is very personal and that I will probably have to figure it out. Then having said that he offers a few possible explanations. He tells me that the area where we are sitting used to be a Native American encampment. He says perhaps the ancestors were just trying to test my resolve, to come and see if I was worthy of a greater vision on my next time out. I think about this as he says it and remember having to experience the vision several times before accepting it as such. Would this be considered worthy? I wonder.

"But the people, as far as I can remember, were not Native Americans," I point out. He says it is still possible. He tells me perhaps they just took a different form so I could more easily relate to them. He tells me it could also be a message about my own tribe, my own group. I consider this as I munch on an apple.

We sit and eat and alternate between silence and casual conversation. I soon get my fill of bread and fruit and we pack up to head down off the hill and back into civilization. We pour some water on the fire and Brian packs up the remaining fruit while I collect my things. I hand Marcus back his knife and tobacco pouch, telling him the knife remained unused. We turn and start down the hill.

I get a few feet and tell them I'll catch up and run back into the clearing. I stoop down and pick up a few of my collection of rocks from the circle, the ones I added over the past few days. Acting on impulse of feeling, I thought I would need them to remind me. I stand back up to follow them down the hill but pause a moment to look around. I can't see him anywhere. Rabbit didn't come to see me off. I then remember I forgot to tell Marcus about Rabbit and ask him if he held any significance. I decide not to either. I already know the answer to that one. He did hold great significance. To me. And that's all that mattered.

Back in the Thunder Cloud Center's parking lot we say our goodbyes to Marcus. I thank him and hope I express how much his help has meant to me. It's sometimes difficult to do so. Someone who was a complete stranger days ago helped in one of those life experiences that stay with you forever. Standing there and thanking him I feel he does get it, perhaps seeing it in my eyes. Something new, something missing.

Brian and I drive back toward Sheridan; he is anxious to hear more and tell more. He quickly begins to ask me questions. They are the questions we thought up together the day I left for the hill. Things we thought we'd like to know but would forget to ask, and then I would forget the answers if they weren't asked immediately. But as the questions hit me we both knew I didn't want to answer. I preferred just to be still. So Brian filled the gap with his tales of adventure. He tells me about tours of the city, things found on the satellite dish, feasts in local restaurants.

As I listen we pull along side a mini-mart and I ask Brian to pull into its parking lot. I get out and walk inside, wondering what I must look like (and smell like) to everyone, suddenly thankful for it being so early in the morning. I roam around the store and collect a basket full of purchases and head for the cashier where I lay out:

2 Snapple lemonades
1 two-liter bottle of Vernor's Ginger Ale
1 Starbucks ice coffee
1 gallon of water
1 bottle Lipton's ice tea
2 bottles Stewart's creme soda
…and one bright blue flavored Flav-O-Ice freezer pop (Yes!)

THE HUNT FOR
SEMI-RETIREMENT

◆

It is never too late to be what you might have been.

George Eliot

"Wow."

The lights to the room come on, and we are both overwhelmed. I have not seen such a grand collection of dead things since my visit to Washington DC's Museum of Natural History as a boy. It even bests the Mint Bar's collection. And to think these were all bagged by just one man.

I slowly look around the room. Lining the walls and filling spaces along the floor were elk, deer, gazelles, antelopes, moose, mountain goats, a female lion (a lion!), zebra, cheetah, and countless others. An incredible display of one man's passion for hunting big game.

Richard Rhoades continues to show us around the room as we listen to accounts of how different animals were acquired. I can't help but be impressed by the freakish collection. He gives the saying 'a room full of stuffed animals' a whole new meaning. I make a nervous sweep of the room upon first entering. Nope, Rabbit isn't here.

At first glance Richard looks like someone out of an old western. The Wild Bill Cody type: lean and strong with piercing eyes and untamed shoulder length hair and beard. Upon meeting him you wonder if he shot the animals or just wrestled them to the ground. But when he talks you can see a lighter side, a family man who is just out to enjoy life for what it is. That's Richard Rhoades: successful taxidermist, big game hunter, and herb rancher.

Richard was born in Indiana and moved to Wyoming at the age of 18 where he began a career in taxidermy. He worked for nearly eight years learning the trade before opening his own taxidermy shop, which he ran for over 12 years. His work has been commissioned by the Smithsonian Institute in Washington, DC, and from people all over the world. In addition to his taxidermy business, he has traveled the globe hunting big game, some of his prized catches on display here in his home's trophy room. Now, at the age of 42, he spends his time as an herb farmer in Wyoming selling his culinary herbs to local restaurants.

We finish the tour of the game trophies and take a seat on the sofa in the center of the room. Richard lights up the first in a long chain of cigarettes and tells us about how he came to be on his current career path.

"As far as taxidermy is concerned, it was something that I had played with as a little kid. I probably started playing with that when I was around ten or so. So I guess in a way it was a little bit of planning and some part luck, but I had a part in the direction I went and any jobs I took or pursued. I had control over the type of jobs. With my interests I was in the right place at the right time to get a job that interested me and after working for another taxidermist for seven and a half years there wasn't anything he was doing that I couldn't do on my own. From then on I pretty much have done what I wished." Richard takes a drag off his cigarette then continues.

"I watched a lot of people, my Dad included, work for the same place for twenty-some years and absolutely hate it. If I had to, I could get a job tomorrow working for somebody else, but unless I get real desperate I won't do it. If you're going to work, you should do something you enjoy, and it doesn't hurt to be able to do a couple of things. Probably the simplest thing to do to find your path would be to take a hobby that you really enjoy and find a way to make money at it. If you enjoy anything, crafts, hobbies, riding a bicycle, anything, there's a way you can find a market for it, somehow. Basically just find out what you enjoy doing and find a way to make a living at it and be persistent about it."

"Do you think there are regional differences on how people perceive success?" Brian asks from underneath the watchful eyes of a mountain goat.

"Definitely! Here in Wyoming things are more laid back. We don't worry so much about the God Almighty Dollar. In the east it's a cutthroat thing where they have to have the dollar. I really don't worry about it. Whatever can be done today can damn sure be put off another day or two. Back there they are trying to shove 36 hours into 24, and it can't be done."

"Is there anything you'd tell people in the east about how they can ease up a bit?" Brian asks.

"Keep in mind that this is coming from a guy who doesn't really worry about much of anything. If it's going to happen and you can do something to prevent it, then you do your best. But if there's nothing you can do, then don't worry about it. Just slow down and relax. Your life isn't work. I've always said that if you work too hard, people may think you like it." I look over at Brian at this and we both chuckle. "I've been semi-retired since I was about 25 and I don't make a whole hell of a lot of money, but I do have fun. I've traveled to Africa, England, Ireland and Wales, Mexico, Canada, and Alaska. I think you have to play as hard as you work, if not a little harder."

"So what are the secrets of being semi-retired by 25?" I ask, ready to take notes.

"How do you become semi-retired by the age of 25? By not having to have everything, not worrying if I have $150,000 in the bank, that's how.

For the things I wanted to do, like going out to shoot big game, I knew I could physically do it at 25, or 35, or now, but you don't know if you'll get the chance to do it later because you could die tomorrow. As long as it doesn't take away from the family or anything like that, if you can afford to do it and you have the time, do it! There's no doubt in my mind that you'll damn sure regret it if you don't. Nobody says when they're dying, 'Wow I wish I would have worked harder.' When you're born you should play and have fun until about 50, then you should have to go to work."

I think about this and remember my dad saying the exact same thing to me when we were just considering making this trip. Richard carries the thought even further.

"My wife says, 'Have dessert first, because life is so uncertain.' I think everybody worries too much about money. I think if you use your head and have common sense and not get totally carried away with the play aspect of it, most people don't need the amount of money that they think they do, and you can have just as much fun as anybody else. Have fun with what you're doing and enjoy life."

"That's sound advice. What other words of wisdom would you offer people struggling with their choices in life?" Brian says.

"Follow your heart. In some instances, not all cases, I think college is probably a waste. That may not go over well with a lot of people. If you want to be a doctor or lawyer or something like that you have to do it, but in a lot of other cases where you go just to party for four years, you're better off working for those years to try to put something together. In some cases, it's a lot of unnecessary expense. I know one woman who went to college to be a teacher, and she ended getting married and never taught again, so for her it may have been a waste of four years. It may be nice to have the degree, and I never went, but I'm not sure it would have been worth the money. There are other ways to pick up the same information if you're ambitious to do it. A lot of the people that I've talked to around here who went to college basically partied for four years."

I consider this while listening to Richard. Sure, I had a great time in college and there were lots of parties, but I learned stuff too, didn't I? I find myself agreeing with him, however. There are many who have "made it" without the aid of a college degree. And yet so many of us are told that it is a requirement, something needed to survive. But not everyone has the luxury of a college education and, as Richard points out, not everyone really needs one.

"Follow your heart. I think for most people in order to do a real good job, you have to be happy with what you're doing. Anybody can do a job for eight hours a day, but in order to do a job that you and everyone around you is proud of, you have to enjoy what you're doing."

Watching Richard speak and looking around at his hobby collection, I can see he enjoys what he does greatly. A little boy with dreams of growing up to be the Great White Hunter he has become. Dreams realized and dreamer dreaming.

We thank Richard for his time and for the tour. He tells us we're welcome back any time in true Western fashion and sees us out to the Jeep. As we head across his gravel driveway an army of grasshoppers jump and dive out of our way. It's like walking through a fancy water fountain, only with insects. Richard walks back to his house as we drive away.

"That was different. I can't say I've ever been in a more interesting sitting room than that!" I say pulling back onto the road that will lead us back to Craig's.

"Another interesting story as well. Some one just enjoying their hobbies enough to make them a career. I guess it is possible." Brian adds.

"Possible, yes. I guess in his case the geography issue really came into play. I can't really see his career and lifestyle taking off in say, the streets of New York."

"Yeah, I guess we were right in our initial assumptions that where you live plays a big part on how you live. It seems it not only affects your choices of what you do but how you live and view the world as well. That must be why we hear of all these disgruntled bankers and traders moving out to buy a farm somewhere and get lost in obscurity."

"What a neat guy." I hear myself saying, Brian's comments lost among my own thinking. "It's really amazing that we've been able to meet so many interesting people. Total strangers willing to speak to us, and everyone seems to have their own take on everything."

"True," Brian agrees. "It's funny how some people look at our topic and take it directly as a career focused discussion. While others talk more about life and happiness. I'm not sure if it's an issue of their priorities or their understanding of what it is we want to hear."

"Probably a little of both. It's obvious the two are intertwined, so I think it would be difficult to talk about one without the other: career or happiness. People probably just choose which is in the forefront of their discussion by how comfortable they are opening up to us or by how we present what it is we are looking at. It could be just some arbitrary factor that sets it in one direction, or maybe a reflection of where they are in their lives at the time." I look over at Brian, "I'm not a psychologist but I play one on TV..."

We both laugh and sit back and enjoy the ride through Wyoming.

SLIGHT SEEING

♦

We often rob tomorrow's memories
by today's economies.

John Mason Brown

Our trip through the northwestern part of the country is taking us through areas of the nation I have never been. And though our quest is one for knowledge, our Creed directs us to have fun and enjoy the journey as well. So we have decide while we aren't on a tourist vacation we would still take the chance from time to time to stop off and see some of the sights as we pass through the area. Thus the tour of Seattle and the stop at the Craters of the Moon.

On the Drive out of Wyoming and through the Dakotas we set off on a series of stops we can only describe as "Slight Seeing". It's a new word, one you won't find in the dictionary. But if you did it would probably read something like this:

slight see*ing: *n* 1: to pay brief visit to historical or geological wonder, the sole purpose to snap a photo and say "I was there" 2: the act of carelessly or inadequately appreciating tourist site or activity **3**: the get in, grab a look, and get–the–hell–out method of tourism

It begins with a brief visit to Devil's Tower in eastern Wyoming. We knew wanted to see it when we were planning our trip and since we are driving by so close it is silly not to. Devil's Tower, that weird rock mountain sculpted in mash potatoes and visited by aliens in the movie *Close Encounters of the Third Kind*. And if that wasn't enough to get us driving out there, Marcus had given us a bit of history on it during our chat with him days ago. He told us it was one of the Native Americans' most sacred sites. To them it was known as Great Horn Butte. According to Indian legend, four sisters were playing with their brother one day when suddenly the brother turned into a giant bear and began to chase them. The sisters ran and ran until they found the stump of a great tree. They climbed up onto the stump and prayed to the gods to save them. And as the great bear approached bearing its claws the trunk began to grow and grow and raise the sisters up into the sky. The bear tried to get to them, tried to climb up the stump, but kept sliding down. Thus the odd marks in the side of the butte. The sisters, finding themselves so high, had nowhere to go but up. So they leapt into the evening sky and became stars, making up part of the Big Dipper.

That's what we think of this morning as we stand road side and look at the strange rocky butte in the distance. It does, indeed, look like a giant stump with claw marks on the side. We look at it, discuss it, take some photos, and move on.

More driving and then Mount Rushmore. We try to get there on time, but as fast as we drive the day slips away from us and the sun is packing up for its journey to the other side of the globe by the time we arrive. We have choices. Stay for the night to see it in the morning or see it now in the fading light and move on. As we approach the entrance still undecided we see the hordes of people and lines of cars. It is, after all, the peak of tourist season. Without knowing it we find ourselves in the entrance line, cars ahead and behind. Still undecided at the window a round man in a Smokey Bear hat asks us for eight dollars to park. Eight dollars for less than thirty minutes of sunlight after a long day of driving. All of sudden it is an easy decision.

Brian tells the man we ended up in the line by accident and are trying to turn around. He directs us to drive up and around, keeping to the right and out of the parking area. We thank him and move along. Keeping right and driving around brings us directly to the entrance of the monument and there in the not so distant distance are the great stone faces of the somber looking presidents. Brian, who had seen the monument before as a kid, quickly looks behind him and pulls over. I catch his meaning, grab our cameras, and head out the door. Fifty feet out and in good photo range I snap a few shots, pay my respects (but not eight bucks) to such a fine work of art, and am back in the Jeep and we are on our way. A new slight seeing record: Mount Rushmore in 3 minutes 17 seconds.

The event captured on film in memory, we drive back down the hill and onward, further into South Dakota. We still have many sights to slight.

People could use many words to describe our actions. Pathetic, sad, shameful, "why bother," are just a few that spring to mind. And I admit slight seeing isn't for everyone. Hell, I would say it isn't even for me if we had more time and resources (i.e. cash flow). But it is all just part of our quest.

What did our rush save us, you wonder? Not much. We make it to a rest area by nightfall and sleep in the Jeep. All the camping grounds are full by the time we finally decide to stop for the day. A lesson in trying to cram too much into 24 hours. So we sleep—or try to—uncomfortably in the same seats we had ridden uncomfortably in for the past 14 hours.

The next day takes us slight seeing some more. A stop at Wall Drug in Wall, South Dakota, for free coffee (yes, the highway billboards suck us in) and curious window shopping. Then a slight-seeing trip through the Badlands National Park—one of the nation's most spectacular natural wonders becoming little more than a drive through attraction. Then driving onward and upward into the night, we trace our itinerary on the map and make it just outside Bismarck where we settle in for the night at the Lincoln Park and Campgrounds.

And here we lie in our tent, listening to the creatures of the night play out their symphony of sounds. Thinking back now on the events of the last few days I wonder if we will reach a day in the near future where we have time to spare. Where we will sit around doing nothing and say to ourselves, we could have spent this day at the Badlands. I guess there's just no way of knowing. The day is gone, the past is behind us. Did we slight anything, I wonder, but ourselves?

A DAY AT THE OFFICE

◆

When men are rightly occupied,
their amusement grows out of their work,
as the color-petals out of a fruitful flower.

John Ruskin

We wake to the sound of birds chirping, water flowing, and mosquitoes buzzing in our ears: the alarm clock of nature. I sit up in my sleeping bag and see Brian is already awake as well, he's just trying his best to ignore that fact. With the water flowing just behind the tent and the birds singing to the rising sun, the sides of the tent glowing from the sunbeams bouncing off their stark exterior, I think of how romantic it could all be if only it were the woman of my dreams and not Brian lying there beside me. Brian moans and rolls over to face the other direction. He must be thinking the same thing.

Once we are both wide awake, we discuss our immediate plans for the day. We decide on a quick run and then a day at the office getting caught up on our web work. Having set our game plan we crawl out of the tent (skipping the camp break down since we'll be staying another night) and dress for our morning run.

Our run takes us down a paved path by the river on the edge of the campsite. Slowly our muscles wake up and begin to enjoy the much needed stretch and work out. Sitting in a Jeep for hours on end, day after day, eating nothing but junk food can take its toll on the human body. We decided before we set off on our adventure that we would need to battle off the slack somehow and decided running was the only feasible way.

We reach the end of the campgrounds, passing waking campers as we do. One man is already up and practicing a kung fu sword kata by his tent with a stick. Another sleepily exits his tent carrying a Frisbee and heads over to where his dog is tied to a tree. The world of summer travelers coming alive. We reach the end of the paved trail and head off onto a dirt path and into the woods along the river, we still have a long way to go.

Shave, shower, and back on the road heading into Bismarck. We pass several viable offices on the way but decide to get into city proper before stopping. We finally pull into a McDonald's in the heart of one of the city's commercial areas, right next to a mall should a break in the day's work be required. We prefer local grease spoons for breakfast and usually we will hunt one out, but not today. First see first go. We pull into the McDonald's parking lot next to a blue sedan with a bumper sticker reading: Ladies Sewing Circle & Terrorist Society.

We gather our office gear and go in to find a table with wall outlet access. We luck out and find a large booth by the window, quickly jumping to overtake it and explode our contents of wires and gadgets, letting them grow over the table and down the walls like crazed, techno-vines in a table top garden of electronics. Our machines hum to life, Brian lit in the green light of the Newton while I am lit blue by the PowerBook. Sony mini-recorders climb from bag to table followed by mini headsets. Everything shrunken to fit the mobile office requirements. In no time the table is full and we have little room for our food trays as we take turns going and ordering our McBreakfasts.

Trays teetering on the edge of the table, hot coffee steaming from styrene cups, greasy meals waiting consumption, the work day has begun.

Brian sits and transcribes our last few interviews for the web while I work on making new additions to the web site. It's part of the division of labor that has formed on the trip. He does the transcribing, I do most or all of the web work. We seem to be happy with the arrangement. So I add photos and interviews and journal entries, typing in HTML and working Photoshop skills to alter and edit photographs. Every once in a while we will want to take a team photo and there will be no one to take it for us or nowhere to steady the camera for a self-timer shot. So we will each take a shot of the other and I will then seamlessly blend the two together into a team shot. I'm tackling such a task this morning with a shot of the South Dakota border. Each time I composite a shot I wonder if anyone ever catches it when they reach the web.

It's the typical workday for two road warriors on the Internet super highway. We can work from anywhere. With our equipment we can compose and create in our fully digital world. Our only challenge is in the upload. Since we don't have access to a digital roaming cellular phone service we have to connect locally to phone lines to send our creations to the World Wide Web. Up to this point it hasn't been a problem since we've been staying with friends and family and have had access to their phones and our ISP's roaming dial up service. But here in the lonely stretches of the Dakotas where we are without friend or family we have been faced with the daily challenges of no dial up access and no (gasp) daily email.

The lack of email has been hard to handle. Even in our previous lives as working stiffs Brian and I were email addicts. I can admit it, I check in a minimum of twice a day but usually more like three or four times. And yes I have multiple accounts to check too. No less than three. Always ready in case one would go down. And as important as email is to a techno-junky in normal life it is even more so out here in the great beyond of the blue and red highways of America. If we ever needed to connect with friends and family and strangers now was the time. Email could provide that touch with home, that daily normalcy, that moral and emotional support that is needed from time to time. But not here, not now. We were high and dry and all alone in Bismarck.

"Oh, I didn't show you the latest web report did I?" Brian asks. "It's saved on the desktop if you want to look at it."

I click and call the report up on screen. We get weekly reports on our web site traffic from our ISP and try to check it on a regular basis. It lets us know how many people are coming to our site, how long they stay, what they view, what day and time of day is the most active, and—my favorite part—from what countries and cities they visit.

I see this week's report welcomes viewers from Sweden, Columbia, Japan, and Kenya. I'm still amazed to see this, even after weeks' worth of reports, each with new countries. The thought that someone in Kenya clicked in and rode along on our quest, no matter how brief a visit, is exciting. So far we've had foreign visitors from England, China, Malaysia, Indonesia, Australia, Germany, Holland, Belgium, Canada, and Greenland. Amazing.

The web site has brought us new penpals and opportunities for chance encounters as well. We have already made several new web friends, a few that were sending us constant support via occasional emails and some who were looking forward to meeting us somewhere along our path. There is Kevin in California, Jennifer in Chicago, Mayer in New Jersey, Julie in New York, and Traci in Atlanta. All complete strangers weeks ago that were now friends out there in cyberspace.

I close the web log and think about returning to the work of photograph editing but decide to first head to the coffee machine for another refill. On the way back to our booth I pass a table full of elderly patrons sipping coffee and tea and discussing the secrets of the universe. It makes me pause and look around the room. No one present but the unemployed and retired. It makes me wonder where we fit in. I head back to the office and get back to work.

HOMERUN KING,
THE MALL, A DOG, AND
A PRIZE PIG

◆

The poor man is not he who is without a cent,
But he who is without a dream.

Harry Kemp

We hop through several states over the next few days, taking time to try to absorb some of the sites, meet some natives, and continue our quest. From Bismarck we head east, stopping briefly in Fargo. Craig had joined the Full Tank Club and sponsored the trek through Fargo. As his requested photo we were to take a shot in front of the Roger Maris Museum. So we drive across I-94, North Dakota's only highway, to Fargo and sought out the tribute to the home run king.

We decide to stop in a Taco Bell (visit number 13) first to grab our usual road lunch (the #4 combo for Brian, 7-layer burrito for me). When we enter we notice immediately that things are a little different in this Taco Bell. I feel like I just entered some nether world of the Twilight Zone. The restaurant sports the same decor as all the others, but everyone in the restaurant is blonde. Everyone! The two cashiers, the three cooks, the three postal workers enjoying their lunch, the family of five (blonde parents fighting with their blonde kids to eat), the young couple in the corner, everybody. In a room of 30 plus patrons, Brian and I are the sole non-blondes.

Blondes, blondes, everywhere blondes! I had heard that the Northern states of the Dakotas and Minnesota where full of Scandinavian stock but I had no idea…I have seen more blondes here in the past few days than I could ever hope to see in Norway and Sweden combined. Perhaps the Scandinavians export most of their blondes to this area, some sort of trade agreement with the US that no one knows about.

And it isn't just Taco Bell. When we finish up our vanilla coated lunch and head out in search of Roger Maris the body count continues. Flashes of blonde and white are everywhere. Another of America's little oddities that you really have to see to believe.

We find the museum almost by chance. Craig told us it was in a shopping mall and gave us a general idea of where so we exit where the map said there is a mall and pay it a visit. With luck it is the right one, and we find the museum there inside. It turns out to be more of a display than a museum, a glass enclosed wall case displaying old jerseys and uniforms and bats and balls and other memorabilia. Tribute to a man who is soon to be dethroned by a younger generation, McGwire and Sosa in hot pursuit. We snap a few digital photos before getting back onto the highways of America.

We leave the Dakotas behind and head for Minneapolis. Here we spend a few days seeing the area and inspecting the Mall of America, the world's largest shopping center.

Upon entering the mall I decide if the world were to collide with a meteor tomorrow, I want to be in Minneapolis' Mall of America. Surely this awesome super structure would survive such a blast. And if the world outside became uninhabitable, so be it. Inside I would have 520 stores to shop in, tons of restaurants to eat in, the Knott's Camp Snoopy (an indoor amusement park complete with roller coaster and water flume ride), movies, popcorn, and thousands of fellow tourists to repopulate with (the brochures are proud to boast that the Mall Of America receives more visitors each year than the Grand Canyon or Disneyland).

I would set up my home in the Pottery Barn store, sampling all of their latest in sleeping comfort. For breakfast I would stroll several city blocks around the mall to the Coffee Caribou for a jolt of morning espresso. In the afternoon I would hit a round of golf at Golf Mountain or perhaps design the future landscape of the reborn Earth in the LEGO Imagination Center. My wardrobe would come from the Gap, Abercrombie and Fitch, and the Old Navy. My meals would come from Panda Express, Taco Bell, and 1-Potato-2. I would hunt for dates on the promenade and take them out to dinner at the Odyssey Cafe's Atlantis Room before hitting the General Cinema to see one of the last films ever made on earth for the sixteenth time. My days would be full in the Mall of America. If the world were going to hell, that's where I want to be.

All malled out and no place to go, we find ourselves a few days later in our Jeep again and headed across to Wisconsin. An old friend of Brian's, Gregg Christensen, has invited us to speak about our quest to his marketing class. We arrive in Menomonie, Wisconsin, late in the evening and are up early the next morning to greet his class of two dozen college students. It is strange to speak to a class full of students, especially when you're not sure which side of the podium you really belong. Shouldn't I be sitting there listening instead of here speaking? It's another weird age thing, that hiccup in time between student and responsible adult.

We talk and ask questions and listen and offer answers. At the onset of the student participation one of the students voices an opinion that she would be viewing us and our quest totally different if we weren't from a so-called successful background. She pointed out that since

Brian and I had followed society's normal road map and achieved success in the corporate world, our opinions and the project had validity in their eyes. Whereas if we were just someone off the street, they would probably pay no heed to our questions or ideas.

This comment took us both by surprise. It was something we hadn't thought of or considered. I thought it highly possible that someone could come to realizations about life and the world around them at an early age and embark on a life that is personally successful and fulfilling without ever obtaining social success. But is it true? Would the views of such a person be scoffed at? Do we need to come from a socially acceptable position in order to have credibility? Or is this society talking again and not ourselves?

It reminds me of a travel journal entry we uploaded onto our website a little earlier on the trip. It read:

Look Who's Talking

Titles are everywhere. And unfortunately we use them here in our site as well. We as a society are so hooked on what a person does and what their title is. We need the title to try to associate with that person: Is she a doctor? Is he a fisherman? Is she an accountant? This is how we relate.

Unfortunately, we all have preconceptions about what these titles represent. When we hear them we automatically conjure up our own images and ideas about that person based on what they "do". Whatever our individual backgrounds and upbringing dictate, that is how we initially perceive that person.

And what do titles really say anyway? They tell you how that person makes his money to do the things he needs to do to survive. Titles often say little about the person, their hopes or dreams, personality, and inner self.

I have no answer to this problem, I wish I did. I wish I could say: John Doe, great father, caring son, compassionate community member. How different an image would this create than saying "salesman."

So when you read our interviews and see the titles listed by the person's name, please take a moment to toss the title aside and listen to them as you would a friend, not a random _____ you met on the street. The titles are not important, it's the person behind them that counts.

Thinking about it a little further, I remember some earlier comments we received from others during the planning stage of our present quest. Some of our friends told us it would be nice to hear the stories and insights of people like them and not high-powered executives and CEOs. They, like Brian and I, wanted to know how their neighbors down the street or the woman living upstairs were dealing with the issues and challenges of life. Someone they could relate to. Not someone who has obtained successes and excesses they would never realize. This seemed to directly contradict what we were hearing here.

The class over and the road beckoning, Gregg takes us to dinner at one of Menomonie's strangest attractions: the Bolo Inn. This eclectic restaurant is decorated floor to ceiling with the image of Bolo, the owner's once faithful black Labrador retriever long since passed away. It is a shrine to his memory with dog patterned carpets, china, and tablecloths. Portraits and photos stare down at diners from the walls, all of Bolo in peak hunting dog performance. Statues of the sleek dog fill corners and nooks. Bolo's presence is everywhere, even on the menu where one can order the Bolo steak. I decide not to ask what is in it, suddenly happy to be a vegetarian.

We leave Wisconsin the next day and drive back through Minnesota on the way south to Iowa and Nebraska. In Iowa we stop off for the Iowa state fair, inspecting prize cattle and pigs and sampling the wares of countless food vendors. Brian again calculates the options of owning a corn booth, though now fixated on the funnel cake business. We eat several for research purposes. We watch shows with lumberjacks, peek in on carnival acts, and inspect the art of local artisans. A day at the state fair has something to please everyone. We head out before the crowd and arrive at Brian's mother's house in Waverly, Nebraska, by nightfall.

SCULPTING WITH SPIRIT

◆

Failure is not a person,
Failure is an event in a person's life.

David Belitz

We get to the coffee shop ahead of schedule and settle into a corner table with a couple of steamy cups. David wanted to meet us here so he could show us some of his work in the gallery just next door. Brian's friend Debrah had suggested the meeting with David telling us he would be a great person to talk with and she even made the arrangements for us.

It's easy for us to spot each other when David enters, there is no one else in the small coffee shop. We stand and meet him half way into the room, exchange the usual salutations, and offer him a seat. David quickly produces several examples of his latest wire sculptures as well as a bundle of wire and some pliers with which he starts to work as we talk. We watch amazed that he can sculpt, think, and speak at the same time, something Brian or I would no doubt have trouble with.

David begins with telling us a bit about his past. David, 29, grew up in Bellevue, Nebraska. In his younger years, David spent much of his free time doodling and drawing, and more of it getting into trouble. This led to years of substance abuse and roaming in search of direction. Almost six years ago David began to turn his life around and went to work for Kellogg's. He worked there for several years but remained frustrated with the way his life was going. David decided to welcome religion into his life and open himself up to new direction. He found himself fired from Kellogg's just two days later, an event he describes as pure inspiration. Finding himself unemployed, David turned to his artistic talents and took up sculpting and has excelled on his path ever since. Now a successful wire sculptor in Omaha, Nebraska, David has found a path that brings him happiness and contentment.

I kick off our conversation by asking David how he made the decision to become a sculptor.

"It's a funny story," David says, twisting a piece from the bundle of wire he brought with him around his pliers. "A friend of mine handed me a pair of needle-nose pliers. He's a painter here in Omaha. His name is Bob Donlan and he's a really talented painter. He said to me, 'Do a wire sculpture. You draw in never-ending lines. I'm watching you do these wire sculptures on paper.' I said: 'You're crazy, I could never do a wire sculpture even if I tried.' I laughed at him for a while and he kept asking me and I said no. Then he walked out of the room to make a phone call and I picked up the wire and the pliers and I made a nine or ten inch sculpture of the crucifixion of Jesus on the cross. That was the first thing that came out. It was the weirdest thing. It was really strange because it was also the first thing I remember drawing as a child. I pulled out a Bible and found this abstract picture of Jesus on the cross and I drew it. It was the weirdest thing because I was raised with no faith whatsoever. Bob came back into the room, looked down, and said, 'You're a genius at this. You should be doing this for a living.'"

His hands continue to work the wire as he goes on. "Less than two weeks later I was down here in the Old Market sitting in front of a coffee shop making a three-dimensional sculpture of a dolphin. A gallery owner walked by and said hello. She asked if I sold my work and I said: 'Yeah, I guess so.' So we set up an appointment and I was making a living that month. It started out as piecemeal but soon I was rocking and rolling. I was doing sculpture all the time. I couldn't stop doing it. I brought it everywhere I went. I was doing sculpture on the street. I've been in recovery for five and a half years and I took it to 12-step meetings. Everywhere people were buying it and it was incredible. I get chills even thinking about it. Now here I am, I've shown and sold my work in nine different states. I sell on a web site now. Now I'm doing large steel work. I have a welder and a plasma cutter to cut large steel. I do life-sized people, abstracts, things that have sold for thousands of dollars a piece. I sculpt for three companies in town, and this has happened in just two years and two months from when I first got into sculpture. So it's really been an amazing trip and it just keeps getting better."

"Is this something you've always wanted to do? Did you grow up with dreams of being an artist?" I ask.

"No, growing up I had a huge fear of it. I was always filled with fear. Fear of failure, fear of success. If I were to start succeeding, I might fail, so I never started in the first place. My art was only used to try to grab other people's attention, to gain acceptance from other people. I used to do caricatures of people and I was very good. I was good at grasping a feature in a person and exaggerating it, like a principal or teacher so I could gain negative attention. And boy did it work. I got kicked out of school several times. So the art was like a joke. I never saw it for the gift that it is. Now I'm using it to make other people happy and to make God happy and to make a living. When I get selfish with my work or when I do it just for the money is when I succeed the least. When I sell the least. It's amazing how that works. It's beyond me why it works that way. It seems when people do things selflessly and not for selfish purposes they can succeed much more greatly and they have an inner contentment and peace. At least I do."

"Where do you think these fears of success or failure came from? How did you overcome it?"

"Fear of failure usually comes from parents instilling a lot of perfectionist expectations on you, that you needed to do everything to perfection, whether it was wrestling or football or art or anything else. Their kid had to be the best. That of course led to failure in my life. I would never feel good enough, you never feel good enough. And when you don't feel good about yourself, you do things to try to cover up the way you feel. My art got lost there somewhere in the middle. But somehow I was able to get over those fears and get back into it. I never ever thought I'd be doing this for a living, ever! EVER! Even two years and three months ago, because I started doing this two years and two months ago. It's scary. In fact I was telling a friend on the phone this morning that last night I felt like just running away. I felt like selling everything I have, all my equipment, and just running. I was so afraid of success. I basically took an inventory in my head and asked myself: What am I afraid of? I'm afraid of success. I'm afraid I'm going to fail if I start to succeed. And what I know today is that failure is not a person, failure is an event in a person's life. And those events will happen your whole life. They happen less and less as I take more action, but they will happen."

"You just defined failure, how would you define success?" Brian asks.

"Success for me is not financial. I think there is a piece of that in there. The world expects financial success for you to be a success. For me it's being content with my life today, being happy with who I am and what I have. And that's hard enough to grasp. I'm pretty darn happy with who I am and pretty darn happy with what I have, materially and things like that. Of course I want a little more. Success for me is being closer to God as I understand him, being spiritual. It's looking for that strength and guidance. I think success comes from within, it's not an outside thing. You can look successful all you want, but I know people who look very successful and drive $100,000 cars and their lives are a mess inside. And today I have this inside job of success, of being at peace in my heart and content with where I'm at and knowing that my life isn't totally unmanageable and I'm just hiding it from everybody."

"One of the reasons we decided to do this project is we talked with a lot of our friends and colleagues who were kind of in your position from the stand point that they were confused with their path in life, and questioned if they were doing the right thing. We wanted to put this project together to help people who were struggling over finding who they are and what they want to be. Are there words of wisdom or hints you can share on this?" Brian asks. The sculpture in David's hands is slowly taking form.

"Well I can only speak from my experience and tell what has worked for me. When I took the control out of my hands and asked other people and asked God as I understand him for help, it's when all this happened. It's when everything seemed to fall into place exactly the opposite of the way I thought it would. God put all these billions of people on this earth for a reason. It's to help each other. And I never wanted that, I always had to do it on my own power and with my own self-will. The only thing that ever worked for me is when I reached out to God and other people and said: 'What do I do? I'm kinda lost here.' Instead of being all prideful and standing by yourself and never succeeding, it's feeling truly at peace with what you're doing. I could have just kept going on and on and on working at Kellogg's and doing the things I didn't want to do. There are days when I don't want to do this, this sculpture. That's just me getting in the way. I know I love it. I wouldn't trade it for the world. The only time that things started to work for me is when I prayed and when I looked to others for help. That is the foundation of it and if I continue to do that, it continues to grow. It continues to build. It continues to work. And it's a fact that it works in my life. I'm an example of that spiritual aspect working."

"What do you find drives you? How do you find your passion and what makes you get out there and do what it is you do?" Brian asks.

"My spiritual rebirth. Ever since that happened when I get up every-day I try to get up with a different attitude. That's one of the most important things in my life today, my attitude. I have the choice to have a good or bad attitude today. It's like a friend of mine always says: 'Have a good day unless you've already made other plans.' And that's so true, because you can make a plan to have a bad day the moment you get up. It doesn't matter what happened the day before, I have a choice on a daily basis. And today because I have a real hope and a real God to serve and real friends and real people to make happy with my artwork, I can go and enjoy the day and actually stop and smell a flower or admire how people built this building or whatever. It's amazing. It's not all about me any more. It's about other people and how I can help them and how I can serve them. That's what drives me on a daily basis. It's life itself. I can live life on life's terms today. I can enjoy the beauty in life today, for the most part everyday. It's not all about self-seeking anymore. That's why I never succeeded in the past. It was all about me, all about David Belitz, and how he's going to get what he wants. That never got me any-where. Today I guess living for other people and for God is what gives me my daily drive to do what I do and do my work today."

"Apart from your spiritual beliefs, are there any other factors that have been key in achieving your success and happiness?"

"Taking action," David says looking up from his wire. "Something I'm famous for is that I can think my way into or out of something. It's like thinking myself into going and starting my car. I can think about it all day, but if I don't take the action, if I don't take my keys out and start the car, I'm never going to go anywhere. And it's the same thing with anything I do in my life, it doesn't matter if it's my art or my laundry, or anything. I have to constantly take action. You can sit there and think about anything you want but it will never get you anywhere unless you take the action to back it up. And that's integrity. I have integrity today in what I do and I'm always taking action. Or I'm trying to. Believe me there are days when I'm frozen in my apartment and I can't leave! If I'm always taking action in my art I'm going to make a living. It's all about taking action, like what you guys are doing. You're out taking action."

"*This* time," I agree. "But there are many times when we haven't."

He puts down the pliers and looks up holding the finished sculpture in his hand high in the air for us to see it clearly. It's the wire outline of a man wearing reading glasses and holding a book.

"Here, this is for you. I hope it will inspire you to continue your quest and share whatever you find with others. Maybe in their reading about what you're doing they will somehow be touched. I know I have been." He says and hands the sculpture to Brian.

"Thanks!" Brian says taking it gently in his hands. "We'll hang it from our rearview mirror where we can see it every day."

"Thanks David. For the sculpture and your time. It was great talking with you." I say as David packs up his wire and tools into his tote bag.

"I enjoyed it. So, would you like to see my other work in the gallery?" He asks.

We insist on it and gather our things to follow him out of the cafe.

KARMA BOOMERANG

◆

No man is a failure who has friends.

Clarence the Angel in "It's A Wonderful Life"

"It's ready," Brian's mother calls from the dining room. Others know her as Diane, to us she's always just been Mom.

It takes a moment for us to react. We remain motionless in front of the TV. The remote is tightly clenched in Brian's hand. He won the latest King Of The Remote contest and got control over the TV and our viewing choices. It's amazing how we can go weeks, even months, without a TV around and be perfectly fine. We spend time writing, or reading, or drawing, or talking, or whatever. But as soon as the idiot box gets turned on, it takes a lot of effort to just walk away and ignore it. And when there's cable or satellite involved, with over 50 channels to choose, look out! The box demands attention, and here at Mom's house in Waverly, it is getting all the attention it wants.

"Boys!" Brian's Mom says again. We both jump up and Brian switches off the TV. We are children again eager to avoid the wrath of an upset parent at any cost.

We all sit down at the table, Brian and me and Mom and Gary and Chelsea, the little yappy terrier hopping up and down at our feet in hopes of scraps. Dishes are passed in family fashion, clockwise, around the table and food is heaped onto plates. My eyes almost tear up at the sight of such beautiful home cooked food. Something that isn't being served to us by a waiter or handed through a drive-thru window (thankyouhaveanicedaygoodbye).

"So how was the interview today?" Brian's Mom asks.

"It went well, a really interesting guy," I say as I dish more food onto my plate.

"It was the artist, right?" She asks.

"Yes, a sculptor. He had some really interesting insights as well. A very spiritual person, religion was prominent in everything he discussed." Brian says forking a mouthful of roasted beast.

"That's not surprising. This is the Bible Belt remember." Mom says.

"No, I know. Actually I was expecting to hear more religious comment during our talks with others."

"That's true, I was too," I say. "But it hasn't really come up that often. And when it has, it has been more of a vague spirituality thing rather than talk of religion. Though we do keep getting asked if we are doing our quest for some particular church or religious organization. It seems to be the first thing on many people's minds when we tell them about what we're doing. But usually I can't tell if they're disappointed or relieved when we tell them we're not." I say from behind green beans.

I'm actually thankful the question always ends with our comment of being nonrepresentational. We're trying our best to be unbiased and open during our quest and don't want to exclude or alienate anyone, especially due to any particular religious belief. We remain open minded and hope others to be the same. And besides, if someone probed further and did ask about our own convictions how would I answer? I'm of the new breed of religious seekers, the kind they don't have a box for on most forms. "Other", I guess. Christian, Buddhist, Taoist, I'm not sure. God? Yes. Hell? Maybe. I'm just not sure.

This is probably another side effect from my overseas exposure. Raised with Western religious beliefs, when I hit Asia I was interested in learning more about the philosophies and religions behind their art and culture. Many of their beliefs made sense to me, a few hit an accord. More options, more to think about. From it all, I've formed my own opinions, my own beliefs, my own box to check.

"I've noticed though that the people we talked to that had some kind of religious or spiritual conviction had a little more grasp on their happiness. Maybe not in a knowing what they want with their life way, but in a happy with the situation or contentment with where they are sort of way." Brian says.

I bounce my head in agreement with a few chews. "It kind of makes you wonder doesn't it. Maybe there's something to it all."

"I know there is," Brian says. "It's just part of the big picture. Regardless of the belief, I think the belief in something, anything, plays a big part in one's overall happiness."

We sit and chew and enjoy the dinner. The food tastes incredible.

"What did you do with the rest of your day?" Brian's Mom asks.

"We worked a bit," I say. "And we ate at Stella's for lunch!" I enthuse, remembering lunch in Bellevue's tastiest and greasiest restaurant. "Then we toured around Omaha and Bellevue, stopping in and visiting the old sites: the stores, the restaurants, the comic shop…"

"That reminds me Brian. When we moved down from Bellevue I found an old box of your comics. It's up in the attic." Brian's Mom says as a side note.

"It's there." I say turning and looking at Brian with a smile spreading across my face like a sudden sunrise. The comment makes me jump a little in my chair.

"It's not. Don't get all excited, the box must be my brother's. I sold mine, remember?" He says shoveling another spoonful of mashed potatoes into his mouth.

"What's there?" Mom asks.

"My Spider-man 100. Don't you remember?" I ask in disbelief.
"No."

"It's a comic Chris gave me once." Brian says with full mouth.

"It's more than that, it was a defining moment in history. You see…"

And I recount the tale for them. I tell them of a little boy and his best friend making plans to visit the soon-to-be-open comic shop, Huntington's first, on opening day the coming weekend. Both boys were hoping to find the coveted Spider-man 100, the comic that would add greatly to their youthful, growing collections. I tell them how an unplanned visit downtown that Friday brought one of the boys (me) to the parking lot across from the not-yet-opened shop, and how the boy begged his mom to let him go look in the window while she ran into the pharmacy to get what she needed. She agreed and he rushed across the street.

The boy stood, stooped over the window, hands clasped to the side of his face, and peered into boyhood nirvana. There a young couple worked frantically to set up and order and align millions of boxes of comics, each moving with super speed and strength in perfect harmony. The boy watched as the man mysteriously sensed his presence and called up to him, inviting him into his lair. Captivated, compelled, and excited beyond belief the little boy ran to the door where the man pointed and slowly crept in, unsure if it was all real.

Inside the smell hit him first, the wonderful, beautiful smell of old comics. The smell of dried ink on frayed paper locked in plastic baggies that gets under your skin and locks childhood memories there, gluing them to your DNA. The boy said something to the couple, thanks maybe, gibberish probably, and was pointed in the direction of the boxes marked Spider-man. He marched over to them and began to leaf through, amazed at what he was seeing. Such old issues, such treasure! And then the little boy's eyes fell upon it, the ark of the covenant, the king's ransom, the holy grail: *Spider-man 100*. He looked behind it, but there was just the one. Only one. He pulled it from the box. He stood and held it in his hand and stared. And stared. And stared.

At some point the stasis was broken when the little boy's mom came in just a tad bit worried. Relieved to find her son, she was in the ripe mood to buy him anything the little boy would ask for, and he knew it. He pleaded for the money and he won. The prize was his!

He bounced off the walls of the station wagon on the ride home, so excited was he to have landed such a prize. Once home the little boy ran to the phone (ran!) to call up his bestest friend and tell him the news. He wanted to tell him he had secured the issue and that his friend could read it as soon as possible. It was such a great day and would be so much greater once he could share it with his best friend.

The phone rang and the line was picked up. The boy excitedly told his story and then…silence. The question: *You got it?* The answer: Yes, yes, I have it! Another question: *Was there another one?* A hesitant answer: No, I don't think so.

Silence. And then a dead line.

The little boy could not understand what was happening. This was the happiest day of his life, the happiest day ever! But his best friend wasn't sharing in his happiness. He seemed angry. The little boy learned a lesson in jealousy that day. His mother sat him down and explained to him that perhaps to keep the friendship he should give his friend the comic. No! Unbelievable! The comic had been his for less than a day and now he would just let it go. To choose between his best friend and the prize of all prizes was such an incredible burden on such a little boy. What to do, what to do. But the answer was obvious and the comic was gone as easily as it had arrived.

I came to a decision that day that friendship is worth even more than comic books. And our friendship was saved by the mighty power of Spider-man.

"So then years later in high school Brian and I are reminiscing and I tell him that if he ever decided to sell his comics I wanted that one back.

You know, for old time sake." I carry on with the tale, pausing briefly for a sip of lemonade. "And he says to me, 'Oh, I already sold all of them last year.' I haven't forgiven him ever since. But now, well, now it's in your attic and all is right in the universe once again."

"I don't know what's in the box," Brian's Mom confesses, a bit sorry perhaps for bringing it all up.

"It's not there Chris, you're getting riled up for nothing." Brian says.

But for some reason I felt it was. I knew it was. I don't know why, it just seemed to make perfect sense to me. A silly sort of poetic karma.

"Well there's only one way to find out. Ready?" I say pushing back from an empty plate. Brian does the same and we head into the garage and pull down the ladder from the attic.

I climb up into the attic and am a kid again. A great explorer entering a lost tomb in search of hidden treasure. At the top of the ladder Brian hands me a light and I wave it around in the darkness until it falls on the familiar white cardboard of a comic box. "Found it!" I yell down and then crawl over to it and drag it to the cubby hole where I hand it down to Brian.

We go inside the house for the opening. Brian sets it down on the carpet and sits back away from it. I slump down next to the tattered box and take a big whiff. Comic smell. I trace the edge of the lid with my fingers thinking of how it seems everyone who ever collected comics as a child has a story. Usually it involves a mother throwing out a box of "funny books" that at present day value would buy a college education. Everyone always dreams of finding the box in the dark recesses of the attic someday. Could this really be happening?

And I open the box. And the smell of comics hits me harder. And it is there. IT IS THERE! The box is full of Spider-mans, a hundred of them or more! I flip through the comics in sequential order and find it right there between 99 and 103. An old friend returned to me, a missing limb restored.

Speechless I sit back and slowly open the plastic baggy and remove it from its vinyl sarcophagus. I slowly turn the pages and stroll down memory lane. Brian in the meantime looks through the box confused.

"I thought I sold these long ago," he says. "I guess I decided to keep this box and forgot all about it."

Forgot or not, I didn't know what was going on and I didn't care. I only knew that it was there again and things really *were* right in the universe, for this moment anyway. Some strange event has taken this away and brought it back to me. I try to fathom the secret meaning behind it all, try to find a reason for it to be happening. But I can think of nothing. There's no great secret or clandestine plot behind it. It's just the ultimate case of good karma coming back wrapped in plastic and scented with nostalgia.

I look up and see Brian is looking at the box and then at me. He leans forward and pushes the edge of the box, sliding the box over to me.

"Merry Christmas."

We were kids again and the karma has returned with interest. All is right in the universe.

I WRITE THE SONGS

◆

*Most people die with their music
still locked up inside of them.*

Benjamin Disraeli

We wait for our next chance meeting in the Cinnabon shop in one of Omaha's many malls. So many people in such a variety of places. I begin to think we should have struck up a deal with Starbucks or Taco Bell, making them the *official meeting place of the Quest-4 adventure*. I could just see the advertisements plastered around the country displaying our smiling faces and the benefits of the corporate sell out now. I mention it to Brian and he suggests we send them a letter. We add it to our ToDoList.

We have that giddy feeling of anticipation that comes with a first contact again. Someone will walk through that door in a minute and sit down and talk with us about life. Their life. A complete stranger with a new story, a new outlook. The thought of it still blows me away, even after many weeks on the road. Each time we sit and wait and watch the crowd and the faces and wonder, is that her? Faces come and go, each with their own story to tell. I wonder if they would like to share.

Brian and I often talk about how hard it will be when this is all over to go back to anonymity. To return to the world where people are closed, where they don't open up to talk about the world around them. With our quest and our current state of mind we have reason and purpose to go and meet people. We have something to ask, something to talk about, and people are responding to that. We have met handfuls of wonderful people on the trip because of this. But when it is over will it return to talk about the weather or current politics and avoidance of strangers in the distance?

A face smiles to us from the crowded mallway and enters the shop. It's Jenny Bowen, our latest and newest friend. A woman in her forties, Jenny is dressed in business attire with pleasant, round features sculpted around her smile. As she reaches us, she begins apologizing for being late and introducing herself. She's the kind of person you like right away.

We sit and go through the background of our journey with her in the usual fashion. I think that by now we should be doing it differently. Perhaps Brian and I should start saying every other sentence. Kind of a broken stereo effect. Or maybe we should put it to music and sing the quest's history in perfect harmony. Something to stir it up and make the speech more interesting. Maybe next time.

We know a little about Jenny from speaking with her on the phone, and she fills us in on the rest. An actuary by trade, a song writer by passion, and a veterinarian hospital administrator through marriage, Jenny Bowen has found a way to manage these professions and passions in a manner that brings meaning and fulfillment to herself and those around her. Jenny grew up in Ohio, went to college in Iowa and has lived everywhere from Kansas City to France. With a bachelor's degree in mathematics with minor in physics, Jenny went on to become an actuary after college and has pursued this for over 20 years. Along with her husband, she went on to develop a second career when they built an animal hospital to allow her husband to pursue his passion for veterinarian medicine. Then at 45, Jenny found her true passion, song writing, after writing a song for a relative's anniversary. She now balances all three "careers" and loves every minute of it.

"Once you found your passion," Brian begins, "did everything else fall into place?"

"Finding my passion, which is song writing, opened me up to more and more positive viewpoints," Jenny says. "The more you're open to positive viewpoints, the more you can see and the more you can see the positive in everything."

"Taking actuarial exams for 20 years really stunted my growth as a human," she says with a laugh. "Being an actuary in the most traditional sense is not nearly as much of who I am as I am a song writer. So the time I spent studying for exams was time taken away from my life. So I think that may be one thing that helps me to now see things better.

"How did you get into your actuary career?" I ask.

"I wanted to do the hardest thing that would most impress people. And then I spent the next 20 years feeling like I needed validation from other people from having made that decision. I feel that I have success now because I know that my life is how I choose it to be, and I revel in that knowledge. I feel like I have the power to define my life. Success is realizing that you have that power and being happy about it and continuing to channel your energy into that journey."

"Do you feel your past decisions have been based on external factors?"

"Definitely! I have spent a lot of my life being needy in different ways, and I think the only way to minimize that is to discover that source that you have and that's available to everyone to create your own life."

Brian asks: "How does the animal clinic fall into your path?"

"I feel blessed that my husband and I share that dream. I think that's quite rare. We've been married for 22 years and we just went into business together last year. I really think it has made our marriage stronger and happier because it's been a way for both of us to achieve a goal that we wanted. We both really believe in the service we provide to the animals and, even better, we agree on the philosophy of the type of hospital that we want: a high-tech sophisticated hospital that provides really good care, but also is a very caring and nurturing environment. We don't compete in the roles we play. Our talents complement each other well, but the vision is the same."

"Is that your husband's passion?"

"My husband has always wanted to be a veterinarian. In fact a year into it he said, 'Jennifer, this is the way I always dreamed it would be.' I was jealous of him for a long time that he knew since he was five years old what he wanted to do. He had some obstacles to overcome towards meeting that goal, but he had a passion. I thought life was good and there were a lot of things I could do well, but until I discovered song writing, I never knew what that was like. Now I do."

I find myself relating to this comment and the mystery of hidden passions, wondering if she experienced a Shamzara event the day she discovered song writing. I ask, "How does someone go about finding that passion?"

"I was 45 years old when I discovered it. However looking back, I can see there were a lot of things that created a situation such that at 45 I could step back. I was fortunate that my parents were very supportive when we were growing up. They didn't push me into a certain career. Although my father really, really wanted me to go to medical school. But other than that, they encouraged every interest that I expressed. I took guitar and organ and piano and violin lessons when I was younger. I took art lessons and sewing lessons. When I decided to be an exchange student, they supported that. That was hard for them to do, to send a 17-year-old off to live with another family in another country. So I'm glad they encouraged me to follow every interest that I had, but also I exercised the discipline when I did try those things. I practiced the piano and organ and guitar. I did a lot of sewing. I made all my clothes in high school. I think it's important to realize that no matter what your passion is, you'll get more out of it if you exercise the discipline to learn from other people and do research and investigate. If it's something that you really love it doesn't seem like work."

She thinks for a second and decides to elaborate further. "For example, every hour that I spent studying for actuarial exams seemed like work and took me away from what I wanted to do. Although I was glad that it had a positive effect on my career and that was important to me, and certainly money is important. But when I compare the time I spent studying for those exams with how I felt when I was practicing piano or sewing or reading books in French, those activities were much more enjoyable to me. But I felt that if I wanted to make money and advance in a career, I would have to take this time away from my real life. Now I realize that you can have both."

"Did you do anything in particular to pinpoint your passion?" Brian asks.

"I would say an important element in finding your passion is to stop turning off the messages that your inner self is trying to tell you. I knew that I loved music and language and art, and I forced myself to ignore it. So I think the most important things in your life are right there under your nose, but we work so hard to not know it. I think that's all a part of the path. I think of part of the path as opening yourself to see the energy that's available and around you. If you try to turn off those self-created things that block you from your path and decide to go with the flow more, then many important things are easy to see. I guess for me the art of finding the important things in life is to quit trying so hard not to find them."

"Did you suffer any lows during the search?" I ask.

"I've had some lows, but I'm a Type A person who is driven to succeed. If I'm low or lost, I revert to that automatic drive to achieve, achieve, achieve. I think that has been good for me at times, because there were years I wasn't advancing as a human because I was always studying and working at my job, but with my drive to achieve it resulted in leaving me in a much better financial position now. Perhaps even if I hadn't been so driven, I still wouldn't have been ready earlier to do the things that I'm doing now. I have something to show for those years. By putting 22 years into the insurance industry means that now I have a nice job that I can finance these other paths."

"Have you found that a lot of your peers have discovered their paths?" Brian asks.

"I think a lot of people are struggling with finding their paths. For one thing, I don't have any children, and it has left us with more freedom as to how we'd like to spend and enjoy our time," Jenny says, and then is quick to add, "Not that parents don't enjoy their children, but more of their waking hours are programmed for them."

"Any regrets, things you would change, or words of wisdom?" I ask her.

"When I look back at all the things I've done and the choices I've made, the only moments that stick out as moments of regret are times when I was unkind. I think that if you don't step on other people's toes and you can find love in your heart for everyone, then there are no bad choices. I think the things you try and find out you don't like, help you figure out more about what you do like. Who knows, I may come up with a new passion. I mean if I was 45 when I figured out I should be a songwriter, what will I know at 55? My father gave me good advice about choosing a career. He said, 'Study the subjects that you really love and you will find a path that makes sense to you.' That's what has happened to me. I'm a songwriting, hospital administrating, actuary. Who'd have thought?"

*   *   *

"I don't know Bri, waiting until I'm forty to find my passion…" I point to the store front of the *World Of Wind Up Toys*. "Let's go in here."

The place is wall to wall noise. Planes and trains and trucks and animals crank and creen and clang. Anything and everything with moving parts to annoy and excite is found here inside. The motion and commotion is enough to send even the non-epileptic into a seizure.

"But she found it. It took a while, but it hit. I thought you'd be happy, it seemed we just got living proof of the Shamzara Effect." Brian says lifting a crawling panda from the display case where it's been walking in circles for 17 panda years.

"I *am* happy," I say as I stroll further into the store. "I think it's great. If anything it shows that there is a different path for everyone and that things happen at different times in your life. Different stages. For example, there's Mark who knew from childhood he wanted to be a film maker. And there's Greg, who slowly developed his passions for his career as weaver and carpenter. And then here's Jenny, who BOOM! One day it just hits her out of the blue."

"Like a bolt of lightning." Brian adds.

"Like a bolt of lightning, yeah. So there are these different ways, these three at least, of finding your passion and your path. I guess the real problem comes when you try to fit yourself into one of the other two slots, or when you try to rush the process. For instance, if you haven't known from childhood what you want to do and yet you still torture yourself over that. Don't just accept it and move on. Or if, maybe like me, you try to seek out the lightning and catch it, harness it in a bottle. It's just not done. Life doesn't play along."

"So maybe you just have to relax and be the *reed*." Brian says. He's quoting me on this. It's something I always say when I feel myself being too stubborn or concentrating too much on my own expectation rather than the moment at hand. It comes from an old Zen saying:

During the tempest the mighty oak stands proud and strong, rigid in its ways. The heavy winds come and rip the oak apart, tearing off branches, uprooting and over turning the great tree. While there beside, the lowly reed bends and bows in the wind, dancing and delighting in the change of weather. The reed rides out the storm and remains to see another day.

Be flexible. Be the reed. It's funny how often I tell myself these simple words. Wack. A flexible disk of nerf hits me on the side of the head. Brian has found a missile launcher, the Disk Flyer, and is taking aim for another shot. I spy another loaded weapon on the display case and make a run for it. Missiles whip and wizz past me as I grab the other gun and begin to fire back. Hundreds of wind up toys look on as the battle ensues, they pang and pong their cheers and jeers. Two gladiators in an arena of toys, forgetting the mysteries of the universe for a moment of fun. Two reeds blowing in the wind.

IN BETWEEN

◆

There comes over one an absolute necessity to move.
And what is more, to move in some particular direction.
A double necessity then: to get on the move, and to know whither.

D. H. Lawrence

Departures are the best part of any long journey. Not the moments leading up to them, or even the long travels ahead, but that moment of release, the moment when you step away from the old and embrace the new. It's a time of pure potentiality, of thriving opportunity, where anything can happen.

Leaving a place behind can be difficult, especially if you have stayed long enough to get comfortable or if you are leaving friends and loved ones behind. The packing, the hugs, the good-byes and farewells, they are all pre-show activities for the actual departure. But then the departure hits and all is well. It comes the moment when you know you are on the road again, and the world is ahead of you waiting.

The journey can vary. The moment of departure can linger for miles and miles, perhaps even to your next destination. Or it can fade quickly and leave you with the arduous road and task of traveling along it. But it is the journey that makes the quest. The journey offers the pitfalls and challenges to test your resolve. It offers the time for mental turmoil and reconsideration, inner demons to see if you are worthy.

Then there are the destinations. Some can be glorious, others a disappointment. Arriving at a place is a grab bag of sensations. It can offer a sense of relief and satisfaction for the weary traveler, or maybe wonder for those unexpecting. The chance to settle in and explore and meet and taste and experience.

Many enjoy the arrival the best. Not me. I like the departures. I like to stare into space and say: Okay, what's next?

We depart from Nebraska in the early morning and have that sense of freedom the road offers as we spin off gravel roads, onto back roads and onto highways facing east. It's a sunny, summer day with a near cloudless sheet of blue above and spinning wheels below and it's a great day to be alive.

We pass farms and corn fields on the way to Kansas City. On the edge of Nebraska we see Nebraska's Faux Mountain Range off in the distance. It consists of a gathering of low clouds resembling a series of distant snow capped peaks. The only mountains this land will ever see.

Departure, journey, arrival. Kansas City offers a look at something new. Brian has been here many times before during his life in Nebraska. For me it's all fresh. The self proclaimed *City of Fountains* with the graceful Spanish architecture and tree lined streets and green parks and smiling people. It's a city that appeals to me at first glance. We tour the city, meet people, catch a Royals game, and absorb as much as we can. And then we move on. We depart.

And we're back in the veins of America. Flat land and a short drive and the mighty Mississippi! Reaching the 'ole Miss is another of the milestones of a cross country trip. Heading east there is the stop at the Pacific, the crossing of the Rockies, the continental divide, the Mississippi River, and then the long stretch to the Atlantic Ocean. We're now passing our last hashmark and are on the way to the goal.

This marker is a popular one for anyone east or south. I'd heard
about it all the time growing up in West Virginia. People would comment: "I've never been west of the Mississippi." Signs would read: *Best
chicken east of the Mississippi*! The river was called upon for so many
reasons that as a child it made you wonder if there was anything west
that held any worth at all.

And here it is! I have seen it before. I've driven over it several times.
But I still can't help being excited as we loop around St. Louis and edge
the flowing beast. Arrival: St. Louis. Another day, another city. We pay a
visit to the Budweiser Brewery (best brewery tour west of the
Mississippi), tour the city, dine at Union Station, stroll the botanical
gardens, explore Washington University, and marvel at the famous
Gateway Arch.

I'm impressed by the different flavors of the cities we hit. They all
seem to have something special to offer, something unique. This varies
so greatly from what we've experienced in suburbia America. All across
the country outside the cities we find we are seeing the same place over
and over. The mass-produced, over-planned, bubble world of American
Suburbia. Suburbia is the same, whether it be in Kansas or Missouri or
Nebraska or elsewhere. The same design, same stores, same food offer-
ings. The same vision of outskirts utopia anchored down by Borders
and Best Buy and Walmart.

I guess the bubble worlds could be comforting. As you pack up and
move from one bubble to the other across the nation you know what to
expect. Your living is the same, so just chose your surrounding area and
the city of interest. And I have to admit we have benefited from the bubbles on our journey thus far. We've lounged in the overstuffed chairs at
Barnes & Nobles while reading magazines or the latest releases, our vir-
tual living room while on the road. We've listened to new music. We visited Circuit City to catch some TV shows on their wall of models. And
when rushed for time, we've visited the same restaurants and received
the same service and the same food at relatively the same price. The

bubble worlds offer the traveler a home away from home. But as nice as they can be while on the road there is something sinister in their proliferation across the nation. They are like relentless cancers that absorb and eliminate originality. The bubbles grow and the little stores die. The tiny book shops, the homemade ice creams, the friendly boutiques, all shut out and strangled in the shadows of the corporate behemoths.

So it is always pleasant to see a thriving city. One that still offers a downtown, an option away from the bubbles of suburbia. A city with spice and pizzazz, its own step, its own tastes and smells. St. Louis definitely fits this bill.

We're in the city only a couple of days before we head out again. We say good-bye to the Arch and cross the river in search of the *best things east of the Mississippi*. Back on the road we suffer from our first road casualty. While out in the streets of St. Louie the relentless heat of the sun tore through the windshield of the Quest-Mobile and melted off our rear view mirror. Not knowing where to find the repair tools needed in this city, we decide to wait till familiar grounds in Indiana to put it back on. So for this next stretch we are making a go at it without its aid. I'm amazed at how often I tend to check behind me while moving ahead. The journey seems different now when concentrating on what is in front of me and paying less attention to what has fallen behind.

Our first stretch of Illinois sprints by us as Indiana comes to greet us. We slide through the gate and into her southern recesses and climb the hills to Bloomington, Indiana.

BACK TO INDIANA

◆

Happiness does not depend on outward things,
but on the way we see them.

Leo Tolstoy

"Are we there yet?" I hear from the passenger seat.

"Just about," I say and turn to where Brian is sitting. Only it isn't Brian. It's an old man, wrinkled and worn and glaring back at me impatiently. The sight startles me and sends me swerving off the road in reaction.

"Hey, what are you doing, trying to get us all killed?" The Old Man exclaims.

I steady the Jeep and pull back onto the road from the soft shoulder where we had strayed.

"Who are you?! Where's Brian?" I say stealing another glance in his direction. This answers the first question before he has the chance to. I've seen the face before, somewhere. On another inspection it seems even more familiar. It's the Old Man from the hill, from my vision. The fuzzy, blurred vision of a man is now here in the flesh and clear as the evening star. Small and stout, with paper white hair receding back on sun speckled pink skin and looking at me through faded blue-green eyes.

"Don't worry about Brian. He'll be back. Now let's just enjoy the drive for a while why don't we." He says and slides down a bit more in the seat beside me, feeling for the most comfortable posture. "I don't see how you can stand riding around in this Jeep days on end. I'd think you'd both have hemorrhoids by now."

"It's not that bad, really. I...Hey, sorry for being so rude and all, but just who the hell are you and what are you doing in my car?"

"Not important. What is important is your reaction."

Great. Here I am on the back roads of Illinois and suddenly some crazed old man shows up mysteriously in the Jeep thinking he's Yoda.

I want to pull over and demand answers or explanation, or perhaps eject him from the vehicle. But I feel compelled to keep driving and do as he suggested, just enjoy the drive for a while.

"So, heading back to Indiana are you?"

"Yep." *That's it, short and sweet answers. Let him do the talking.*

"Ah, Indiana. Lots of memories there eh? So tell me, learned a lot on this trip have you?" The old man says as he reaches out and touches the wire sculpture hanging from our rear view mirror. His hand looks like it's wearing a freckled skin glove that is several sizes too big, extra bunches of flesh sagging in pools around his wrist and knuckles.

"Yeah, I have. It's amazing that..."

"It's amazing," he begins, interrupting me and turning my direction, "that you could learn a whole lot more if you'd only start paying attention a bit more! Really listening. Really hearing. Really experiencing." He seems anxious in saying this, agitated. "People are talking to you and you're off talking to yourself. Wake up and enjoy the ride boy. Forget about the search and pay attention to the finds."

The old guy is speaking with a new zest and passion, poking the air between us with his fingers as if providing punctuation for each remark. I'm waiting for him to start telling me about the *Force*.

"See, right there. There you go again. Don't anticipate, just listen."

And then I'm a bit frightened. Not only was he right, but he was right along with my thoughts. He seemed to know what I am thinking.

"Not important right now." He says waving his hand and the eerie feeling returns. "And something else. Look at who you're with. Look around you. Feel for it."

His voice is wavering and I hear a word spoken very faint. *Friends*. At least I think that is what it is. The voice is distant, miles away. I don't have time to really think on this. The man is speaking to me again, something about a border.

"…to miss the border." I hear him say.

I turn around and look at him through eyes that have suddenly grown misty. "What?"

"I said, you're going to miss the Indiana border. It's coming up in two miles. Want to stop for a photo?"

It's Brian talking. It's Brian driving. I shake the clouds from my head and look out the windshield at the trees and grass and tired homes. I then sit up in the passenger seat with a jerk and turn around to look into the back of the Jeep. Nothing but piles of travel gear covered with the stench of weeks of road use. I look back at Brian and it slowly makes sense to me where I am. A silly dream. I tell him to go ahead and stop at the border and slide down a bit more in my seat, feeling for the most comfortable posture.

I'd been sleeping. Just a really weird dream. But for some reason that doesn't stick. I feel like it was something more. Something I should pay attention to, listen to. I take a moment to try to recall what was said and tuck it away into the hard disk of my mind for easy access later.

At the border we pull the Quest Mobile in front of the bright red, white, and blue sign that welcomes us to Indiana, the "Crossroads of America." We walk over to the sign and I position myself underneath it, my turn to be in the photo. Brian lines up the shot, I manage a crooked grin, and he snaps the lens. We then head back to the Jeep and enter the lands of yesterday.

ENVIRONMENTAL PROTECTION

———————————— ◆ ————————————

Who is the happiest of men?
He who values the merits of others,
and in their pleasure takes joy,
even as though it were his own.

Johann con Goethe

We hit the outer banks of Bloomington, Indiana, and begin to drive through the city at a slow pace, passing old ghosts and forgotten memories. I'm driving now. I wanted to navigate my own return to the place that was so special to me in the past. My alma mater, my college town.

It's been nearly ten years since I left Indiana for far away places, but not much here has changed since then. A few new shops, a few renamed bars and restaurants, a little bit different landscaping. But for the most part it's still the place I remember. It's me that has changed.

We drive in off 46 and past the football stadium, stopping briefly at a convenient mart just beside my old apartment across the way. There I call our Bloomington hosts and tell them we will be arriving shortly, after a quick drive around town. We then cruise campus, past the HPER (school of Health, Physical Education, and Recreation) and student union, down Third, around the courthouse, up Kirkwood and Tenth. We make a complete driving tour of my old haunts and Brian patiently listens as I stroll down memory lane and regale him with tales of past adventures

Indiana University is one of those places that is close to my heart, a place that is a big part of who I am. It is the place I stepped out of my old life of small town America. It's where I shed old identities and expectations and entered a new world with head high and ready for anything. I met new people, made new friends, and learned about the world, life, and my place in it. Maybe college is like that for everyone, I don't know. Maybe others find themselves elsewhere. I found myself here in Bloomington. I think back to Richard Rhoades' comment about college not being for everyone. I can see now that it was definitely for me.

Kim Dingess and Eric Eckhart greet us at their door with hugs and hellos. Brian exchanges long looks with them; they haven't seen each other since junior high school. A lot has changed since then.

I have known Kim since as long as I remember. I can still recall our kindergarten class photo with Kim standing there right beside me. Eric and I have been friends since junior high school. My friendship with the two really kicked off in high school, and we have grown closer ever since. We immediately fall into conversation and begin catching up on each other's lives. There is a definite comfort and security in being around people who you have known for so long, who have seen you at your best and worst, and still choose to associate themselves with you.

We share stories of our quest, and they tell us tales of their current lives. Kim, a doctoral student in the anthropology department here at IU, tells us about recent field trips to the neo-tropics of Costa Rica and some results from her studies of howler monkeys there. Eric skips right past details of his wage-winning work and goes right for the stereo. He loads a CD into the player and cranks up the volume. It's his

latest creation and true passion, his self written, produced, and per-
formed music CD. I am impressed, but Brian is amazed. He knew Eric
before his musical talents developed and he is taken by surprise by the
level of Eric's gifts.

"Wow, that's all *you*?" Brian asks enthralled by the music.

"Yeah," Eric answers in a voice far too modest. The music sounds
incredible, better than most of the stuff we heard on radio stations from
L.A. to Indiana.

"You know Eric, I noticed that guitar and mike down in the base-
ment…" I say, my implication is quickly picked up on.

"Want to hear some live?"

"Thought you'd never ask!"

We move the evening downstairs and put it to music, Brian and I taking turns singing backup and once in a while making up our own lyrics.

In spending time with my friends I find myself feeding areas of my
brain and passions that I haven't used much in the past years. In an earlier life as a college student I minored in anthropology, once having
dreams of rain forests and field studies myself. Dreams that were tossed
aside at some point, lost in a world of practicality. But now I get to live
vicariously through the exploits of Kim. And with Eric I find my artistic
elements sparked and kindled. As the music flows through the room I
can't help but feel the creative energy. I feel like picking up pen and
paper or brush and pallet and returning to my days of studio art.

The visit makes me realize how important the environment can be in
nurturing a person's individual successes and encouraging them to follow their dreams. While success may be internally conceived and created, being around close friends and a friendly environment can lend a
big hand of assistance in getting there. Here in Bloomington not only
do I have friends to bounce ideas off of and tell dreams to, but I also
have inspiration to learn about past passions and pursue creative ventures. Here I have the love and support of close friends urging me to use
my talents and abilities and follow my own path, be that what it may.

People who will tell me when I'm being foolish, or making poor decisions, who will pick me up when I'm down and fly along with me when I soar. Friends who will offer constructive criticism and welcomed advice and a world of support.

I once read that you should take a good look at the language of the business you are considering for a career. Look to see if the terminology is something you want to hear and use on a daily basis. It made sense to me then, and now I can see how to take this a step further, looking not only at what is being said but at who is saying it. Even outside the business world, if the people around you are talking about the things you love, passionately, positively, and in an inspiring way, how could you not be thrilled to take action?

I've heard it said and thought about it much, but never has it been so blatantly demonstrated to me. Or maybe I'm just paying attention to it for the first time. It's so important to look hard at our environments, the people we surround ourselves with, and add that into the melting pot of figuring out this thing called life. And maybe we could all get by with a little help from our friends.

WINDY CITY

◆

*I'd rather be a failure at something I enjoy
than a success at something I hate.*

George Burns

"…dress is a bevel of excess."

"What!?" I scream over the blaring horn and screeching bus and try to make out what Jeff just said. My only hope is to have him repeat himself. All of a sudden our quiet little corner of Chicago has become far too noisy. But as quickly as the noise struck it fades away and we are surrounded by pleasantness again, all part of the dynamic of city dwelling.

"I said, I guess there's many different levels to success." Jeff repeats himself without competition this time.

"The first level is being happy with what we do and just enjoying it." His wife, Blythe, adds.

That's Blythe and Jeff Veltman, our newest additions to our club of fellow seekers. Blythe is an old friend of mine from my days at Indiana University. She was one of the kind souls that helped me to break out of the craziness once in a while to just sit and have long talks over coffee. A stable island in the sea of chaos. But since graduation we lost touch with each other and haven't made contact in years. But as our quest brought

us closer to Chicago I remembered she was headed here after graduation and decided to make the effort to find her. With a bit of luck and
the power of the Internet (it is amazing what and *who* you can find
online) we managed to make contact again. Now sitting here with her
and her husband Jeff it seems like little time has gone by since our last
meeting.

"So do you think you have achieved that success?" I ask.

"I think we have definitely obtained success to some degree," Jeff tells
us. "For so long I had this feeling—as a lot of my friends have—of what
the hell are we doing here? I bounced around from different jobs and
tried to find what I was able to do well, and I think I feel like I've succeeded in that sense, just using the tools we have upstairs, the computers, we have succeeded. At least with being happy with what we do. But
then there is obviously financial success which I don't know if we'll ever
really understand what that's all about."

Jeff smiles an infectious smile and we all laugh as Blythe quantifies
this a bit, "As long as we just have enough to make ends meet, go camping, travel around, that's all that really counts."

"To make ends meet is success for me." Jeff adds.

"Yeah, if you can do that now a days you're golden!" Blythe says.

"I guess the real trick is you get a little bit and you want a little more.
The thing is when you do make more your needs grow, so trying to find
your balance with that is the real trick." Jeff says and breaks off for a sip
of tea.

About the Veltmans. Blythe was born and raised in a suburb of
Chicago, and received a degree in telecommunications from Indiana
University. After graduation Blythe's path led her to freelance production work in Chicago and San Francisco, and a period as general manager for an architecture firm in the Windy City where she learned the
"business side" of life. It was during this period she met Jeff…

Jeff hails from Wilmette, IL and received a degree in political science
from the University of Wisconsin—Madison. After graduating, he

stayed in the area for 2 years and worked for a lobbying group before moving to Chicago. In Chicago Jeff explored all sides of the music industry from working in record stores to interning at recording studios. He eventually ended up working for a market research firm and was there when he met Blythe...

Jeff and Blythe were engaged when Blythe was diagnosed with Hodgkin's disease. During treatment (she is now in full remission and doing great) they took the opportunity to learn more about the Internet and the software involved and found a shared passion for all things multi-media. They jumped into the industry with both feet and sat up their own multi-media production company in Chicago, Jevou B'shert Interaction (or JBInteraction) where they have found their path to success and happiness.

"So do you both feel like you're on your right path now?" I ask.

"Yes, it's *B'Shert*," Blythe explains. "B'Shert means soul mate destined to be. And we actually feel we have found this, that this is what we really want to do. It's funny, you think about it all your life: What the hell *am* I going to do? We still have a lot of friends that are still saying that. But it kinda hit us like a ton of bricks. You can search forever but you know what, it finds you. You can't find it. When I was sick I had nothing to do, I couldn't concentrate on reading a book. So we decided to find something that would use my brain a little bit so it wouldn't turn to mush. I decided to learn some computer software."

"Did your illness really affect the way you view things?" I ask.

"It's funny you ask that; we were just having a conversation about that last night with some one." Blythe says.

"Damn, and I thought I was being original here." I say and force a look of disappointment.

"Sorry," Blythe says, ignoring my long face. "But yeah, being ill puts your priorities into perspective. As horrible as it is, going through chemotherapy and all that in a sense is also the best thing that could happen. You realize that life is not just work, not I gotta be at the top, gotta make my $100,000 every 6 months, whatever. It's family, friends. It's let's go traveling and check out this country, explore the world. Of course work and business is important, but it's not number one on the list. You're only here for so long, if you want to do something, then go do it."

"What is it like to find your path together?" I ask.

"It's quite eye opening and inspiring," Jeff says. "We all know what it feels like to discover something you're talented at and really find rewarding, but to have both of you feel the same way is awesome. It's like having the power of the world at your fingertips and at times you feel invincible—no one can talk you out of your positive mood. Granted, finding that path was not easy, it never is, but it all falls in place."

"Many people ask us how we are able to spend 24 hours with each other and we always smile and shrug our shoulders," Blythe tells us. "It's the love we have for each other and the same passion for mutual interests that keep snowballing into something bigger. Of course you have a bit of compromise on both sides for different issues, but you discuss all points of view and agree on the best solution. And you also learn from each other's mistakes. Mistakes always have a good outcome—never view them as negative—even if you don't realize it until 6 months later."

"Do you feel you both also have individual passions and paths that will need to be pursued later?" Brian asks.

"Of course we have individual passions and paths," Blythe explains. "As much as we have common interests and act as one, we still have independence from each other. It's quite Taoistic. Each of us is an independent person with our own dreams but together we are complete and whole and will achieve those individual dreams and combined dreams together. All these individual paths will be discovered in time with the help of the other."

"So how do you go about finding that path, or that something you want to do?" I ask them after waiting for another loud city bus to pass.

"Reevaluate the fears that you think are real. You look at it and cate-gorize these fears in terms of importance, and in terms of their *realness*," Jeff says and looks over at his wife who picks up from him to continue the thought.

"Right, you confront your fears. If you find you're afraid of it, then you go and do it. That's the only way you're going to overcome it, and once you overcome the fear you look at it and say: Hey, that wasn't so bad. I know it's easier said than done, but..."

"It's kind of a hard thing to explain," Jeff say in turn. "We were talk-ing to our friends when we were going through trying to decide what to do, it's the kind of the thing you just have to go through sometimes to really understand it. You can share stories but everyone's got to find it for themselves."

"Another thing that has helped me personally is traveling and seeing what is out there," Blythe says. "One of my passions is traveling. It's an easy way to procrastinate too. It's: 'Gee, what can we do with the money we made this year? Let's go to...' But I'm so glad I did spend that money and go traveling because I wouldn't trade it in for the world. Well, I guess I *did* trade it in for the world! And you have to still be a kid at heart. Always ask questions, have fun. If you're not a kid, if you're too much of an adult, it's just no fun."

I feel like a kid right now, just sitting and having fun with friends. We talk more about life and plans for the future. We talk about the past and remember old times, try to recall former classmates, and share more stories of what has happened to us between college and the present. When the time comes for the two of them to get back to work, it is dif-ficult to say good-bye. But I rest assured that I know where to find them now and can keep in better contact, realizing once again what an important element friends are in the equation of happiness.

We leave the Veltmans and begin our exploration of the city. We browse the art collection at the Art Institute Of Chicago, wander about the architecture of the downtown loop from both ground level and the top of the Sears Tower, hit the Navy Pier, and enjoy Chicago style pizza at Gino's East. A full day's adventure that comes close to wearing us out for the evening's entertainment we have already planned.

Tonight we are off on a blind date. Well, not a date really, more like an arranged meeting. Brian and I knew what a blind date was, having suffered through one the summer I spent in Nebraska. We doubled with two girls that summer, one Brian had been out with once before and her friend, my date for the evening. It has since been recorded in the annals of the biggest dating disasters of all time, the evening resulting in the girls not speaking to us. But that's another story.

Tonight, this was not a date. It was an Internet rendezvous. One of our web site readers noticed we were going to Chicago and offered to put us in touch with his soon-to-be-sister-in-law to show us around the city. We, as our Creed dictates, jumped at the chance to meet somebody new, and emails and phone numbers were exchanged. Upon arriving in the city we made a few calls and Jennifer volunteered to show us a taste of the Chicago nightlife, inviting us to try our hand (or feet) at swing dancing in one of Chicago's swing clubs.

We wait outside the club for our tour guide and chat about the movie *Fatal Attraction* for no reason at all. We watch as people walk by or enter the club and wonder if one of them is Jennifer. One young woman walks by, enters the club briefly, and then walks out and off in the opposite direction. I point this out to Brian and we question if that wasn't Jennifer who arrived, saw us, and then decided against the evening and deserted us. But just as we begin to build on the hypothesis, another young woman approaches us to say hello.

Jennifer is as young and spirited as she sounded on the phone, all smiles and warmth. With shoulder length curly blonde hair and porcelain skin she immediately brings up mixed images of Grace Kelly with a bit of a young Shirley Temple. There is no awkward introduction stage, we fall right into conversation.

We enter the club and have a talk about our quest that carries us through the entrance, across the dance floor, and to a table in the corner where we let it grow until the dancing begins. Just as she had told us on the phone, the evening was beginning with a quick lesson for all new comers like Brian and I. As we file onto the dance floor with everyone else in the room, we see why she said our ratio of two guys and one girl wouldn't be a problem.

On the dance floor men and women are divided into separate groups as we learn our initial steps. From here we form lines facing the opposite sex across the dance floor. Slowly we learn to dance with a partner across from us and just as we are getting the hang of the move and dancing partner we are rotated to a new woman and taught a new dance step. The cycle continues with new moves and new partners, and we meet as many different women as dance steps learned.

I struggle with the moves, trying to learn the new ones, memorize the old ones, put them all together, and not bruise my partner along the way. I can just see the headlines now:

Cross Country Quest Results In Shin Bruise Epidemic
At Local Dance Club

We pair off with our current partners now to try out the choreography of steps we have learned up to this point. I see next to me that Brian has lucked out and matched up with Jennifer by rotation. I, on the other hand, would be dancing with Diane, a friendly enough woman who is patient with my ineptitude but is, unfortunately, an Amazon. She stands a good half head taller than me and the rest of the men in the room, making the spinning moves a real challenge. As the music begins and we are in the rhythm of movement I quietly say a prayer for her shins.

TALKING 'BOUT MY GENERATION

——————————————— ◆ ———————————————

The way we imagine ourselves to appear
to another person is an essential element
in our conception of ourselves.
In other words, I am not what I think I am,
and I am not what you think I am.
I am what I think you think I am.

Robert Bierstedt

We have been looking forward to tonight for some time, weeks maybe. Ever since Brian's Dad, Bruce, contacted us via email and told us he thought he could arrange another focus group. Seeing how the group in Sacramento went so well and our discussion with the college class in Wisconsin was so much fun, we were anxious to have the chance for another group setting.

Our discussions with a group have such a different dynamic than our one-on-one meetings. Both play a valuable part in seeing what is out there, what people are really thinking. In a group setting we are no longer the interviewers but moderators in a discussion that takes on a life of it's own. We may ask a question, but where it goes from there is up to the evening's participants. They decide what is important to them and what they want to discuss. We are just along for the ride.

Our evening here in Columbus does not disappoint. Already the group is feeling comfortable with themselves, and the topics of discussion, and everyone is opening up to one another. It may help that some of them know each other already, either personally or professionally. Or perhaps that is an obstacle to their free speech. It's hard to tell what goes on in the mind of another. Here, like in our past groups, they are all bound together by one factor, this time the fact that they all know Bruce.

We sit in a haphazardly formed circle in the back yard of one of Bruce's friend's home in downtown Columbus. The conversation is fueled on cheese and shrimp cocktail and an underlying sense of excitement. In attendance with us are: Moishe Appelbaum (25) student, computer consultant, camera sales; Sarah Arnold Behrens (35) medical student, actress; Robert Behrens (36) speech and theater teacher, actor, director, choreographer; Kae Denino (27) English instructor, writer; Steve Kaczmarek (30) English teacher, consultant; Mathew Moran (27) attorney; and Keith R. Newton (25) music instructor, musician.

As the casual discussion slowly dies down and the shrimp disappear from plates, we begin to ask our guests about their thoughts on successful living, beginning with the question of finding a life's path. I notice Keith looks slowly around the gathering before deciding to jump in a start.

"I'm one of those guys," Keith begins, "that, from what people tell me, can do a lot of things, so consequently I don't know what the hell I'm doing! For me success is getting my goals met, but for me that can change at any time."

"Do you think the plethora of choices we have out there is one of the problems our generation has with making choices and finding their individual path?" I ask, following up on Keith's comment, but directing the comment to the crowd.

"I found it very difficult when I got to college to choose what I wanted to study," Steve says. "I saw relationships between this and that, and it seemed like if you focus in on one thing you would miss the big picture."

"I'm in that position right now," Moishe says and scans the circle, suddenly aware he is the youngest among us.

"Are you?" Steve asks.

"Yes. I'm in my third year and I don't have a major yet," Moishe confesses.

"And every body has told you that it's bad," Steve says directly to Moishe and then expands his attention back to the group. "Take your time. The focus of education is really in a bubble. You finish your degree and it's not really work oriented at all, so you really don't know what you're studying, unless you as a student are motivated and go into the work place to see how your major will apply to the industry. You just hope that your degree will apply to something. It's backasswards. It used to be you had a mentor who would be practicing in the industry of interest and you would watch and learn. The world doesn't work in such segmented ways any more. You don't study one thing and stay in it. During the three and a half years I worked in industry, people were fired, downsized, shifted around, whatever, back and forth."

Sarah steps into the conversation. "We do have so many opportunities in America. More often that not we get our needs met, so then you have to decide where and how you want to go. I think the broader you go the more you are enriched as far as success is concerned, at least in my experience. I need to have the broad experience, and I needed to decide that. However, that may not be acceptable if you measure success with money. I won't have the time to put in 15 hours a day to become a nurse, for example. For me it's more important to have the time to be able to do many things. So for me that's success. I define success as freedom. It's having the time to do what you want to do."

"You have to have time to enjoy the fruits of your labor," Robert adds in true married couple fashion, obviously thinking on the same page as his wife. "If you're just out there to sow the fields and that's all you do, and you never get to see fruits, then why bother."

"I think most people of our generation are sitting in three spots," Keith says. "There are really, really psychotic workers who want to work beyond all recognition of time. There are people who are in the middle, who want to work just hard enough to get what they want. And then there are people who just don't want to do crap at all, and still want to get it all."

Keith pauses for a moment for a glance at everyone, then decides to carry his thought further.

"I think everybody watched growing up, and saw all the cars and everything and thought, 'This is pretty good, look at all these folks, they're pretty young, I can have all that.' They thought, 'I want to figure out something I can do to make money really fast and then go and do something else.' So you either make your money real fast then go off and do something else until you run out of money. Or you get into this mode where you make the money, make the money, and then just as you're starting to plan to go off and do what you really want to you think, 'Wait a minute, but if I work this much more, I can go and do this.' So you become one of those workaholics. You become either completely crazy, or you say screw it, I'm not doing anything at all."

There is a nervous laughter that floats around the room, as if Keith has hit on something we all have thought at one time but have tried to push it out of our grown up, responsible minds. His comments make me think of the "golden handcuffs" theory, the theory of getting tied to a job you don't like because of its financial rewards. You become stuck, unable to give up the lifestyle the job offers while at the same time making you so miserable.

Keith continues, "Right now I'm in the position in my life where I'm confused as hell. I'm trying to figure out what it is that I want to do. I took something because I wanted to have a certain quality of life and to use it to get to where I wanted to go. And I'm doing that now, and I'm finding that with the challenges and everything with that I'm going completely nuts. I'm trying to do that *and* what I want to do, rather than just what I want to do. I guess if I was more of a risk taker I'd go out and live real poor and just do what I want to do until I decide I can't do that any more."

I know he's talking about the conflict between following his passion of being a musician or his career choice as a teacher. It seems we see this internal conflict frequently in people with artistic talents and interests, the dilemma between pursuing a passion based on talent versus a career anchored in security and social norm.

"It's a difficult question. I know that by the time I'm 25 I want to know what I want to do. I don't want to be 30 or 31 and not know." Moishe says.

"I'm 35 and I'm still confused." Sarah advises.

"I thought I knew what I wanted to do," Keith goes on. "I thought I knew for sure, dammit this is what I want to do. But now I'm going completely nuts out of my mind. I know I'm doing this, but I know I also want to try *that*, but I can't do that because I'm doing *this*. If I'd just taken the risk earlier, then I think I'd know a lot more clearly now what I want to do versus trying to do everything just so I have a cushion. I'd say find what you think you want to do and just take the risk."

The conversation has caught in an interesting circuit between Moishe, Keith, and Sarah. Each offering their own stories and perspective while trying to assist each other with their questions on life. It's amazing to watch and listen, to see strangers helping each other, communicating on personal issues. I can't help but wonder what it would be like if we were all so open and caring in our day to day lives. And I can empathize with their feelings of being lost, their comments hit close to home. I know I, for one, expected to have it all figured out by now.

Moishe begins again, "I think it's very important to forget what success is to people in movies and on television, and what successful means to your parents and whatever else you've been taught in school. You have to forget all that. You have to search your own mind and your own heart, in an intellectual and an emotional way to find what your version of success is. In some ways I feel I am successful. I'm where I want to be right now. In some senses you have to realize not to get too hard on yourself. Just existing, just being here, just making it through the day, just not taking the easy way out, that's an achievement. We are all successful to a large extent whether we feel it or not."

Sarah's turn: "Take it in small steps. Try not to get overwhelmed. For myself, a lot of time there are so many options and so many things that I feel I should be doing that I get stuck just with the thought of all the things I need to be doing. Taking small steps, accomplishing just a little something every day. That can give you the confidence and motivation and small successes to get you going."

And then Steve jumps into the discussion.

"I think one of the worst things we do in this country is we point a gun at your head at 17 or 18 years old and say, 'decide what it is you're going to do for the rest of your life.' And I don't know if at 17 or 18, or even 30, you necessarily know. Life is evolution, we're constantly learning new things about ourselves, and you may change. The wonderful thing about Gen-X out of all past generations is that we're the one group that probably has the most opportunity to change. We can re-invent ourselves at any turn in the path that we want to."

"I think if you're going to be successful," Matt Says, "then rather than asking yourself what profession do I want to be, ask yourself what would you do if you really had the opportunity to do whatever the hell you wanted to do. What is it that makes you happy? If you could find a profession or something that matches that, and a lifestyle that goes with it, then you are probably going to be successful."

"Unfortunately, we measure by material things because that is the easiest thing to do," Steve says. "And the funniest thing is most people I know who are happy don't become unhappy until they go to a party and meet somebody who starts telling them of all the things that they're doing. Up to that point they were satisfied. But then they come home and say, 'Damn, that guy's doing...' So you have to look inward, you can't look outside for that answer. You have to know it."

A few take a moment to make a break for the food table and contemplate the discussion over cocktail sauce, cheesy Ritz, and Ranch covered veggies.

"So what should a person do to try to deal with finding a path and making the right choices?" Brian asks as people begin to rejoin the circle.

Matt offers his opinion: "I think you have to be somewhat realistic. I think one problem with our generation is everyone wants to have the career, kids, perfect marriage, some time for themselves. But you have to be realistic. Maybe you have to work for five years, ten years, not have kids, earn some money, get the right position, and then you can have kids. You can't have everything at once and I think our generation has problems with that. You have to sacrifice."

There is momentary silence as people munch and think. Matt picks up again where he left off.

"You also have to watch with comparisons. For example, I could be a successful attorney but not in a million years would I be a billionaire like the guys who founded Yahoo. I went to an Ivy League school and had a lot of friends who are engineers, who are starting companies, who are just getting successful, who tomorrow someone could come in and offer them 25 million dollars for their company and then all of a sudden they're multi-millionaires. I could look at that and think, 'Gee, am I going to be able to do that?' But wait a minute, I'm not an engineer. I don't have those skills. You can't just jump up and create a company! A lot of time you look at the entrepreneurs or investment bankers or whoever in our generation is making tons of money and try to compare yourself to them. But if you don't have that training or background or *interests* it's useless to compare yourself to them. If you're going to compare yourself, compare yourself to people who are doctors or lawyers or whatever it is you are doing. If you have to compare yourself, at least stay within something that is realistic."

"I think a lot of comparisons come from outside pressures. Many people have pressures, for instance, with their parents," Moishe says. "They're not necessarily going to be happy until their parents are satisfied at some point with what you're doing. There's something in your mind that says, 'I was raised to do this, and so I do this. Until I do this I won't be successful, I won't be happy.' Many people's happiness is still somewhat based on society and their parents."

"That's true," Steve agrees, "but when you look at our generation compared to that of our parents you see totally different worlds. My mother is from Korea and when she was five years old she had to face the Korean War. Her generation had different struggles than ours, so our expectations should be different. It's really remarkable; Gen-X is the most fortunate generation in American history. We haven't had to face a major war, a lot of the major diseases have been wiped out and the ones that haven't, not all but some, we can avoid getting if we're careful. We have more information and education than any other group of people. We can expect to live longer. We haven't had to experience the kind of physical and societal turmoil of previous generations."

"However," Steve continues, "we live in the shadow of the 60s and all the things that were supposed to be changed socially. We have value systems that have become embedded in our psyche that may not necessarily be what we want. We are coming out of a situation where the divorce rate is 50 percent of marriages, and where the traditional family is like, what, four percent? We have these problems that have turned inward, it's sort of caved in on itself. We have eliminated or easily avoided many external problems of society, but on the other hand, it's like we can't survive without creating our own turmoil in some way."

Steve leans forward as if to continue but Matt has already begun speaking.

"I think that's part of our problem, our generation has had everything given to us so that now when people are leaving school and they get one job offer they get all upset. They want three or four. If you're not getting the newest and greatest, the best new game, the vacation to Florida every year, or whatever it is, many bitch and complain. Thank God we don't have a major war, our generation would not be able to handle it!"

Laughter echoes around the room again as everyone shifts in their seats and throw out jokes about our generation's lack of real conflict. I've heard comments on this from friends before, but never in such heated debate.

"Do you think you have to reach some sort of personal or major world conflict to do self-reflection and try to figure things out?" Brian asks. I immediately think of all the people I've heard of, or who we have talked to recently, that made big life changes after a sudden crisis, be it a fire or illness or other life upheaval.

"I think so," Steve answers. "Many people will not make significant changes in their lives until they sense there is a real definite crisis. Most people, when they're faced with crisis feel that they're either not prepared for it or, for whatever reason, don't want to accept it and try to avoid it. And that's not necessarily a bad thing, it's a survival instinct. That's what people do. But I think people who look back on their lives and see more success than failure are the ones who anticipated the crisis before it happened and said, 'What am I going to do? I have a choice.' You can't have it all. You can make $75-80,000 dollars a year at a job you don't really like, or you can go and spend 35-40 of your most productive years doing something that you enjoy. Maybe you don't get the big house, maybe you don't get the big car, but maybe at the end of it all you're happy. Or you can sit back and say I can marry somebody that I respect as a human being, I love and I want to spend time with, or I'll marry the supermodel. You have your choices. And I think the people who are successful are the people who plan and make goals and have an idea."

"It's difficult to be happy at times," Sarah says, picking up from Steve. "And maybe that's just me being negative. I don't think everybody's happy all the time. And I think you can have everything and still not be happy. And sometimes that's okay. As long as you know happiness at times throughout your life, it's okay. Every once in awhile, be dissatisfied. It makes you check on things, it makes you take stock in life."

"If I haven't been to the lowest of low," Robert adds, "if I haven't seen a relative die, if I hadn't been in serious trouble, if I hadn't had breakups in relationships, then how am I going to know when things are good? Human beings have to struggle, we have to have crisis. It's how we measure our lives, it's how we define ourselves. Without it we'd fall apart."

"I agree," Moishe says. "I feel that way right now. In a large sense, in my mind, I'm saying to myself, 'I'm not going to be happy until this struggle is over.' But I have to take a step back and realize I need this, I need to be problem solving. I need to be helping my family, my world, my country, my whatever. I need to be doing this and be content while I'm struggling."

"You also have to stop measuring success in what you've done, like it's over," Robert says, and then with a smile adds, "I blame this on television, I know that's bad, but on TV life wraps up in half an hour or an hour. The story is over and done, the struggles gone, and everyone's happy. We're trained to say this process is done, and once it's done I should never have to do it again, and I should be happy. But that's not real. It's an ongoing continuous process. And we don't like that kind of maintenance. It will never be over until we die, and then you don't want it to be over. So we should enjoy the process more than the results."

"The process takes the weight off of the goal, for instance wanting to have it all figured out by the time you're 25. I had hoped for that too," Sarah says and looks in Moise's direction. "But it didn't work out that way. If you concentrate more on the process of it, then even if you never necessarily have it all figured out, it's okay."

"But it's also important not to keep striving all the time," Matt says. "You should be happy with the success that you've already achieved. Looking for conflict or something else sometimes just opens you up to failure or more stress in your life. Or perhaps you sacrifice your family, or some other aspect of your life, to achieve new career goals, and then you find you're all of a sudden not content again. Now you want this job or that job and you continue to sacrifice. And I think that's a problem many have with achieving success, they're never really satisfied. Be satisfied. If you realistically and subjectively look at what you have and say it's successful, if you've already completed the amount of schooling you wanted, or have that job you want, and can be really happy, then be satisfied. If you feel you're successful, be satisfied. Don't allow yourself or your family or whoever it is tell you you're not a success."

Matt continues to offer his perspective. "I think a lot of people say if you're not always trying to better yourself, or do something else, you're not successful. I think that's a bunch of crap. I know I personally don't want to have conflict all my life. I don't want to keep thinking I have to do something better, do something different. The hell with that, I want to enjoy life. Be satisfied. There's nothing wrong with that. If you've already achieved your idea of success, why keep struggling to do better just because other people think you need to."

As we have talked the day has run out on us and the evening has creeped in. Our discussion now lit by the flickering glow of mosquito candles. With this gathering, like all our one-on-one meetings, it is difficult to draw it to a close. We are so interested to see where it will lead and how it will play itself out that we want to let it go on until it's own momentum ends it. But we don't. We know it's best to cut it off while the interest is still there, or as they say in show business, to go out while still on top. And that's what we do. We thank the participants and move into the casual discussion, closing part of the evening. If the conversations continue past this point it's due to personal choice.

A few rush off, a few stay and talk. But soon the yard is empty save for Brian and me. We circle the area gathering up empty cups and plates and begin carrying them inside.

"It's pretty amazing the differences in opinions we hear from people. I mean there are similar core issues, but still such a wide variety of insights." Brian says stacking plastic plates.

"What do you mean?" I ask.

"Well tonight, that whole society conflict thing that reared its head. This group seemed really tuned into it."

"Yeah. I wonder how much of that is from being a group of young scholars," I say, balancing the dip bowl and a pile of glasses in one hand and reaching for more with the other.

"Could be," Brian says. "I thought some of the comments about enjoying what you have were interesting. Who was it, I think it was Matt, that was saying he thought to constantly struggle and try to do something different was sometimes foolish, that you should just accept success when you get it. It was an interesting take. I always thought, and still feel, that you need to constantly improve and change in order to grow and realize your highest potential. Kind of the opposite from his viewpoint I guess. But then, he probably meant to not keep striving for other people, or for your career, that if you are changing and striving for yourself it is okay."

"I think that's more of what he meant. Hey, I just had a thought. What is the difference between a success and a failure?" I ask.

"What?"

"Someone's opinion. That's my quote of the day."

We carry our handfuls of plates and cups into the kitchen. In the next room Brian's Dad is talking with our host and a few friends. We leave them to their conversation and head back out for the remains of the finger food, taking a quiet moment to let the thoughts of the evening's event sink in.

HOMECOMING

◆

This above all: to thine own self be true.

William Shakespeare

Someone once said you can never go home again. I don't remember who, maybe the director of the witness protection program?

I think of this as I make the drive from Columbus to Huntington, West Virginia, solo. Brian's Uncle Kevin was in Columbus and heading to Pittsburgh—our next stop on our itinerary—in a few days and volunteered to give Brian a lift if I wanted to head home on my own. We talked about it and decided to take him up on his offer. This way Brian will be in Pittsburgh with his family (grandparents, cousins, aunts, and uncles) for a few days without me, and I'll be in Huntington on my own with my family. It's been many weeks since our last break from each other during my vision quest and we thought we were due for another.

Driving south from Ohio alone the Jeep seems bigger, more spacious. I reach down and switch the radio in mid-song, scan for songs I want to hear and make haphazard adjustments to the dial and volume. The little things you can't do when traveling with someone. Actions requiring a totally selfish, self-centered environment.

People are still asking us if we have wanted to kill each other yet. It's one of the FAQ we should add to our T-shirt if we ever have it printed. It would read something like

No problems yet, we're getting along just fine!

But now, almost three months on the road, there has been only the occasional squabble or argument. How could there not be? And yes, some little things—actions or habits—have started to annoy. But usually only in the confines of our box, only when clumped inside the Jeep. But the griping and whining and nagging that has gone on has been very slight. We remain amazingly upbeat and are still getting along royally. Our earlier joke about killing a friendship with a cross-country journey proves just that: a joke.

And as I command the vessel on my own, flipping dials and swapping CDs, and thinking my own thoughts, and singing my own make-believe lyrics I find the Jeep bigger. And empty. And missing an important element. My friend.

Our stay in Columbus was a good one. We were able to get together with old friends living in the area and catch up with them on the past few years' events, longer for Brian. More of the group of friends I kept and he lost with his move to the Great Plains. We also met some fresh faces in the city, were interviewed by the local newspaper, and made new friends through our quest. One of these meetings still lingers in my head.

His name is Gordon Brooks, an English Teacher at one of the local colleges who had once held the world record for long distance running back in his early days when he ran from New York to Los Angeles. It wasn't something he planned but some thing that just fell together. As he explained it:

"I'd run every morning, 10 to 15 miles, and then when I came home from teaching in the evenings, I'd run another 10, 15, 20 miles. I think I was going through a depressive stage in my life. I didn't consciously say, 'Well if I run, that'll get rid of the depression,' I just started running, kinda like Forrest Gump. So I was running a whole lot, between 20 and 40 miles a day and I swear I was just in a book store and happened to pick up a Guinness Book of World Records. I was just leafing through it and happened to open it up and it said: 'John Lee of England ran across the United States in 60 days.' And I thought to myself that an Englishman shouldn't own an American record. I thought that I was running between 20 and 40 miles a day and I was teaching all day long and if I had 24 hours a day to run, I could beat that record—a crazy thought."

His crazy thought took him across the country and into the record books. And as if one time wasn't enough, Gordon told us he ended up running it again when asked by Dick Gregory—the comedian, political / civil rights activist, and anti-Vietnam protester—to help him make the run for charity for the 1976 bicentennial, this time running the opposite direction from LA to New York.

But the comment that keeps playing out in my mind from the interview came when Brian asked Gordon if the run was the defining moment in his life. To this Gordon told us:

"Umm, I think to be honest with you I was still disappointed because I thought that with an effort like that I might see the light. And it didn't happen. Reflecting back, I learned a lot. I think sometimes—and I'm sure I can't speak for all of us—when we're younger, maybe it's especially true with males, we think that if we do something spectacular enough, or if we study enough, or read enough, or do something like run across the US that we'll somehow see the light. And it didn't happen. I thought I'd run that experience and then I'd see the light, and then I could sit down and be a writer because I wanted to be a writer. I didn't want to be a teacher anymore. I wanted to be a writer. It just didn't happen the way I expected it. I think what we do as young men, or at least some of us, is that we put our expectations too high concerning somethings that may be philosophical, spiritual, or even romantic. I was even disappointed in my first marriage because it wasn't 'romantic' enough. It wasn't enough for me. Nothing was enough until I finally got some maturity under my belt. I think eventually I said to myself, 'Look, you are who you are and that's good enough, and that's going to have to do.'"

It made me think. It made me wonder. Was he looking for lightning to strike, looking for the Shamzara? And did he find it or did he give up on the search? Questions that remained un-asked during the interview but come back to haunt me now as I drive a few hours in solitude.

It's a question that has plagued me, the contrast between non-action and acceptance and pro-action and striving. The Eastern philosophies of stillness and looking inward and the Western principle of go, go, go and making the drive for your dreams. Is it a question of settling versus seeking? Or is there a natural order in all this mess that I am just not seeing.

Scattered thoughts on a lonely drive. If Brian were here I'd ask him about it, get his input and opinions. Instead I'm left with my own thoughts and

visions?

Sitting next to me in the passenger seat a young boy scribbles into a notebook. No, not scribbling, drawing. I cautiously set the Jeep to cruise control and split one eye on the road and the other on him, bouncing back and forth until I get a good look at him. It's the boy from the hill, the boy from my vision. The sight of him isn't as startling as I would expect. It seems almost natural to look down at him there, as if he was expected. But expected or not he is definitely welcome. I look at his drawing of a person, a super-hero maybe, and he holds it up for me to see better.

"See, he's flying over to here where the bad guy is." The Boy says.

"I can see that. It's good." And it was. The legs a little too big proportionally, but quite good for someone his age. His age, what, seven maybe? It's hard to tell. At one glance he seems really young and the next he seems a teenager. It's as if the laws of time can't decide how to place him into my reality.

"Do you like to draw?" the Boy asks me, his attention turned back to the page.

"Yes, sometimes. I don't do it much any more though."

"I like it. I'm going to be an artist when I grow up. An artist and a writer and a movie star."

"Wow, that's quite a list. You know those are all hard careers to break into. You may want to think about something a little more practical, something easier to make a living off of." I hear myself say it, but it's as if off in the distance. An echoing, ethereal, disembodied voice.

"You think? Yeah, maybe." The Boy looks older now, back in his teenager guise. Then he's a little boy again. "Maybe I'll be an explorer, like Indiana Jones!"

I can't help but chuckle at the innocence of childhood dreams.

"That'd be fun. But you still need money to buy all those whips and leather jackets and plane tickets!" Where is that voice coming from, from me? It sounds so distant, almost as if I'm listening rather than speaking.

"Yeah." The older Boy again. "So what are you going to be when you grow up mister?"

"Me? I…"

And I stare out at the rolling asphalt of Highway 23. The Jeep seems to be driving itself now, an unfortunate circumstance that leaves me faced with the question at hand. *What the hell am I going to be when I grow up?* That's really what it's all about isn't it, this quest. This search for discovery, trying to find my path and passions. *What am I…*I still have no idea.

"When you get there you should really look at it mister." The Boy is speaking again, stirring up my thoughts. "Is it what you thought it was? When you get there look at it for me, will ya?"

"Look at what? Where?"

The questions, the words, they tumble around in my head as a crack in my world begins to form out the window. It splits my world into horizontal halves and a strange light begins to flood in accompanied by the sound of music.

Now everybody's got advice they just keep on giving
Doesn't mean too much to me
Lot's of people out to make-believe they're living
Can't decide who they should be.

The light has overrun my world and I see nothing but a field of white as the music plays on.

I understand about indecision
But I don't care if I get behind
People living in competition
All I want is to have my peace of mind.

I blink and move my eyes from the stark white ceiling and around the room, remembering where I am. Home. I roll over in the bed and seek out the source of the music, groping for the clock radio beside the bed.

"That was Boston and *Peace Of Mind*. It's eight o'clock here on WKEE and we've got…"

I slap my hand against the top of the clock and the announcer blinks off. I roll back over and sit up in bed and glance around my room. No, not my room. My sisters' room. My room is now an office with desk, and shelves and computer. And this, I guess it's a guest room now. It hasn't been Heidi and Gretchen's since the twins moved out years ago. Guest room / art gallery. It's weird seeing my old high school drawings and paintings spread around the walls and tucked in here and there. Seeing them mixed with the high school photo collage on the wall and the *Planet Of The Apes* trashcan in the corner acts like a bizarre time capsule. I wonder how much of this is packed up and put away after I leave only to be displayed again upon my return. But I know the answer already. The room remains the same. A shrine to an earlier time, something only a mother could do. I get up and step out of the capsule and head downstairs to greet my family.

*   *   *

I walk out onto the back deck to join the rest of my over-fed siblings. It's typical for a meal at the Moeller household. Mom cooks and bakes and feeds us until we are overflowing with food. And we, being that we usually have to fend for ourselves, dig in with reckless abandon. A vicious cycle of American abundance, resulting in bellies stretched to the outmost extremities shutting down vital physical systems in hopes to digest the cargo lying inside.

On the back deck we all sit around with coffee and sodas and let the digestion process commence. I sit on the swing next to sister Gretchen and sister-in-law Debbie who are swinging their baby girls, Olivia and Zoe. With Frank and Eric and Heidi and Dad sitting all around enjoying the afternoon, it is a slice out of Southern American life.

Southern. Technically West Virginia is not part of the South if you judge based on Civil War allegiance. The state was formed when it sided with the North to abolish slavery and split from Virginia. But ask anyone from the area and you'll hear pledges of Southern pride offered through accented vocabulary. We're South, just not *deep* South.

"So," Frank asks from a plastic deck chair beside me, "where was the neatest place you've been so far."

Ahhh, another of our Frequently Asked Questions. More ammo for the T-shirt: What was your favorite place you visited? What was your least favorite place? Unfortunately these were harder to answer on a shirt. The trip was not over and the answers may yet change. And they are so difficult to answer anyway. It seems so many places had their good and bad points, how could we choose just one?

"It's difficult to say. I really liked the ruggedness of Idaho. It was totally unexpected. I think maybe that's why it made such an impression on me, because it was a huge surprise. Minneapolis and Chicago were nice too though. But then we didn't see them in the winter so that makes the difference."

"Find any place you want to move to?" Gretchen asks. I know she, like the rest of my family, secretly wish I would chose someplace closer to home. She and Heidi both live in the area and Frank not far away across the border in Virginia. But me, I seem to have been as far away as possible ever since moving away for college.

"Not really. I like San Francisco, and Portland, and Seattle. And Chicago, like I said, was nice, but it gets too cold there. And I guess Portland and Seattle get too rainy. And Columbus wasn't too bad. I guess I'm still undecided."

I give a nudge at the baby swing and push Olivia back into the air only to come swinging back at us. It would be nice to be closer to home, to be nearer to family. It was one of the things in the back of my mind when we set off on the road, something to look into along the way. I guess when it comes down to choosing a location you have to weigh your options and make the decision based on your priorities. You have to discover what is really important to you. Is it weather, or entertainment options, or the environment, or the people close to you?

I could see myself enjoying being closer to my family. But the rest of the package isn't here. I seem to be drawn to places that are far away and things that life here at home cannot offer. I tell myself it's a timing issue. That perhaps someday things will look better for me here. But for now my place is elsewhere. A trade-off I need to come to terms with.

But choosing a location isn't the only trade off in life. There are many. Watching my nieces giggle and smile in their swings it makes me think about the stages of life we all go through. I always thought I would be ready for that "family" stage by the time I was thirty. I thought I'd be here with the rest of my siblings bouncing babies and talking about pre-school. But my life has gone in different directions and pulled me away from that world.

It's something I've been contemplating on our journey, the fact that we all go through a series of *life stages*. A progressive development into who it is we are and who we want to be. From student to career to family to retirement, there is a path there set out for us by ourselves, friends and family, and society. How we progress on the path, however, is up to our choosing.

I think maybe that up to now I was being led along my life stages by a road map I was carrying inside my head that was long out of date. I've thought about it here and there along our journey but it seems clear sitting here now. I must have created visions, plans, and preconceptions of how my life was to be while only a child, and it seems I am still using these expectations to guide and judge my life. Based on what I had observed around me growing up—my parents, the media, etc.—I developed ideas and plans for what I would "do" as an adult, what kind of job I would hold and what its day to day activities would consist of, where I would live, when and who I would marry...the list continues. Maybe not extensively detailed plans, but quite elaborate for such an early age. They did, however, provide me with mental checkpoints and guideposts for how I was to lead my life.

What I didn't account for as a child dreaming the dreams of adulthood was all the changes that would take place in myself and the world around me as I aged. I had no idea how the world would open up for me, or how it would grow to be so vast and yet so small. There was no way to foresee the opportunities that I would face, the challenges, the changes in opinion, dreams, and personality. And yet as I grew and my life's patterns and paths changed, my road map did not. I've realized recently that I was still judging my progress on the route from my childhood.

Perhaps this perceived steering "off course" has been the root of much of my apprehension, confusion and stress; a big part of my feeling earlier that something in my life was off. I was turning thirty and had yet to reach my benchmarks of solid career, house, and marriage. Not only had I not reached them, but I was thousands of miles away from even being close! I was literally off the map. It's easy to see how this could lead to stress. My life was "not going as planned."

This must have been my state of thinking that pushed me to embark on this adventure. I was lost, I was off track, and I was looking for answers. But now by crossing the country we have met friends and strangers in various stages of life. We have seen people of all ages and backgrounds in various states of marriage, singledom, parenthood, social status, financial security, and career achievement. With each person I saw someone traveling down their individual path, a road that has led them to many great adventures and is sure to take them toward the happiness they crave.

I guess in the back of my mind as we talked to others I began to look a little closer at my own map that I had steered so wildly from. We've visited with friends who had families, families at the age I was expecting myself to have one. Families like my brother's and sister's here with me now. They look so happy. But is it for me? Am I ready for the settled down, married with children lifestyle?

The answer comes quickly from my heart and gut alike: no. But how is that possible? Hadn't I expected, even planned from early on to be there when I reached the age of thirty? Perhaps, but that is not who I am. That adventure will have to wait a while longer, wait until I am prepared for that stage of life. At present I guess I'm just still too content with the fluid lifestyle I have.

I realize this sitting here, and it makes me look at my road map even closer. If I was wrong about this, what other unrealistic expectations do I have heaped upon my own shoulders? My bet is that many of my pre-conceptions of career, lifestyle, and material / financial success are out of line with my current ideas and philosophies. If this is the case it's no wonder I've missed all the benchmarks I laid out for myself. They were planted for a person I no longer am. I have changed and grown in ways that make the old road map obsolete.

It's odd when life creeps up on you and slaps you in the face. When circuits spark or gears click. But that's what has just hit me. Suddenly I feel as if a great burden had been lifted. And ironically the burden that has weighed heavily on me for the past several years was placed there by my own expectations. How easy it would have been to remove so much earlier.

I can take a look at my life now, this time not from the eyes of a child but from my current place in life. I can clearly see how I've grown, how I've changed, and all the accomplishments I have achieved. I can see the struggles and challenges and how I faced them and how they have made me a better person. My past decisions that led me to where I am today seem much clearer, and I can appreciate them for making me who I am. Present life all of a sudden makes more sense in light of my new found perspective.

Maybe that's part of what I was meant to learn out here on the road. I guess we are all meant to move from stage to stage when we are ready. But many of us jump too soon, either because we force it upon our-selves out of our own expectations for our life or because it is dictated by those around us, either explicitly or implied. We are quick to jump into or hold onto relationships in order to move on to the next stage. Relationships not only with others, but with our careers and material status as well. We buy the home that is beyond our means because it is "time" to be a homeowner. We stay in a job ill-suited for us because we "need" to begin to build a career or make the final choice of occupation.

We stay with a mate because we feel it is "necessary" to hurry and start a family. But how many times do these jumps to the next stage result in stress, health problems, unhappiness, financial instability, and divorce?

Maybe I have been trying to push myself ahead to the next stage too soon. I was putting heavy expectations on myself that I would not be happy with even if I had achieved them. It's like trying to force a square peg into a round hole, I was trying to go somewhere I just didn't fit into yet. I am sure I will someday be ready for each stage, but who knows, perhaps the playing field will change again. But sitting here in the familiar surroundings of my family home I feel comfortable enough with who I am and where I am going to enjoy the process of life a little more and to be prepared to redraw my life's map when necessary.

PITTSBURGH

◆

Destiny is not a matter of chance,
it is a matter of choice;
it is not a thing to be waited for,
it is a thing to be achieved

William Jennings Bryan

Just another day at the office. Only this time the office is in downtown Pittsburgh in the heart of the university district in a booth by the front window of *Friar Tuck's*. Our work as cyber road warriors continues. I'm prepping the web site and spicing up photos for the site. The photos take more time now. Ever since learning that others—not only friends and family, but complete strangers—are going to our photo album when first visiting the web site we've been taking more care in the photo shoots. We now offer photo collages instead of the one photo per screen ratio we were before. More stunning visual bang for your download buck.

Brian is sitting across from me and transcribing an interview I did with a white water rafting guide named Squirrel while in West Virginia. We thought since he missed out on the actual interview it would be good for him to hear it. Brian listens as Squirrel tells how he had absolutely no exposure to white water rafting while growing up in Smithers, WV, and thoughts of actually being a river guide never entered his mind. But at the suggestion of a friend Squirrel took a trip down West Virginia's Gauley River and was hooked. He worked part time as a guide during college, and after college, as he worked in medical sales his thoughts were still of the river. Squirrel made the decision to follow his passions for rafting, quit a job as a sales manager, and has been on the river ever since. Pursuing his own path to success, over the past 16 years Squirrel has had the opportunity to live the vacation others only dream of.

Brian's fingers fly across the tiny keyboard of his Newton computer as he transcribes the interview for the web.

Chris:
You said you had never thought about being a rafting guide, was there something else you had planned on doing?

Squirrel:
No, when I went to college I didn't have a lot of direction with what I wanted to do as a career. And, truthfully, even towards the end I had hundreds of semester hours and had been going to school for a long time, and I still didn't have too many ideas of what I wanted to do. There wasn't an occupation out there where I said, 'Oooh, I want to be that.' So that never really happened for me.

Chris:
Do you feel that rafting is your passion now?

Squirrel
I know I can do a lot of different things. I really enjoyed it when I started and I've always liked it, not necessarily the rafting part of it. It's a big part of it. It's a lot of fun. I'm really good at it so that obviously

makes you comfortable in what you're doing. I love it, enjoy it, and am good at it, but what I really like is the people. I really like talking and spending the day with all these people. It's kind of funny how you make a difference in their life in just a five or six hour period. They treat you like family. They get close to you. You end up developing relationships. I've taken some of the same people year after year after year. It's a job that really makes you feel good. In so many things you don't have a positive impact on that down-to-earth scale with somebody. I don't know, spending the day with them, giving them a thrill or experience, it makes you feel good. What can I tell you? It's a great feeling. People appreciate you putting out the effort to do an exceptional job. People can pick up on whether you are really trying hard to make sure they have a good time. Everybody's a winner. I'm a winner, they're a winner.

Chris:
So is that a big part of how you define success?

Squirrel:
Success is happiness. I'm really happy with what I'm doing. There are a lot of other things that give you a lot of free time at different times of the year that gives you a chance to pursue other things—travel, fish, hunt. It gives me the opportunity to do that.

It's different for everybody. I don't define it as wealth or position. To me it's about enjoying life and what I'm doing affords me the opportunity to enjoy my life. I'm not going to look back and say, "I didn't do this or I didn't do that." I'm making other people happy and that makes me happy. I think that makes me feel successful. In my peer group I know they respect me. Maybe comfort is it, I don't know. I'm very comfortable and I know that's out of the norm maybe. I raft in the Spring, Summer, and Fall. I hunt and fish. I ski patrol in the Wintertime. My life is almost somebody else's recreation. Other than not ever becoming rich from it, it's the perfect occupation. I'm happy every single day I come to work. I look forward to it. That's success. I'm happy. I'm proud of the job I do. Life is good.

Chris:
What where some of the challenges you've had to face getting to where you are today?

Squirrel:
I'm really happy that things didn't work out in what most people would call my last *real* job as sales manager. In those positions, I felt that I was doing what anybody would do to elevate themselves in that career path: more money, power, control over what's going on. But that didn't make me happy. Funny how things work out because there are different situations where I might still be doing that, and I'm real confident that I wouldn't be enjoying life as much as I am now.

Good things are happening all the time. Of course over the next couple of years things could happen to lead me off into a different path. I mean if that happens, I'll go with it, but I'm not actively pursuing another lifestyle. Why would I? I'm enjoying life. I'm doing okay financially and all that. Other people may not be as comfortable with the amount of money that I make, but for me I'm comfortable with it. If I had a personal relationship and family, which I don't have, I'm single, things may be different.

Chris:
Do you see yourself living for the moment? Do you plan ahead or take it as it goes?

Squirrel
I do plan ahead, but I do take it as it goes at the same time. I know what to expect next year. So I have to plan my lifestyle around what I'm going to accomplish financially through the occupations that I'm doing. I mean, yeah I look ahead and everything, but I don't look ahead and say 'I want a quarter of a million dollars in the bank at this time in my life.' I think more in terms of home, personal relationships with other people. I just don't have a burning desire to worry about a lot of money. If I win the lottery, I'll keep doing the same thing that I'm doing. Other than taking some of my friends on some nice trips, it won't change my life.

I think a lot of people worry a lot about what other people think. You need to live your own life and not take into consideration or at least put a lot of weight on what society thinks you should do, or what people around you think you should do. It's kind of funny that I'm surrounded by people who took the norm—engineers, lawyers and such—and I'm fairly confident that I've enjoyed life and am a lot happier than they are. I don't know. All I ever hear from them all the time is: "Boy I wish I did what you did." I don't ever say "I wish I did what they did." So don't let other people dictate your future. You've got to be smart and reasonable in whatever you're doing, don't worry about what other people think.

Brian pulls the headphones off and wiggles his fingers above the table to give them a break from the long task of transcription.

"Sounds like a fun guy. Did you get to go rafting?"

"No!" I say with obvious frustration. "I really wanted to but due to my poor planning I just happened to be there on their busiest day of the year. It was opening season for the Upper Gauley and that's one of the biggest days for white water in the world. Their boats had been booked months in advance. So no such luck, maybe next time."

I look at my watch and mention that the others should be here soon. We both begin to shut down our computers. We were nearly finished with the day's work anyway, so might as well call it quits while we're in a lull.

The others are Brian's brother Nick and a few of his friends, all graduate students here at the University of Pittsburgh. We had told him earlier that we would be in the area working today, and he suggested we meet up with him after class for drinks.

We both pull wires from walls and begin to roll up and pack away all the accessories and extremities we had spread across the table. Nick and Claire arrive just as we are zipping up the overstuffed bags and stashing them on the floor underneath us.

Nick introduces Claire as a fellow masters student in English at the university who has dreams of working in a museum after graduation. We are introduced to Claire as Nick's brother and his brother's friend, the "two that used to abuse and beat me up when we were kids." He says it with a chuckle. And yes, it's true. I admit it. Like all older brothers and their friends, we were living hell to the poor kid. And since I didn't have a little brother myself, Nick always got my hazing and chiding as well as Brian's. He was my surrogate little brother. But that was over two decades ago and it was always in good fun. He couldn't still hold a grudge could he? But I know he doesn't, it's just his turn to turn the tables and haze *us*.

"Great to meet you Claire," I say trying to make the best impression possible after such an introduction. Brian swerves around to my side of the table so they can slip in together on the other. Once seated Nick goes on to explain in detail our quest and what we were doing here in their fine city.

"Oh, I see. This isn't going to be some sort of interview is it?" She asks.

"We hadn't planned on it. But now that you mention it we're always open to hearing from others if there is anything you want to share." Brian offers.

"Yeah, I want to hear this. Tell us Claire, are you on your right path in life?" Nick eggs on.

Claire, who seemed interested in our project and what we have found along our travels lights up and decides to play along.

"Well, I think I've figured it out in the last year. I always thought I was going to head towards some one goal and I needed to find what that goal was. I thought it was this big hassle: Oh God, what is this goal going to be. And I thought as soon as I found it everything would be all right 'cause I could begin working toward it."

Shamzara, I think to myself. She was looking for her career Shamzara.

"But that never happened. Instead what happened is I realized that okay, I have this vague goal. I think what is important is to have an open mind and keep an eye out for all these pathways that you can keep going down. Up until last year I thought I would be doing something totally different with my life and where I would be this year. And now I'm here and I'm ecstatic, and I'm so happy about where I am and where I'm going and what I'm doing. So I think, for me anyways, it's just keeping an incredibly open mind."

"So you found your goal once you got here to school?" Nick asks her, and I wonder if our meeting isn't just a secret way to learn more about his friends.

"Yeah, I think I did. It's been sort of vague but I'm happy with that. I think people get really locked into things. It's, 'I'm going to be a teacher!' But what if you don't? What if it doesn't work out? You have no other options and you're destroyed. I have all these things that I want to do so I can pick and choose some of them. I think some people just have one goal, they want to be just one certain thing and they're missing out on too much."

We're interrupted by the arrival of another of Nick's friends. He introduces Louisa, a fellow classmate who is getting her masters in poetry at the university. She's welcomed into our group and brought up to speed by Nick as I place another order with our waitress. He defers to Brian for a quick synopsis of our quest and a recap of what we were discussing before her arrival.

"So back to what you were saying Claire, what do you think limits people from achieving their highest potential?" Brian asks, but it is Louisa who jumps in with an answer.

"I got a comment on that," Louisa says and looks around the table checking if it is okay to continue. "I think the idea that success is linked with stability is incorrect. You are going to change until you die. And maybe then you are going to change some more! The thought that success is having enough money to have your house whatever size, and your car whatever size, and not having to worry about paying the bills, well, I don't find that from a lot of people I know—having done a lot of tax returns in a former life as an accountant. It's not really aligned that way. I know people who have a tremendous amount of money who can't pay their bills. And yet to others they would appear successful. I think that stability is a erroneous concept. I think you probably have to learn to be at ease with chaos."

"Settling," Nick offers his opinion. "I think out of fear people decide: This is good enough. Or you reach a certain age where you say: Okay, that is not going to happen and I need to stop thinking that is going to happen and I need to instead content myself with this. Instead of saying: This is my dream and I'm going to keep going for it even if I'm 63. That seems to be a cultural phenomenon."

"Interesting…" I begin to try to contrast this with what Claire said earlier about being stuck on one thing. But Louisa is more ready to step in than I.

"I used to agree with you Nick. I would look at my ex-husband's friends that were in his peer group, and he was 34, who all of a sudden hit that magical age where they had to get married. And I always thought it was so terribly unfortunate that they decided it was time to get married and the next person they met, they married. I don't think that's such a tragedy anymore. I now have a view that maybe they couldn't meet the person they should have married when they were younger because they weren't ready to marry. In a way, when you're in the twenties looking ahead you kind of say 'gee that's settling.' But when you're in your thirties and forties side of it looking back you see it as having maturity enough that you can actually get married."

"Do you think this is the same for a career or a path?" I ask. "That you have certain dreams and goals and then you get to a certain age where you think: Well, this is as good as I can do. And then you settle."

"It's an interesting parallel," Louisa says, "because I think the settling thing from the twenties part of it brings on the same kind of myth. But I think once you get past that and you look back on it you have a different kind of view. And you realize the people you think were settling from your perspective as a 25-year-old were not settling at all. I think it's kind of a myth in a way."

"So the whole idea of the calling, path, lifestyle thing is a myth?" Nick asks.

"No, I very much agree with it. But I think what we consider is the 'soul mate' is probably not the soul mate, what we think is our calling in life probably is not it. My calling in life might have been to pull a four-year-old off a street. If my sole purpose in life was to do that and I did it, then I'm done. I don't think you get to know those things."

"So it may be there but just forget about it and move on." Claire adds, not really a comment or a question, just an undefined statement that glides around the table.

"The soul mate isn't in the other person, it's in you," Louisa continues. "It's when you get to the point that it unlocks in you that the next person you find could be it. Since you're happy with yourself you'll be able to be happy with someone else. Same with the calling, once you're happy with yourself you'll be happy doing whatever it is you're doing."

"So what you're saying," Brian says trying to get it all sorted out, "is instead of constantly going out and looking for the perfect job, perfect occupation, perfect path, instead make an inward search and whatever you find will just happen to be it?"

"I think the process is more important than the actual nugget of information." Louisa continues. "I think you have to come up with your own rules, sort of come as you are and do as yourself. The people that always seem to land on their feet are the people with those coping skills. The answers don't come in a box."

I let the conversation float around me and sink in. It seems in line with what I was thinking earlier in the trip about life stages, that when you are ready to move on to the next level it will happen, and not before. But I never really thought of it this way, in relation to finding the right path or soul mate. I had thought about the soul mate theory before though. I decided it was too limiting to think there was just one person out of billions that you have to somehow find. Instead, my theory is that people are like that children's clothing line *Geranimals*. There are all these sets of people in the world—spread out all over America and Asia and Africa and wherever—and you can match up with anyone from your set. Green rhinos with green rhinos. Blue monkeys with blue monkeys. As long as the tags match, the couple matches.

"So speaking of soul mates fellas, have either of you met yours along your travels?" Louisa asks.

It's another of our FAQ. We didn't get it so much during our first leg up the West Coast (though someone in Sacramento did ask if we were looking along the way). But since turning toward the East we have been asked this at every stop. And strangely enough, it is always a woman who asks. Another line on our T-shirt:

Haven't met the woman of my dreams yet, but I'm still looking...

"No, unfortunately not." Brian answers. "Women is one of the areas this trip has been severely lacking. It's difficult when you are in town for only a few nights and then moving on to possibly never return."

"I guess. And I bet if you do meet someone you two would be fighting over her." Nick observes.

"Maybe, but probably not. We have different tastes in women. But the trip is young and so are we." I say and then drift off and let Brian field the questions.

I have a lot to consider from this evening. Our discussion has made a valiant effort in destroying the Shamzara theory. Claire with her talk of career paths and Louisa's theories of soul mates, both work as alternates to the Shamzara effect. Thoughts and ideas that just fuel my passion for exploring further down our road.

IN THE BIG CITY MOOD

◆

I am seeking,
I am striving,
I am in it with all my heart.

Vincent Van Gogh

Whenever I hear Glen Miller's *In the Mood* I think of New York City. It's my fault. When I flew into the city once as a child I had it playing on my Walkman as we descended from the clouds and saw the incredible skyline off in the distance. Horns and saxophones bopped and crooned as the World Trade Center grew closer and closer. The image of Manhattan was etched in my brain along with the tune, forever forged into one entity.

And that song from my personal soundtrack is playing over and over now. As the F train carries us into the city, passing Lady Liberty off to our left in the distance, and we see the skyline for the first time, Glen Miller is there playing for me, getting me in the mood.

We spill out of the train at the Citicorp Center along with millions of others, just two more gears in the great American machine. A long escalator carries us out of the city's circulation system and tosses us onto the city sidewalks of glorious New York. And BOOM! We are jazzed. This is New York City!

We've been excited about seeing places on the trip, even thrilled, but this is something else. We can feel the pulse of the city sweep us up and carry us along and we just give ourselves over to it. This is the coast, the edge of the world, and we have made it. Coast to coast across America, we have made it!

As I said, I've been to the city before as a young boy, a visit with my Dad and brothers. The city holds a special place for me because of that. It was my first trip *away*. My first glance at the real world outside of the South. So full of life and people and so many new and exciting things, it was quick to capture my imagination. This is where it all took place. I'd seen the movies, everything happened here. Everything!

Brian, on the other hand, has been here only once before and that was on a two day business trip. His enthusiasm is of a different sort. It has a freshness and an element of suspense, of wonder. And together we are bouncing.

We begin walking west and notice our pace has stepped up a notch. Whether it is to keep pace with the city folk or out of our own sheer excitement to be here, we are speed walking through the city, looking all around us and trying to soak everything in. And the first thing we notice is the wonderful abundance of absolutely beautiful women.

Maybe it comes from sitting in a Jeep with another guy for way too long, or perhaps our new arrival enthusiasm for the city. But everywhere we turn there seems to be a tall, leggy uberbabe strolling by or smiling at us as we pass. So many in fact that we pull over to the side of the sidewalk to glance around and see if we are perhaps standing on the corner of the fashion district, wondering if the world headquarters for the Vogue, or Ford, or Elite modeling agencies were somewhere right in front of us. Nope. Just an average city street corner in the Big Apple with the average city pedestrians. Wow. We're going to love New York!

We slowly get over the constant flow of natural beauty around us and focus instead on the man-made sights of the city. We knew we would want to spend some serious time here in the city and are fortunate enough to have a kind host to allow us just that. Our buddy Michelle Jaeger was quick to offer accommodation when she heard about our journey, almost as quick as we were to accept. So when we drove in from Philadelphia we dumped the Quest-Mobile outside her place in Brooklyn and now seek out her office somewhere here in the heart of the city. Our plan for our stay is simple, we will split our time right down the middle: fun first, work later. So for now all we have to do is kick back and enjoy the ride.

And what a ride it is.

Uptown, downtown, midtown, Greenwich, Soho, Noho, Chinatown. Eastside, Westside, Riverside, subway rides, buses and screaming cabbies. Hotdog carts and coffee shops, thin crusted pizza, bagels and lox. Stocks, the financial district, Wallstreet, the New York Stock Exchange. Central park, Prospect Park, and the Staten Island Ferry.

"Spare a quarter."

"Go Yankees!"

"Do you have the time?"

Times Square, neon lights, colossal billboards, McVeggie burgers that taste like cardboard, and the New York Public Library. Macy's, Trump Tower, the Plaza Hotel. Brooklyn Heights, the Brooklyn Bridge, and the skyline reflected in the murky waters of the East River. Coney Island and the Atlantic Ocean.

And the Atlantic Ocean.

"We made it." Brian says staring off at the watery horizon.

"We sure did. There to here. Amazing." We both squat down to feel the cool water and sand.

It's a good feeling standing here at the end of the earth. We have achieved something, we have completed half of our journey. The last of the cross country milestones. At one point during our planning stage we considered making New York our final destination, a one way trip coast to coast. But the more we talked about and considered alternatives we decided we really needed to make a full loop. There were just too many places and too many people south of the Mason Dixon line to ignore. Thus we decided on our jagged around-the-country loop.

But even still, our arrival here is something special, and we just dig our toes into the sand and savor the moment.

TAKING THE PLUNGE

◆

Fear not that thy life shall come to an end,
but rather that it shall never have a beginning.

John Henry Cardinal Newman

Our first "working" day in the big city we have a full schedule. No more sight seeing, it is time get back on track and meet with some of the city's residents. We have two meetings scheduled for this afternoon and we're racing through the subway system to get to the first one on time.

Her name is Stephanie Dowling and she works for the NBC Nightly News right in the heart of the city at Rockefeller Center. She comes to us as a friend of a friend of a friend, but highly recommended as someone we should speak to. Brian's friend who made the suggestion told us a bit about Stephanie already. He told us Stephanie, 25, grew up in South Dakota, and after graduating from college got a job in Washington DC working in politics. During school, she was very active in politics and television, and this job was an extension of one of these interests. But after this exposure to the world of politics, Stephanie decided to pursue her other interest in television news instead, and ended up working at one of the premiere studios in one of the biggest markets in the world.

We make it to Rockefeller Center just barely on time, the big city environs playing havoc on our usual early arrivals. We locate our meeting place just above a large golden statue of Prometheus hovering over a vacant and iceless ice skating rink and wait. We don't wait long. Stephanie appears right on time and walks up to us waving, she has no doubt seen us on the web and recognizes us right away. She fits right in with her New York counterparts, a beautiful brunette with an intoxicating smile. We exchange introductions and decide to head over to the nearby *Dean & DeLuca* cafe to chat.

We find a quiet table upstairs and find ourselves already too engaged in conversation to order anything. Instead we just turn our attention to Stephanie as she tells us about finding her path.

"I originally thought my calling was to work in politics until I woke up in the middle of the night and decided that's not what I wanted to do with my life. So I decided to move to London. Within the next two weeks I had a plane ticket. In hindsight it was so naive. I didn't have a place to stay or a job. I didn't have anything except a work permit and my passport. I got there and basically wandered the streets for a few days looking for a place to live and a job. My luggage didn't come over with me and I had to wear the same clothes for a week. It was pouring rain and at that point, it was the most shocking thing in my life. I think at that point, I'll never forget it because it changed my life, my world all of a sudden became huge. I realized how sheltered I had been in South Dakota."

"That whole experience just started it all. I finally got a job and found a place to live. I ended up spending six months over there and it was wonderful. I came back and went straight to New York, where I ended up house sitting for a family I had never met before. I think I've gotten extremely lucky, but I also think it has to do with when you put your mind to something things just happen to work out. I really believe that they do. I don't know if that's a naive way of looking at things, but I just keep my mind open."

"Right now," she continues, "I'm a Researcher for NBC Nightly News, and I'm lucky enough to work closely with Tom Brokaw. I'm one of the youngest ones there and I'm proud of that fact. I started as an intern and worked my way up to researcher. We have a really small staff of about 25 people. So it's pretty exciting. I've been there about a year and a half."

"So do you think you have found your calling?" Brian asks.

"I don't think that television news is my calling," Stephanie says. "I'm not sure what my calling is and I've been doing a lot of thinking about it. I just don't know. You're confused at what you want to do because there are so many opportunities that you're overwhelmed with all the possibilities. It is confusing, and you just can't pick one. And yet it's reassuring to know that you can do whatever you want and you're young enough to do it. I think everybody has a calling, but I don't know if it goes along the lines of a career. I don't know what that is or when that comes in your life. I think life's an adventure and that's the meaning of life, to find happiness and do as many things as you can."

"I think one difference between my generation and past generations is that I don't see that I have to pick one career and stick with it the rest of my life. I think that leads to the restless feeling and confusion of what I want to do next. It's kind of an exciting feeling as well because I'm constantly playing a game with myself, asking myself: 'If all of this were to end today, what would I be doing tomorrow?' And I get really creative in the process. Yesterday, I was thinking about going to Germany and becoming a brewmeister. That one doesn't follow a lot of my other ideas. I want to earn my pilot's license, and I want to do all these different things and I'm still young enough to go do it. So I think that's where it differs between our generation and the past. Everything is out there and no one is really telling us that we can't do it. And if they are, then that just fuels the fire."

"When do you know if you're a success?" I ask.

"I define success as if I'm living up to all my dreams. I think your dreams should be more of a reality in your life. What makes me happy is constant change. I like to be challenged and to push myself to the limit. Growing up you're so confused at who you are and you're struggling to find your place and how you fit into the whole big scheme of things. That's how I've defined my 20's. It's the time when I pushed myself to the limit. I think as a female it's a little different. It's not as rare as it used to be, but it's rare for women to take off and be totally independent and fend for themselves. I'm really proud that I've done that. It's been very scary, but I know that no matter what happens I can take care of myself. That's a great feeling."

"So how do you go about finding your path?" Brian asks.

Stephanie thinks for a moment then says, "I'm trying to explore as many different things as possible from one experience to the next. I really enjoy art, and actually I started out as an art major. I like the serene. I like isolation a lot. Sometimes I like to not see people for days, just drive, paint, listen to certain music. At other times I like being around a lot of people. I really feed off other people and learn so much from others. In finding out what my thing in life is going to be, I think I just have to explore every angle and extreme."

"Finding a path is very confusing," she says. "It's almost kind of blinding in a way, because you don't know which way you're going and nothing is really that clear. You almost want someone to come down and tell you what you're supposed to be doing in life so you won't have to worry about it anymore. Everybody's like, 'Why do you want to know your future?' Well, it would be such a great peace of mind to know exactly what you're supposed to be doing. I get really impatient, and I just really want to know and sometimes I feel like I'm in such a hurry to find out what it is. But, it's just a state of mind and you have to slow down and enjoy every single day."

"So what do you do to wade through the choices and pick a path?" Brian asks.

"I think there are an endless amount of possibilities out there," Stephanie answers. "It's important to maintain your own happiness. Push yourself and really live. There are too many people that are content with doing the same thing every single day, and that's fine, but if you're not happy living like that, you need to change it. You can't be afraid of taking that leap. It's like when I was in high school, we had this filling basin in South Dakota right on the Missouri River. We used to go up there and to be cool the guys would jump off the basin into the water. It's a nice long jump. I was there once, and it was the first time I ever thought I was going to act tough. I was with all these other guys and I thought 'I'm going to jump.' I went up there and I stood there for so long that I psyched myself out of jumping and I had to climb down the ladder. I'll never forget that. I should have just jumped. I should have just gone for it. A few years later I went back there and I just jumped in. It felt so great. There was nothing to be afraid of, it was the thought of doing something and making it happen. It was so symbolic of my life. I just had to do it. If you get into that comfort zone, I question whether you'll ever really be able to enjoy life."

At this point we find ourselves needing to make a jump of our own. We still had to meet with Joe yet this afternoon and our scheduled time was rapidly approaching. I mention this to Stephanie and tell her we wished we had more time to talk.

"Are you guys still going to be around tomorrow?"

"Sure are." I say.

"Well if you'd like I can get you in to see a taping of the news broadcast tomorrow night."

"That would be great!" Brian accepts for us. "We'd love to see it. Just tell us when and where."

Stephanie gives us a time and directions, and now it isn't as bad saying good-bye for the day. We'll get to continue our conversation tomorrow in the studio. We head out of the cafe and walk her back to her office en route for the subway. Once again we are on the move, swept up in the fast pace of big city living.

GETTING TO CARNEGIE HALL

◆

So what do we do? Anything. Something.
So long as we just don't sit there.
If we screw it up, start over. Try something else.
If we wait until we've satisfied all the uncertainties,
It may be too late.

Lee Iacocca

We find we're actually not as far from our next destination at Carnegie Hall as we thought. We could even walk it if we had a little more time. But instead we rush over a block to Seventh and hop on the N train heading North. We're up ground level and into the Hall with plenty of time to spare, enough that I'm tempted to head back out onto the street for yet another bag of sweet roasted New York peanuts or another large pretzel. Here such a short time and I've already found my addictions.

We're meeting with Joe Schamaederer, one of the performance managers here at Carnegie Hall, another suggestion that came to us via email. Joe greets us in the reception area of the marketing department and after brief introductions he shows us across the street to a Chinese restaurant where we hold casual conversation over a steaming dish of beef and broccoli, Joe's dinner for the evening. He explains he is due back at the Hall shortly for a concert being held there this evening, and this may be his only chance to grab a bite.

"No problem, we're just glad you are taking the time to meet us. Well we've told you about ourselves and what we're doing out here in your fair city," Brian begins, reminding him of our conversation on the walk over, "why not tell us how you ended up in Carnegie Hall."

"And please don't say 'practice, practice.'" I add, killing the really old, bad joke before it has a chance to fly.

"Well, I ended up coming to New York on a vacation and I absolutely loved it, so I made the decision to move here. And while I was here on vacation I found a job as a manager of Warner Brothers Studio stores. So I said, 'Okay, this is my get-me-to-New York-job.' I figured I could appease my parents by letting them know that I have a job and I'm not just being crazy. I came here and started working, but I wasn't happy because I wasn't really doing what I wanted to be doing. I've always been interested in music. I love music. At one time I wanted to perform, but in the end I studied business because I thought that was a better path for me. But while I was here working my get-to-New York-job I just started sending out applications. Then one day I saw that Carnegie Hall was looking for someone in ticket operations. It wasn't what I wanted to do, but I thought if I can get my foot in the door, then maybe I can get known there. I sent in my application and as luck would have it, the human resources director called and mentioned that they had a position open in their event sales department and would I be interested in that? I said absolutely—my other previous work had been in sales. So I went and met with her and we clicked right away. And that's how I got to Carnegie Hall."

"So I was living in New York for about a year and a half before I found my job at Carnegie Hall," Joe says after a quick steal from his dinner plate. "I considered it ideal for me because I love the fact that during the middle of the day I can duck into the hall and hear an orchestra from Berlin playing. Where else can you do that? I'm just amazed. When I was a little kid studying piano, I never dreamed of working at Carnegie Hall. I never even considered it. I'm just happy that I can work in an environment that combines so many of the things that I love to do."

"Are you happy with it now?" I ask.

"It's not my ideal job, but for this time in my life it is. It's a good learning opportunity for me. I love going to work and that's the main thing. I've had other jobs…I've managed a car rental company and had a company car and good money, but I hated going there. Everything I was doing for that job was for a goal that I didn't even want. I mean I didn't want the next higher position. I had no personal joy in renting cars to people. Now at least I'm in an environment where I feel like I'm learning a lot. I realized in coming here that I don't know a lot about classical music. So when a new conductor comes or a new orchestra comes, I'll listen to the pieces and try to learn about them. It's just a whole interesting process for me and it's exciting. Sometimes I wake up and can't believe I'm living in New York and working at Carnegie Hall while two years ago I was working in a car dealership in Iowa. How did this happen to me? It just blows me away."

Brian starts to say something, to ask another question probably, but Joe continues talking between bites of broccoli.

"It's funny how different people follow their paths in different ways. I have a couple of young friends in the city that offer an interesting contrast in this. One is 20-years-old and moved to the city wanting to be an actor—like almost everyone else, unless they're trying to be musicians—and he's going through a dilemma. He was going to college and left college to pursue acting in New York. Meanwhile he had taken a temp job at a company that makes bath and beauty products, and he did very well and was very successful. They hired him full time. They made him manager of the division. So he's like, 'Joe, I want to be an actor, but now I'm worried about soap products. The problem is I'm making such good money that I can't leave work to audition.' I tried to tell him to go on an audition, but you need money and need to do what's right for you. It's strange because he's at the stage that I was at a few years ago. I gave up the job and took jobs for lower pay because the long term benefit would be better for me."

"The other friend," Joe continues, "works at Carnegie Hall as a temp. He also wants to be an actor and he's very focused in that. Carnegie would offer him a full time job, but he won't take it. He wants the flexibility of saying, 'I can work on Tuesday or Friday, but I have to audition on other days.' His main goal of living in New York is to go to auditions, and he goes on tour every so often. He's more my age, around 28."

"It is interesting when you see different approaches to the same dilemma. We've seen a lot of that talking to people during our travels. It really is a different strokes way of looking at things." Brian says. I notice him eyeing the remaining bits of beef on Joe's plate and am reminded of our dinner appointment.

"So what about you Joe? Are you set on your path now?" I ask.

"I'm in a state of reevaluation now. All my life I've set goals for myself. They started off real small, like to get a department store credit card to establish credit. Then my goal was to go to college. And I did that. Then I had some issues with my own life and I realized that I didn't want the things like getting married and having kids that everybody else did and I had to come to terms with that. When I did come to terms with that it opened my eyes. It made me realize that whatever I wanted to do I could do, but I'd just have to take charge and do it myself."

"That's when I decided I wanted to move. I had friends who had moved to Oklahoma or Dallas but nothing really fit right for me until I got to New York. When I moved to New York I also wanted to be an actor, but I really didn't want to put the effort into it. I didn't really know at the time what I wanted to do, I just knew that I had to move somewhere else. Now that I've been here for two years and I've made it to Carnegie Hall, I've sort of become complacent. I've gone to all the shows and seen all the museums and all that, and now I need to take myself up to the next level. I'm not sure exactly what that is. The more I learn about music, the less I know about it. I thought I knew a lot about it until I started working more with it."

"Five years down the road I don't know what I want to be doing," he says, "but I'm sure it'll be something fabulous. I'm comfortable in the ambiguity of it all. I have a certain comfortable level. I wouldn't just give up my job and health insurance, but I want to continue keeping my eyes open. Looking back at acting I realize now that that is something I'll do on the side for fun, but I don't want to put in the work to make it my profession, and I've accepted that. At one point, and this has happened at a number of times during my life, I thought what I was doing would have been the most fabulous, ideal thing. I've reached that at several times in my life. When it first happens, it's the most fabulous thing for the first six months. Then I'm like, 'Okay, this is great, but where I was in the previous position I never even thought about this. I never knew about that. My life has changed this way...' and it keeps evolving to the next level. Right now I'm at that point. I've been here two years. I've done this. I'm happy with my job and I'm doing well here. Now what am I going to do? I'm kind of at that state."

"So do you feel you're constantly re-evaluating your definition of success?" I ask.

"Success is an evolving thing. Success is being able to say that if I died today, if I went out there and got hit by a car, I wouldn't have any regrets. All the people that are important to me know that they are important to me and I have that secure. I know that what I want to be doing at this point in my life is having this conversation with you. Success is being able to say that if it all ended today where you are as a person is the best person that you can be at that point."

He forks his plate again and collects a few more chunks of food. Brian steals a glance at his watch and knows our time is running short.

He bridges the subject with Joe, "Joe, thanks for meeting with us. We really enjoyed it."

"No, I really enjoyed it, thank *you*. I only wish I didn't have to run off so quickly or I'd give you guys a tour of the Hall. Are you going to be around tomorrow? You could come by for a tour tomorrow." Joe asks.

"We will be," I answer looking sideways over at Brian. "That would be really cool. Especially if I can get on stage and sing an aria."

"Well I'm not sure about that but we'll see what we can do." Joe says.

"Not to worry, I couldn't sing an aria if my life depended on it anyway. But yeah, a tour would be excellent." I say as Brian nods in agreement.

"All right then. How about two o'clock meeting me at the same place" Joe asks.

"Works for us. I guess we'll see you tomorrow."

And just like that in one afternoon our next day's plans are made. We now have opportunities to see and do things we never planned for, tours of Carnegie Hall and NBC news. New adventures waiting for the traveler willing to look for them.

MARVEL

—————◆—————

Imagination is the beginning of creation.
You imagine what you desire;
You will what you imagine;
And at last you create what you will.

George Bernard Shaw

Everyone has their Valhalla, their Asgard, that mystical place in their heart that they are longing to see. It's the place they would go in dreams as a child, or lie awake at night and wonder what it would be like to actually walk through those doors. For some it may be the gates of Yankee Stadium. Others may dream of the White House, or Stone Henge, or the Taj Mahal, or the Great Wall of China. My childhood dreams always took place between the pages and behind the doors of Marvel Comics.

I learned vocabulary looking up words I read in comics, learned to draw mimicking the comic greats. Growing up, Marvel was *the* place to be and today I am going to see it!

During my previous trip to New York City I saw the tourist sites, climbed the Statue of Liberty, peered down from the Empire State Building and World Trade Center, and saw the Rockettes dance. But one thing that eluded me was a visit to the miraculous ivory tower of Marvel Comics. We called to get on their tour list and found we were too late, they were already booked. But that was all about to change. Today those doors were wide open.

"What's up?" Brian asks.

"Oh, nothing," I say looking at the outside of the building again to see if we were indeed in the right place. "It's just that I always had a different picture in my mind of what their building would be like. I was thinking more Trump Tower with glistening walls and sparkling lobby. This…"

"But you said they moved offices recently, right?" He says, stepping back into the lobby from the sidewalk.

"Yeah, they did. That's right. Their old place must have been a gleaming tower of white!" This thought reassures me and massages my expectations.

We walk across the nondescript lobby to where a portly guard is sitting behind a desk reading a newspaper.

"We're here for Marvel Entertainment!" I exclaim with enthusiasm. But the guard just thumbs us in the direction of the elevator without looking up from his paper.

"Eleventh floor," he says as we walk by.

That's it? No handshake or signing in or security check or laminated Visitor Pass?

We head over to the elevator and punch number eleven. As the doors start to close two other guys slide into the elevator with us and press for floor number ten, also a Marvel-ous floor. I glance over at them and try to decide if they were famous artists or writers, but the doors open and they escape before I have made up my mind.

Ding! The doors sound and open the gates of Asgard. It must be the home of the Norse gods, for right there in the room rests Thor's hammer, tucked safely behind glass. Thor's hammer, Doctor Doom's helmet, and walls lined with comic art, posters, Spider-man toys and paraphernalia. I'm ten again in an instant.

"May I help you?"

The voice comes from behind us and we turn to notice for the first time a woman seated behind a desk. *Oh yeah, this is a reception lobby, not a museum.*

"We're here for the ten o'clock tour," Brian explains.

"Fine. Please sign in here and I'll give you a visitor badge. You can wait over there if you like. We'll start as soon as another group gets here." She holds out a clipboard; we each take our turn signing in. She then hands us each a bright green, stick-on Visitor Badge decorated with the visage of 'ole Spidey himself.

We stroll around the room again and take notice of everything before heading to the sofa in the corner where she suggested we park and wait for our glimpse inside.

"Hey, check out the reading material," Brian says and points to a large stack of comics on the end table next to the sofa. "As far as reception areas go, this one definitely kicks ass."

The elevator dings again just as I am getting into the battle between Captain America and the evil reptile people. A swarm of kids explode into the room, shattering into little groups that race for each of the room's attractions. We are just getting used to the new noise when another ding brings another swarm even louder than the first. Our tour group has arrived.

We put down our comics and follow the group of kids through double glass doors frosted with spider webs and into Marvel's conference room. The room, like the lobby, is a museum of Marvel products. The walls are glass covered display cases showing off every product made over the last year and some from earlier times. Action figures, lunch boxes, kites, clocks, everything imaginable. The kids go wild and it takes all their teachers' efforts to get them seated and still.

And then our tour guide enters and the room erupts again. It's Spider-man. The big man himself is here to lead us around the Marvel offices, taking a break from swinging around the city and keeping America safe. Brian and I roll our eyes while kids scream and yell and tug at his costume as he passes by. The innocence may be lost from my older eyes, but I can't help but feel the excitement of the room and see it through the eyes of the younger tourists. For a brief moment, I am there screaming along with them.

Spidey gives a needless self-introduction and then clicks on a slide projector and begins telling us about the history of the company and how comics are made. He walks us through the process and throws out questions to the crowd where they are quickly answered. This is a gathering of fans that knew their stuff.

He then shuts off the projector and leads us into the offices where it all happens. We walk by the *Hall of Covers* where all the covers for next month's new comics are on display. We peek in the offices of editors, see the library where copies of all the Marvel comics ever printed are stored for reference, and have a chat with an editor about an upcoming project. And then we move into the Bullpen.

Here a group of artists is working on cleaning up and coloring covers, all seated behind their own Macintosh and lost in their work. Spidey explains to us how most writers and artists work off site, but these few still operate in office. Our group surrounds the desks and peers in at the works in progress. I join some kids at one desk and try to get a grip on the software being used. At the desk next to me one of the artists is laughing with a group of kids gathering around him. He is younger than the rest of his co-workers and seems to be loving his job. Or at least he is enjoying sharing it with the kids that are overtaking his workspace.

"Sure you can do it," I overhear him say to one of the kids. "Just keep on practicing and drawing."

Words of encouragement from one of the pros. I look at the smiling face of the little girl he is speaking too and wonder what those simple words have just done for her sense of worth. Her smile says it all. I nudge Brian and we stroll over to see what he is working on.

"Hi, how you guys doing." He says as we approach.

"Great. What are you working on here." I ask.

"It's a cover for an upcoming issue of Spider-man. I'm doing the coloring."

"You work in Photoshop?"

"Yeah, uh-huh. You just visiting New York?" He asks looking up from his computer as if he had nothing to do but just sit back and enjoy the afternoon with the office visitors.

"Kind of. We're actually making a cross country trek interviewing people about the meaning of success and how it is defined in America today." I notice that I am out of practice describing our venture, Brian's been telling the tale almost exclusively of late.

"Wow, that sounds like a lot of fun. I bet you've met some interesting people."

"We have. We—hey, any chance we might be able to talk to you? It'd take maybe a half an hour if you have any time." It just hits me that we should talk with him so I decide to extend the invitation. You never know unless you ask.

"Yeah, no, that would be great. When?" His smile grows even bigger and spreads to Brian and I.

"Any time you're free," Brian says and then remembers we haven't been introduced. "I'm Brian, this is Chris." He says and hands over one of our cards as if to prove our identities.

"Hi, I'm Joe Velazquez. Well, if you'd like you can come back up and see me after your tour. I should be able to take a break and talk with you for a while."

"That'd be perfect. Thanks Joe. So I guess we'll see you in a bit," I say and Brian and I go to re-join the tour group that has slowly seeped out of the room.

Back in with the tour we find there isn't much left to see. We head with Spidey back into the lobby where we're each handed a bag full of goodies (comics!) and then the kids follow him outside the building for photos. We go along to snap a shot for the web site and to give Joe a little more time before we barge in on him again. I pose with Spidey as Brian takes a shot. Then we all watch, a bit disappointed, as Spider-man turns to leave us using the front entrance instead of scaling up the wall.

Still wearing our day-glo Visitor Passes we zoom back up in the elevator with authority. We weren't group tourists any longer, we were entering the inner circle and ready to take a glance behind the curtain at the great and powerful wizards that work here. On the floor of the Bullpen we announce ourselves to the receptionist and she calls back for Joe. Joe is at the door in seconds and still smiling with enthusiasm as he greets us. I can't decipher if it is a love for his job or just life itself that radiates from him, but whatever it is it's infecting Brian and me, and soon we are all laughing and having a great time.

Joe leads us around the floor seeking out a quiet spot to talk. He peeks into a conference room in use, finds a few office doors locked, and finally decides on an unused dark room.

"This should work," he says rolling in another chair. "So tell me more about this web site project you're doing."

I defer to Brian again, too enthralled with the surroundings at present to jump into long explanations of our quest. *So this is what it's like to actually work here*, I think as I listen to the familiar story of our journey.

"Wow, that sounds really cool. So how can I help?" Joe asks.

"Well, for starters just give us a little info on who you are and how you ended up to be working here at Marvel." I say.

"Let's see, I was born in Manhattan Infirmary in '72, raised in the projects for 16 years. Then my Mom and I moved out. I had an interest in art growing up, but I wasn't very dedicated in high school. So I ended up going to community college for art and advertising design because one of my best friends went there. From there I had got an internship at Marvel, this was 1991, and I've been here ever since."

"So you went straight from college to Marvel?" Brian confirms.

"Yes, literally. The day I graduated from college, when I finished my internship, a friend of mine who worked here called me and said there was a cheap job here carrying photo stats from one floor to another. It paid $4.25, but even though it paid poorly, I said yes. From there I began to talk to my boss. I let him know I had an associate's degree in art and advertising design. So I took a test they had, passed it, and became freelance paste up and mechanicals. From there I ended up getting on staff and getting into computers. I went to night school to learn to use computers. Now I'm doing cover design and started color separation. I was originally going to go back to get my Bachelor's degree. I haven't abandoned my dream of getting a four-year degree, but I have put it on hold because I had reached my goal of working at Marvel."

"Is this something you have always wanted to do?" I ask, remembering my own childhood dreams.

"When I was small I wanted to be a doctor or a scientist," Joe tells us. "I wanted to be a scientist so that I could be a super hero. I used to tell my mom 'I'm going to be a scientist so I can invent something so you'll never get old!' And then later on as I got older it was I want to be a scientist so I can turn myself into a super hero. So when I figured out that wouldn't work I decided to go into comic books. It's the next best thing I guess. It's not real, but it's as close as you can get!"

I want to stop him and ask what super power he would most want, remembering such discussions from elementary school. But before I get the chance he goes on talking.

"In high school I used to draw and I just ended up here. People in my neighborhood would always keep my drawings and say, 'Yeah, I'm going to keep this so when you become famous, it'll be worth something.'

Well, I'm not a famous penciler, but they love the fact that I work at Marvel. Every time I see them they're like, 'Man you did it, you work at Marvel' and that feels good. I'm not rich, but I'm doing something that they saw I wanted to do and I ended up doing it."

"Do you like doing the computer work or do you wish you were doing something else?" I ask.

"I actually wanted to be a penciler growing up, but I kind of gave up on that…not really gave up, but traded that for computer stuff because I enjoyed doing that more. Penciling I always had a hard time with and computers I didn't, so I just changed priorities. I would get frustrated drawing and I don't get frustrated on the computer ever. If I have a lot of work obviously I get frustrated, but it's just a lot of work. I enjoy solving problems on the computer more than trying to foreshorten an arm!"

"So how would you define success for you personally, Joe?" Brian asks.

"Success for me would be doing what I want to do and something that I enjoy doing. My personal vision of success for me at some point in my future would be doing video games. To be perfectly honest, to be allowed to create video games and take the stuff from my head and watch kids play my games and to think, 'Yeah, I made that!' That would be success. Money is a factor, but not the most important part. I would love to say, 'Hey do you guys like that game?' And when they'd say, 'Whoa.' I could say, 'Yeah, I made that,' and play it with them. With video games it's almost like I get to create a small little universe for kids to mess with. Plus doing it in the right way is important. I'm a born again Christian, so doing things the right way and keeping my faith helps make me successful."

"My real dream is to create." Joe explains further. "While I get to color here, I don't get to create so much. In video games I'll get to create. That's my character and that's my world you're moving around in. Maybe it's an ego thing. So I guess my career has been a natural progression to create new worlds. If I can't pencil them, I'll create them in three dimensions."

"Watching you deal with the kids in the tour group today it seems you really enjoy having them around. What kind of advice do you give kids when they visit?" Brian asks.

"I tell them that you can't hang out with negative people. All my friends growing up were positive. I had the bad friends, but I never did what the bad kids did. Actually, believe it or not, the kids I used to hang out with in the projects wouldn't let me do the things they did. They knew. It was like, 'This kid's not going to be like us. We don't want him to be like us. We want him to do something.' You've got to want to stay away from the negative influences. Like I said I have another faith that drives me to not do the negative things and to be involved with people more like myself and my values. I try to be positive, especially to kids. Right now especially Hispanic kids, not to exclude non-Hispanic kids, but Hispanic kids don't have as many positive role models out there."

"I over heard you giving some words of encouragement to one of the kids on the tour. Do you encourage a lot of the visitors to go into comics?" I ask.

"Sure, if that's their dream," Joe says. "I tell them to be persistent. Don't give up and don't let people tell you you can't. I had college professors who pulled me aside and said, 'Don't go into comics. It doesn't pay. You'll fail. They're too many kids out there who want to get into comic books. Don't try to work for Marvel because I did and it didn't work out. You're better off working in advertising because that's where the money is.' All these things. Now they want me to talk to their classes and are praising us. Don't give up. I think it's a basic principle for everything you do. Look to do what you want to do and never give up. You will at times feel like giving up, but just believe in yourself and what you're doing and you will do it. It may not be in the time frame you want it, but if you keep fighting you'll get it."

"Sounds like very sound advice. I'm sure all the kids that meet you leave here feeling good about themselves. I know we will. But we've probably kept you from your duties for too long." I say and begin to stand.

"No, I really enjoyed it. Hey, best of luck on the rest of your trip. I think what you two are doing is really neat." Joe says with genuine enthusiasm.

"Thanks, and best of luck to you as well. I hope to hang out in one of your video game worlds someday soon." I say.

We step out of Marvel and back onto the streets of New York. I feel satisfied from the visit, finally getting my look behind the scenes.

"So what do you think?" Brian asks as we seek out the nearest subway.

"That was fun. And it's cool we got to speak with Joe. It's interesting seeing it finally, especially with all those kids there. I guess I was about that age last time I visited New York and had hopes of seeing Marvel. I wonder what different effects the tour has on us and them."

Something comes to mind. Forgotten words. The Boy's words to me in my dream:

When you get there you should really look at it mister. Is it what you thought it was? When you get there look at it for me, will ya?

It's funny, I had thought he was talking about being home with the family. But maybe not. Maybe it was Marvel he was talking about. About looking at forgotten dreams and today's realities and trying to balance out the two, decide between one or the other. I guess we all have hidden dreams from childhood. Dreams to be a baseball player or an astronaut or something of the like. Dreams that are discarded with adulthood and the realization that we could never have been that.

But then there are the dreams of the *What If* type. Dreams that could have been achieved, and maybe with a lot of work and dedication still could be. I think working here at Marvel was one of these kinds of dreams for me, hidden in my subconscious but refusing to go away. Our quest has brought me here, has shown me what was waiting. Now it was up to me, action or deletion. Decide now to act upon the dream and move ahead or delete it from my memory and move on in other directions.

Or another option. Keep it as a *What If*. Hold onto it for what it is, the dreams of the child I once was. In my reality my path may be elsewhere, but I'll leave the dreams to the Boy. Who knows where they will lead him.

NEW ENGLAND

◆

Rain rain go away,
Come again some other day

Nursery Rhyme

We head north from New York, a little wiser and bit saddened. We really enjoyed our stay in the city and all the things we did and saw. As promised we got private tours of Carnegie Hall and a look inside the making of a nightly news program. I didn't get to do a number on stage or even read a news report on camera, but that's okay. There's always next time.

Northbound into the glowing foliage of a New England autumn. The changes in season have already begun to take place around us. Growing breezes, cooler nights, falling leaves, all signs that winter is not far around the next bend. Brian's excited about the change, always ready to welcome winter. I'm excited to see the famous colored leaves of the season up north, but could do without the colder weather. I'll be happy to see the countryside, meet the people, and then get the hell out before the cold hits. Spring time in New England, that's more to my liking.

We hug the coast line on I-95 on the way through Connecticut, stopping occasionally in little towns along the way. Our first stop is in

Stamford to pay a visit to one of Brian's former colleagues. A quick look around town, a drive by the corporate headquarters, and lunch with a friend. One of our briefest stops yet. As we pull back out onto the road again I notice Brian is a bit silent.

"Any regrets?" I ask him.

"About the trip you mean?" He says, breaking his silent contemplation.

"The trip and leaving your old life behind," I say. "This is probably where you would have ended up, right? Here at the corporate HQ?"

"Possibly. Probably. But no, no regrets. If anything this just reaffirms my decision. Listening to him talk about office politics and the way the company is headed it seems like I made the right decision. My gut tells me I did anyway." And I can see in his eyes he believes in what he is saying.

"And many people we have met on the trip have said to go with that gut feeling." I remind him.

"Yep. But no, I think my past life is just that, the past. I'm ready to move on to the next stage. This journey was definitely not a mistake." Brian says, probably more for my sake then his own.

"Glad to hear it," I say and look over at him for emphasis, "because we still have a long way to go."

A long way that takes us through Connecticut and into Rhode Island with camping spots here and there and sightseeing stops in the streets of Providence and the elaborately decorated hallways and gardens of Newport's luxurious mansions. We can't resist a look at the opulent "summer cottages" of the Vanderbilts. Although our quest is in search of Everyman's views of success it is time we at least see how the other half lived. So we line up with hundreds of camera touting tourists and file through the halls of Marble House listening about railroad barons and gold leaf ceilings and imported Italian marble. It is another world when you balance your books in the millions. But I wonder if their true definitions of successful living are really that much different from the rest of us. I'll have to remember to ask next time I meet a gazillionaire.

We make a judgment call and decide, though most of the day is behind us, spent swimming in the luxuries of Rich World, we can still make it to Boston. We pull out of Newport late in the afternoon and head north. We tried repeatedly to reach our host in Boston, Brian's friend Ed, to let him know we are on our way. But each call proves unsuccessful. It's one of those evenings where flexibility is a must. We hit the outskirts of Beantown and have no where to go for the night. A quick assessment of our options leads us to catch a movie and wait to see if Ed comes home. He doesn't. We check the map and decide Boston can wait for the return loop and head forward into a cold, rainy night without a destination.

It's the second night we have slept in the Jeep. But this time we are experts at it. We are experienced. We know what to expect: an evening of total lack of sleep and severe discomfort. We are both surprised when we wake up past daybreak the next day and exchange stories of small amounts of fitful sleep. The mysteries of travel never cease to amaze.

It is a little known fact that somewhere just north of Boston there is a tunnel into America's only rainforest. Well, it's not really a forest but a region. A rain region. The region consists of all the New England states and once you enter you will never see the sun again.

That has been our experience. Autumn in New England is wet. Wet, wet, wet.

Good morning and now time for your weather forecast. Today we can expect constant showers followed by severe drizzles. Look for the clouds to get just a bit bleaker tomorrow as rain begins to really fall in force. On Wednesday more rain can be expected with a big ass storm hitting us Thursday followed by much more of the same over the course of the next five weeks.

From our rest area, we drive coastal Maine stopping in many of the small cities along our path. Most stops are for photo shots for my Mom. When she heard of our route through the north she rattled off a list of places she would like to go, many of which were prominent high society stops during her childhood. I guess while we dreamed of partying with supermodels and rockstars in L.A. mansions and Cabo Wabo, she dreamed of Vanderbilt homes, Kennebunkport, and afternoons with the Kennedys.

Five days or so into our endless shower we reach a safe haven on the island of Islesboro off the coast of northern Maine. Stacy, an old high school friend, sent me an email before we began our journey and extended an invitation for us to stay with her parents when passing through Maine. As nice as it sounded to us when we received the invitation, it was a godsend now. Now we would have a place to settle for a day or two and dry out our shoes! The trials of travel seem much more real when you are out fending for yourself without the aid of friendly faces and open doors. At this point we are ready for another dose of hospitality.

We drive to the edge of America and wait patiently in the rain for the ferry to drift us over to the island. The port city is a one streetlight, one minimart sort of place. The kind of place you drive through, not to. It makes us wonder what exactly was waiting for us on the other side of Penobscot Bay.

Ferried across and let loose on the island's quiet little streets, we steer the Quest-4 Mobile through rain and falling leaves, ticking off the directions as we hit each one in turn. *Right at the school house, left at a barn, pass by a yellow house, stay right at the split, you'll see the house with the horses. And if you get lost just ask someone, everyone knows everyone here.* We pull into the driveway and both us and the Jeep let out a sigh of relief at having made it.

It's a different experience meeting the parents of a friend for the first time later in life. I'm used to knowing sets of parents from the time I met their kid. There is usually some history already there. They have seen me as a rambunctious child or unruly teenager, or scolded me once, or heard stories of things I've done. I'm accustomed to meeting parents again later in life and having to dispel past images and expectations. But that isn't the case with Terry and Lois when we meet them. Our slate is clean, and we meet each other more as friends than as former child and friend's parents. Maybe it's just another sign of aging.

It's only the second time in 12,000 miles we've stayed with someone we didn't directly know. The first time was in St. Louis where a friend of my dad's put us up. And just like then, our new hosts welcome us like long lost relatives. Introductions are made, full liberty of the fridge contents is granted, our room—complete with welcome basket of food and drink—is shown to us, and we are told to unwind and unpack and come back to see them whenever we are ready. It's a level of such unsolicited hospitality it leaves Brian and me both speechless.

The kindness of others. We couldn't have made this trip without it. People opening their homes to us, offering words of encouragement or the occasional home-cooked meal, Full Tank Club members helping to fill our vehicle with gas. Sometimes I wonder how it could be that we have been so lucky, that so many are willing to lend a hand with what we are doing. But most of the time I don't even try to figure it all out. I just consider it the true nature of human kindness and accept it at that. There may be a message here about following the right path, or the universe lending a hand when you need it, or something metaphysical. Or it may be that people just really care sometimes. Whatever it is, I have been and remain extremely grateful.

BED & BREAKFAST

◆

You don't get to choose how you're going to die.
Or when.
You can only choose how you're going to live.
Now.

Joan Baez

Louann Bebb grew up in Buckport, Maine, and at an early age was exposed to the hospitality industry that would become her passion later in life. Her grandmother ran a tourist home and as a child Louann often found herself helping out around the house, tending to guests and making their stay more comfortable. She enjoyed this work and knew she wanted to have a tourist home of her own someday.

After high school, Louann moved to Bar Harbor where she met Bill, her husband of 14 years, and saw the birth of their son, Buddy. Bill, a chef, used to rent out parts of their home to hunters, again exposing Louann to the world of New England hospitality. When Bill died in 1989 after a long struggle with cancer, Louann traveled here to Isleboro to stay with friends. She instantly fell in love with the island and returned often over the next several years. A few years later Louann suffered another loss, this time her home to a fire. Then in 1995, she and

Buddy, now 12, decided to get away from it all and moved to Islesboro to buy a house that would eventually be opened in 1997 as *Aunt Laura's Bed & Breakfast.*

We sit in Louann's kitchen and listen as she tells us her story while elbows deep in a cobbler she is making for a party later this afternoon. Pots and pans and dishes and baking materials are spread around the counter top in chaotic precision. Everything is in its place and waiting to be used, or discarded after being used, in a manner that tells us she is an artist at what she is doing. A culinary Van Gogh creating a new masterpiece.

As she stirs and sprinkles, Louann recounts for us her long road to today.

"I did many things before getting to where I am today. I worked for Captain's Grill. I went to school to become an accountant, but I quit. I went to EMT school. I've taken computer courses. I went back to my hometown—not to live, but to work—and worked for Columbus Paper for five years. The money was good, but it was a pressure cooker and it was no place to be working and raising a son. My son was with three different caretakers a day, and it was a lot of money and not worth it. So I quit in 1995 and I found this house. There was nothing really for me there. I didn't have any family there, so I decided to move and do something different. I was tired of the rat race of the mill. I decided I wasn't going to work that way, and I was going have the bed and breakfast that I always wanted."

It's fun watching the baking process and listening to her talk. Especially listening to her talk. We've heard a variety of accents across the country and have enjoyed a lot of them, especially the funny Scandinavian vowels of North Dakota and the O's in the city speak of Pittsburgh. But none have been as distinct as Louann's Maine accent. It's the kind of accent that sounds born from braving too many rainy autumns and cold winters, kind of suppressed yet articulate at the same time. It is even more punctuated by her direct, straight forward manner of speaking.

"So this B&B is a lifelong dream finally realized?" Brian asks as Louann stirs.

"I've always wanted to open a bed and breakfast, but my dream was to live in Central America with my husband and son. This was what we planned on doing. We were going to guide bird watchers and just have fun. That's what I wanted to do. But after Bill died, I probably could have done it, but it wasn't the same."

"I guess that was something we developed together. We used to travel all over the world. Central America is one of my favorite places, Costa Rica especially. When Buddy got to be school age we were going to move down there. Even though we didn't do that, it doesn't mean I can't. I have plenty of time to grow up."

"Are you happy with the way the bed and breakfast here has turned out?" I ask.

"Yes," Louann says dropping more ingredients into the cobbler pan. "I love the way it's turned out. I love people. I like working with the public. I like to cook. They like to eat. It works out great. I'm really happy with how things have turned out, and it's not done yet. There's still a lot of work."

Looking around it's hard to see what work has yet to be done. The place is immaculate and well equipped. It seems the perfect place to hide away from the world for a while, especially on a rainy afternoon such as this one.

"Based on the decisions you've made and the directions your life has gone in, is there any advice you are saving up for your son as he gets older and starts making decisions on what path to follow?" I ask, my eyes back on the birth of the cobbler.

"That's going to be his choice. But ever since Day 1 it's always been college after high school. He's never known any different. So when he's done with high school, he'll be in a college. But beyond that, it's his choice. School's important, it's not everything but...my parents never encouraged me to do anything because they were partially miserable in their own lives. It was, 'get these kids raised and out of the house,' and I'm not like that. I'm behind my son 100 percent. My experiences are that I'm just a happier person than my parents ever thought of being. My father worked in the mill for 43 years and my mother was pregnant at 17 and was just miserable her whole life."

"It seems you have really faced some challenges in your life and have come through shining. How do you do it?" Brian asks.

"You're only given what you can handle. There are times when I feel I can't stand it because I have too much to do or something, but you can't buy your health, so as long as you're healthy and have food...I don't really know tough times. Well, maybe back in the 70's when Bill and I could only afford beans, rice, and stewed tomatoes, and we missed the Bob Dylan and Joan Baez concerts because we couldn't afford $7 a piece! Other than that..." Louann trails off for a moment thinking, "My husband died. That was pretty bad. And then my house burned down. But you know I lived through it and it made me a stronger person. Right now, I've got to concentrate on raising my son. That's the most important thing."

"My son and I weren't hurt in the fire. He was safe at school and I was at work. I had insurance and it was just material things. I had to fight with the insurance guys and the usual hassles that it involves, but we rebuilt the house. It was hard, but we did it. We never went without. Nothing has been that bad. I just chug along. I do take time to stop and smell the flowers. When things get crazy I like to check out nature and that helps."

It's easy for us to see why Lois suggested we speak to Louann. She radiates a strong spirit that pulls you in and lifts you up, a contagious optimism. An incredibly strong, upbeat woman. And a damn good cook. I want to sample the cobbler before it is even baked.

"It seems you've made quite a success of yourself here. How would you suggest others seek out their visions of success?" Brian asks Louann.

"Look at your definitions. I don't care if you have a nickel or a million dollars, I treat you the same. I don't care about that stuff. You cannot buy your health. We tried when Bill was dying of cancer. Money isn't everything. All I want to be is happy and comfortable. That's success: enough food on the table, some money in the bank, and being healthy. If you're not happy with what you're doing, move to an island. Quit. Quit the job. It's not that important. I've never missed a meal since I quit work. We do everything we did before. Actually, I get to do more because now I see my son more."

She stops for a moment to slide the pan of raw cobbler into the oven.

"You have to take one day at a time. Who knows, five years down the road I may not have any guests, but…keep it simple, don't overspend. Keep everything in your life simple and you'll do fine."

MERRY DAY

◆

Nothing that I can do will change the structure of the universe.
But maybe, by raising my voice I can help the greatest of all causes—
goodwill among men and peace on earth.

Albert Einstein

The weather breaks on the day we leave the island in some sort of cruel joke on us. Here we've been on one of the most beautiful islands in the northern Atlantic and have seen next to nothing through the rainfall and cloud cover. And now that it is time to move on we have clear skies and sunshine. We decide to roll with the punches and enjoy it while we can.

We bid our farewells to our kind hosts and drive back through the winding streets to the ferry terminal. On the way we pass the small boat dock we ventured out to last night when trying to see a docked schooner. It ended up being too dark to see much of the boat but in the water by the dock we saw the most amazing display of phosphorescent fish. A tiny school of fish that glowed and sparkled in the murky waters like a brilliant sky of falling and dancing stars. Another example of one of the road's lessons: you go to see one thing and find it's not what you went to see but something totally different, totally unexpected, that captures your attention and stays locked in memory forever.

The drive to the ferry is through scattering leaves and painted trees, a taste of the fall foliage the area is so famous for. I make a silent wish for the sun to stay with us for our drive through New Hampshire and Vermont and grant us a few unobstructed glances at the hills of colored trees.

The ferry is on time and we float back to the "mainland." Our days as islanders are gone for now, but we aren't ready to leave the seafaring world behind just yet. We have an early morning meeting with Barry King, captain of the schooner Mary Day, just around the bend.

We pull into the city of Camden and head straight for the marina. Barry was another suggestion of Lois', "a true New Englander through and through." We find a place to park the Quest-Mobile and stroll along the water trying to spot the majestic schooner we were told to look for. We notice a few masts hanging over the water and walk toward them only to find it isn't the Mary Day. The boat hand on board points us to the opposite side of the marina where a large boat wrapped in a cocoon was resting. The Mary Day being put down for the winter.

We make it around to the other side of the water and find Barry chatting with a few friends, waiting for us. He confirms our observations, they were in process of weather proofing the ship for her dormant season ahead.

Barry looks the part of a schooner captain. With auburn hair and beard, and sun and wind swept skin, all highlighted by the wind breaker he is wearing. He looks right at home in the marina. He has an easiness about him, very approachable and easy to talk to.

"My two second bio, eh? Let's see…" Barry thinks a moment as if trying to remember what has happened in his life before today. "I was born a suburban ghetto brat north of Boston in the town of Marblehead. I lived the first 15 years of my life there and grew up around boats and the ocean. Both my Dad and brother are captains so there

were many family vacations sailing together. Adolescence marked a
time of confusion at which time I decided that I needed to get out of the
suburban ghetto environment, and I was fortunate to have parents who
had the resources to allow me to get away from it. So, I moved to Maine.
And for some reason, I don't know why, Maine felt more like home for
me than the suburbs of Boston ever did. Perhaps that's because I find
more of a sense of identity here than I ever found amidst all the confusion of the suburbs."

"Boats were a natural path to follow. I knew at that point I wanted to
teach environmental education, so I spent three years in a university in
Boston. The city just sucked so much of the life right out of me that I
realized that this was crazy. I'm trying to learn about teaching environmental education, but my own sense of the environment was getting
drowned. At the end of three years there I went on to the Audubon
Expedition Institute. Actually my wife Jenn and I met there. We were
doing graduate work in experiential environmental education. It was a
traveling graduate and undergraduate degree program. We traveled all
over the country. It's kind of 'hunter gatherer' learning, very exciting. It
was perfect for me and I spent a great deal of time backpacking in the
wilderness. I spent a lot of time listening to other people and listening
to the wilderness and found I learned more there than I ever learned in
a typical university."

"I spent a year there as staff and found myself outside my area of
expertise thinking, 'I know I want to teach and I know I want to be
around people sharing what little I may know and learning what lot I
could from them.' So I knew how to drive a boat and here's this great
platform."

"So from there you went into boating?" I ask.

"Yes. After we got out of graduate school, Jenn and I bought our own
little boat, we could take six passengers, and that was graduate school in
business for us. We were the 'granola boat' on the bay. We were vegetarian, macrobiotic. We did yoga cruises and men's cruises and women's

cruises and kind of cutting edge sailing themes. We were doing the Zen of Sailing and promptly went bankrupt. Literally. We realized, and isn't this a life lesson, that being poor was not going to provide any sense of contentment. It looked good from the outside, but after you live for a month on soy beans and carrots—which admittedly is more than many people in Bangladesh have—for our expectations of our lives we realized we were just going backwards. We had dumped every life savings that we had in there and just lost our shirts. We had to sell the boat and get out of that kind of business. See the problem with people who are socially conscious is that they don't make enough money to go on vacation!"

Barry chuckles and looks around the bay, his light-hearted optimism is obvious as he tells us more of his story.

"We meet people from every walk of life imaginable, some I'd care to visit and some I wouldn't care to visit…everybody I meet on that boat has expectations of success or contentment. Some of which would work for me, some of which I wonder if they really even work for them. Even the most successful looking people from our cultural stereotype still have to wrestle with success and contentment, and the two are very different. Success I tend to line up with things. Contentment I line up with my heart."

"So that's where we're at now, trying to take what is still a financially marginal business, and hardly anyone would call it a highly successful business, and make it work. We don't have kids yet, that will undoubtedly change our entire perspective of what success is. But for right now it's okay. We don't make much, but we don't eat much. We don't go on vacation. We work. They call it a lifestyle choice. We work so hard year-round. I mean I'm supposed to be able to take winters off, but it never seems to work out that way. For years we have taken other jobs during the winter and I'll be looking for part time stuff this winter to make ends meet. We're very close to owning the business and we're putting the finishing touches on a buyout plan. We've spent four years busting our butts to make that happen."

Barry's gregarious nature is quickly apparent. It is easy to see how he can keep his guests entertained on a week-long voyage at sea. We do little to prompt our discussion, he seems interested in talking about life and his philosophies on success with or without us.

"You mentioned you see many opinions of success through the guests on the schooner. What would be your personal definition of successful living?" I ask.

"The whole notion of success is a real personal one for everyone. It's a personal decision. My notion of success changes all the time. It's not a static thing by any means. I think especially in Western culture, we're so acculturated by our families, our school systems, by all these institutions that we kind of get on bended knee to. Our teachers say success is this. Our parents have very different ideas of what success is for us. My path to success, and I do consider success as personal fulfillment, is feeling content. It's not about money, obviously. I work on a windjammer, which is a marginal business. As you can see I have a nice view from my office window today," Barry swings his arm out to take in the panorama of the bay. "My only hope is that I come out from all this with some feeling of contentment."

"I'm fairly people focused and I get a lot of satisfaction from being with people. It also fills in the gaps that I can't fill in myself. So playing music with people on the boat, for example, helps fill in some of the gaps in my life. I have fun doing it. They have fun and everyone feels good. Sailing with people is real easy. Even when it's raining, most people just love the thrill of sailing. That's what makes us a fairly positive vacation story for people. It's easy for me to have fun with people sailing, not to say that it isn't work, but it is easy."

"I do get to the end of the season and all those people go away and I still have to face that question of 'how am I doing here.' There's always this withdrawal symptom. Usually I'm fried enough that I don't want to see people and you need a break from the constant barrage of questions. So wintertime is different. It's more of a time to draw back and gather enough energy for the next season. It's more of a time for introspection. It's a nice seasonal thing to regroup, shut down for awhile."

"Is owning the schooner and having your own business your dream or is there something else you are moving toward?" Brian asks.

"I don't have a dream I'm moving towards. Maybe a nightmare! Maybe it's because in some ways…I'm not saying I'm already there, but I'll be blunt. I'm pretty confused with what I want to be when I grow up. The problem is this schooner thing is the only thing I know how to do right now. I'm not a computer programmer. I can do a lot of things, a Jack of all trades, but master of none. I've faced the proposition of career changes. If I have had a dream, it's been to have a family and have a business of our own so that we can have some amount of control over our time. But as anyone who has run their own business will tell you, you have no free time, but at least you're doing something that works."

"My brother is a lawyer in Los Angeles and he loves it and thrives on it. I often think of my brother and I as the same people doing two completely different things, but striving toward the same thing in the end. We're both striving to feel good about ourselves and be content and treat the people around us with dignity and respect. But we're doing it through completely different paths. My path wouldn't work for him and his wouldn't work for me, but we'll both probably end up in the same place."

This makes me think of my own brothers and our differences. We're very similar to Barry and his, I suppose. All different control groups in the experiment of living. Frank the engineer, the homeowner, the husband and father. Me the wayward soul, perpetually single, and forever in flux. And Randy there somewhere in-between.

"So I don't know what my dream is now. I used to dream that I'd have a boat and go sailing but it doesn't feel like a dream anymore. I feel pretty jaded to tell you the truth because it has not been easy to get here.

I used to say that the day I owned this business I'd be jumping up and down and it'd be the greatest thing since sliced bread. Now I say to myself, 'If it happens, good. If it doesn't happen, even better!' I don't feel wistful, dreamy about it. I don't even know if it'll work once we get there. If the economy goes down the tubes and people stop going on vacation, then we really are going to lose it all. So, again, what I come back to is that I hope to be able to feel contentment."

"So through all your experiences have you gained any insight or perhaps developed any that help you seek out the personal contentment you're looking for?" Brian asks.

"I forget where I heard this, I think I heard from some park ranger in some part of Utah, but someone told me two things. One was people spend a lot of time fighting against things, being against something. Wouldn't it be a different place if people were fighting not against something, but for something? Do you see the difference there? It's the difference between saying, 'stop the clear cutting' versus 'let's work to preserve old growth forests.' There's a certain antagonism with going against something, but if you can find the common values to strive towards we should be better off."

"The other thing he told me was, 'start by doing what you're good at.' Everybody is good at something. I don't care who you are. It might be just smiling. It might be as simple as walking down the street and saying good morning and sharing a smile with someone. I'm not talking just about a career path. Find something that you're good at and let that be your springboard into the rest of the world. Find something that you feel good about doing, and I don't know if 'good at' is the right term. Find something you feel good about doing and do it in a way that respects yourself and the rest of life and the planet around you. To me, that is what works."

He sits back and thinks for a moment as if lost in a memory. We can see something brewing so let it sit for a moment. Then the thought hits him and he leans forward again.

"I think about the number of people who come on this boat. I play music with them and we go sailing and we live out in the elements for a whole week and 30 some odd of us—and we do get odd at times—share two heads and shower for the week. I can't tell you how many letters I get every year. I have people walk off that schooner in tears because they had such a good time. My parting comment to everybody is this: I hold up my hands and take a deep breath and I say, 'Walk, don't run back to your vehicles. Take a moment to do what we call Schooner Shivasana.' In yoga at the end of every practice the last posture you do is to lay down. This is the most important thing that you do after bending and stretching and pulling for an hour, you let every bone and muscle in your body relax. The most important part of Shivasana is you take that relaxed feeling and you absorb it into the marrow of your bones and carry it with you into the day ahead. What I tell people on the schooner is to take a deep breath, walk, don't run to your vehicle. Keep breathing. The office will still be there when you get back. If you run off the boat back to your vehicle, you will undo in 10 minutes what it took six days to achieve. Walk, don't run, keep breathing. For most people that one week has to last them an entire year before they get a chance to come on vacation again."

When we finish talking, Barry offers us a tour of the schooner and we follow him on board to get a clearer picture of what life at sea is really like. And then after thanks and good-byes we take his Shivasana advice. We breath deeply and take the insights of our meeting with the schooner captain with us, quietly, walking to the Jeep.

PSYCHOBABBLE

◆

The best way to make your dreams
come true is to wake up.

Paul Valery

We are blessed. The rain has stopped, at least for now. The wet grayness is gone and has been replaced by a brilliant vibrancy of color and light that is just dazzling. This was the New England autumn I've always heard about.

As we cross Maine the leaves explode in an ensemble of hues all around us. Ignited by the new found sunlight and glistening from the recently fallen rains it is as if the forests are on fire. A whole orchard of burning bushes singing of the mysteries of nature. Our simple drive has become a trek across a new and wonderful world.

We glide on sunbeams all the way through Maine and to the border with New Hampshire. We can't resist a chance to jump out of the Jeep and snap some shots for the web. I know they won't turn out, that there is no way to capture this visual ice cream parlor on film, but we have to give it a try anyway. We pose, we shoot, we collect leaves, we wave at passing motorists. After years of serving an unrighteous sentence in a prison of rain we were free to enjoy the sunshine again!

We enter New Hampshire (*one more state, 21 to go*) and pass a sign reading: *Brake for moose, it could save your life.* And then just below it just to drive the point home: *Hundreds of collisions.* Lois told us about the moose situation while we were in Maine. Apparently there are so many moose roaming the woods up here that motorists tend to hit them on a regular basis. So often, in fact, that many of the smaller communities have a list where residents can place their name if interested in obtaining a moose. Each time one of the fine beasts is killed by a passing automobile, the city checks the list and the next person down is called to come and claim their prize. Sunday dinner, mantle place garnish, or mighty large hood ornament, it's their choice.

Our visit here in the remaining stretches of New England is one of small towns and natural beauty. We make a few stops in New Hampshire before heading into Vermont: Gorham, Lancaster, and a look at Mt. Washington. But cold weather is chasing right on our rear bumper and we are in no man's land now, we have to fend for ourselves again. Our time here will have to be brief.

When we cross into Vermont we begin swimming in rain again, the intermission is over, and it's on with the wet, wet show. Montpelier sights, *Ben & Jerry's Ice Cream* factory in Waterbury, and a look at the real life *Sound Of Music* Van Trapps in Stowe. A pocket of tourism, a microcosm of Americana. A few days, a couple states, and a trip south.

We bounce back into New Hampshire on the road south and the clouds clear again. *Is there some rivalry between these two states I don't know about?* Mother Nature seems to think so. The sun flicks the leaves and they burn with the passions of fall once again, glowing red and orange and yellow and purple and green along our path. Magnificent colors blending together in a world of beauty that at once brings us new appreciation to our quest and the magnificence of the world around us. A brilliant dream world to cruise through on our way to Boston.

             *   *   *

"We're not crazy." I say in answer to Allison's question.

"I don't know about that…" she jabs back at me, continuing our habit of constantly jesting with one another.

"Well, maybe we could get a second opinion."

"I thought that's what we were doing here!" Brian jumps in.

We continue walking from the lobby of the Psychiatric Center and into the building's labyrinth of halls in search of Allison's office. That's Allison Lee, a former classmate of mine during my year of study in Hong Kong. She's back in her hometown of Boston now and just a few steps away from a full fledged psychiatrist.

"But seriously, how was your talk with Boris?" Allison asks again, hoping for a more straight forward answer.

"It was great. He was really friendly, informative, had some great opinions." I say.

We're talking about Allison's friend and colleague Boris Vatel whom we had a talk with earlier today. Boris is an intern in psychiatry here in Boston with an interesting background. He was born in the former Soviet Union and moved to the United States in his teens where he settled in Chicago and quickly became swept up in the field of psychiatry.

"So what did he have to say?" Allison seems very interested in hearing what her friends have to say about successful living.

"Quite a bit. Let me see if I can remember some highlights. We asked him about how he goes about planning his life and making the decisions he does." I tell her.

"And he said?" Allison nudges.

"It was something like…"

"I'm kind of a person who it seems has had some kind of unconscious plan or a certain knowledge that things had to be a certain way, but I can't say that I'm a great planner. I ended up in good places in my life, but sometimes I think it's almost in spite of myself. There are people who research a great deal the residency they want to attend, and they know exactly why they want to go there, or they knew exactly why they went to such-and-such medical school, or knew which med school had a good department for this or that. I was never one of those people who planned things out that way. I ended up in good schools and I ended up getting a good education, but it wasn't because I planned to go to these particular places. It's that certain situations presented themselves in certain ways and I took the opportunities when they arose. I was able to get to those opportunities because, once again, I enabled myself or my family enabled me or my intelligence enabled me or something like that, but good things have always come my way. I can't say that I planned them that way."

"In other words, I'm very conscious of the fact that things might very well have been otherwise, but they weren't. I'm a bit of a fatalist. Things were meant for me to be this way. It's what we call in psychiatry *magical thinking*. I really do believe that certain paths are outlined for you and maybe this was outlined for me. I don't know. I'm a great believer in the fact that situations present themselves to people, but people have to be there at the right place and right time. I think it is up to us as to how to react to these situations. You have no control over walking down the street and having a brick fall on your head. You have no control over a job opportunity that opens up next week. Certain things just happen. They are completely outside your locus of control, but it is up to you how you are going to react to the situation. So I think chance determines a lot, but it's not only chance because then you have to make a choice and not making a choice is a choice in itself."

"Magical Thinking. That's interesting, I wouldn't have guessed that about Boris." Allison admits as she continues leading us on a confusing path through the hospital's hallways.

"You'd be pretty amazed what you can learn about your friends when you start talking on the subject of life." I say.

"I think one of the things we discussed with him that was really interesting was society's definitions of success," Brian says. "We asked his opinions on why we all have our individual sense of success, but in almost everyone's definition they are quick to point out that it's not money or financial gain. You'd think if no one believes success is money then where is this coming from. Boris had an interesting opinion on this. He thinks that…"

"It's very difficult to live in this country and not be financially success-ful. I think that the only reason to live in this country is so that you can live comfortably. I came here from Russia, a country where the eco-nomic system was very, very different and the distribution of wealth was very different. The values on what made you a human being were very different. We were all equally poor. My family did not own an auto-mobile and neither did most of my other friends and acquaintances. My parents, despite the fact that both were highly educated professionals, made just enough to live from paycheck to paycheck. We did not have a savings account. Sure people liked things. People wanted to have the bedroom from Czechoslovakia because the Russian bedroom sets sucked. You wanted to have a pair of jeans that cost a month's salary or you wanted to have a pair of shoes that wouldn't fall apart, but there was not such an intense emphasis on things as there is in America."

"This is one of my favorite subjects of mine and I take a somewhat paranoid view of the advertising industry in this country. But the adver-tising industry in this country is one of the most successful propagan-da machines that has yet to be invented by man, it far surpasses any propaganda machine in Nazi Germany or the Soviet Union for the sim-ple reason that people don't think it's a propaganda machine. At least when we saw banners in the Soviet Union that read, 'Long live the Party,' everyone knew that this was a slogan. I think when you are sur-rounded everywhere you go and you see all the ads that are directed to you to drink this coffee and use this antiperspirant and be such and such and tell us we are in the Jeep generation or the Pepsi generation, they sell so much more than a thing. They sell a way of being that will cause you to want to buy this or that thing. It's not only to be content to have bought that thing, but to actually be discontented so that you can buy the next thing they are trying to sell you."

"The reason this is so successful is that people don't realize this is going on. Those people who were born here and who have not had the experience of living in another country think that this is a normal part of reality. All it takes is for you to stop and think about it for a second to realize how scary this is."

"To get back to the original point, with the kind of philosophy that exists in this country that equates success with financial success, that sells you images of bliss everywhere you go and emphasizes endless consumption rather than looking around and smelling the roses, or looking at yourself, or seeing another person, I think it's very difficult to live otherwise. I think one of the reasons America is so seductive is because once you come from a poor country to this one where you can have a hot shower everyday and can use a different shampoo on your hair everyday, where you can have five silk suits and drive the best possible car that money can buy, that kind of thing is very seductive. All of these cost money so I think it's very difficult to live in America and not buy into this, unless you build some kind of electromagnetic wall around you, but then you become alone. If you want to function, if you want to have friends, if you want to be a part of society rather than live in a certain elitist ivory tower, it's very isolating to resist the system. I'm not sure that that is good for one either."

"My path is to find some kind of happy medium and to see the advertising industry for what it is and to decide for myself what I really need. For example, I'm not thirsty for a BMW. I drive a Nissan now and it gets me places and as long as it's in good working order and is clean then I'd be satisfied with buying another Nissan. I'm saying that right now and things change. I'm trying to identify the things in my life where I can say, 'This is enough for me. I don't need more.' The more I can say that to myself that I don't need the latest thing then I can concentrate on other things that are probably more important."

"Now that, *that* sounds like Boris! It looks like your interview with him went very well." Allison says as she directs us up another flight of stairs.

"It did," I say. "He of course had other comments but I'm holding out on you with those. You'll just have to log onto our web site to get them."

"Okay," Allison agrees. "Well I think Maureen will give you a different perspective. Actually, it's about six already, maybe we should head straight to her office. She's expecting you."

And just as we are on the cusp of entering Allison's wing we head back down the stairs and back through the maze of hallways to the door of Maureen Goldmen. Allison taps on it gently and swings it open. Maureen is standing behind her desk with a phone to her ear which she quickly hangs up when she sees us entering.

"I was just calling you," she comes around the desk and approaches, a blonde with a friendly smile and perky step. "Hi. I'm Maureen."

"This is Chris and Brian." Allison beats us to the introduction. "Okay, I'll leave you guys alone. Just send them to my office when you're done, okay Maureen?"

Allison heads out and closes the door behind her and we offer more substantial introductions to Maureen, giving the details of our quest and a few of the highlights of our stay in Boston. She offers us a bit of self-introduction.

She tells us she was born and raised in New York state. From an early age she was expected to do great things, earmarked for an occupation as a doctor by her parents. Maureen did, in fact, turn out to be a doctor but not the doctor everyone had always expected, choosing psychology over her family favored general medicine.

"That must have been difficult choosing a path that went against what your parents or others had in mind for you." Brian comments.

"It's been a problem," Maureen explains, "but only from the standpoint of my family. For my friends it doesn't matter. However, with my family, you have to be a doctor or accountant. So of those two choices, I chose doctor. I wanted to do that for whatever reason when I was little. I probably would have been a teacher had I had no pressures from anything, but I thought that I had to be a doctor. I think it started when I began buying into what my parents wanted me to do. Once you get on that train you can't get off. College, med school, 12 year plan and that's really it. There's no point of exit because you have the school debt and you can't stop to pay them and so you continue."

"But, psychiatry was a exit point for me. I was not supposed to do psychiatry. My parents did not approve because I was supposed to be a family doctor, so it was a break off point. In psychiatry you're 'supposed' to be a therapist. I hate that. So I'm breaking from that and I'm starting to shape my life the way I like it. It's taken me the better part of three years to be okay with what I like about psychiatry. That struggle is an ongoing thing and it's very slow."

"So do you feel you're on your way to making the success of yourself you want?" I ask listening to the echo of my voice off the cavernous concrete walls of the office.

"I imagine that part of success does not include misery," Maureen says and laughs to herself. "I'm miserable, so I can't call myself a success yet. When people just look at me, they may see the 'package': I'm in Boston. I'm in Harvard. I'm in this prestigious residency. I'm a doctor. I have a house, a dog, friends, somewhat of a social life, nice family. All these things look pretty good. I've always had that. Everything has always *looked* good, but it's been sort of unhappy on the way. Now in particular, I'm ready to shift gears. I've put in the work and the misery and now it's time to change."

I appreciate her being so candid with us. I've often wondered as we've traveled around talking with people if they were holding back on their answers to our questions. Or maybe telling us what they want to believe or do believe but don't practice. Just my natural cynicism coming to surface probably. But to hear someone say straight out "I'm miserable" takes a lot of courage. I'm sure there are plenty of people in the world that feel that way. People that feel they have everything they should have, everything that should make them happy and yet aren't happy.

"I guess my measure of success is different," Maureen continues. "I thought a successful person is somebody who does everything and is the best at whatever. So I thought to myself that I would be the best psychiatrist, whatever that means. I thought that they should know my name in other parts of the country because I'm doing something important. That belief has since shifted because it takes too much of your own personal life to achieve."

"Now, success is changing. I think I can start off on a new foot next year. I'll have to develop it, but it's just enjoying everyday instead of being miserable everyday and living for the future. I'm done with that and that's how my definition has changed."

"You have to be able to support yourself. Poverty is not success, but success is figuring out what is important and what makes you content and then doing that. It's not getting caught up in, 'people who are successful have a husband and two kids and a dog and a boat, summer house, whatever.' That may not be important. For example, I may want a little house and I don't really care about my car, and I'd really like to travel or work 9 to 5 and have time for other things. Like I used to dance. If I was dancing or singing or doing something else besides just making money and—this is kind of weird actually—the ultimate success would be if I didn't have to work to support myself. If I won the lottery and could still do psychiatry for fun, then I'd be doing it because I wanted to and not because I needed the money. It takes away from the enjoyment when you do something because you need the money. It's better just having enough and not needing more."

"So what do you do to stay optimistic when you're feeling down or unsuccessful or, as you put it, miserable?" Brian asks.

"It takes different forms," Maureen tells us. "Sometimes I pretend it's not there and just go through the motions. Do what I have to do then come home and relax. That I can do for awhile until I crash. When I crash, I rely on my support from others and try to connect with someone to find out if I'm crazy, or if other people feel or see things the same way. And that helps. You realize it's not the end of the world."

"Is there something you would have changed or is there advice you would give to others to try to steer into a more happy, successful living?" I ask.

"When I was in college I started to see that people are different and not everyone sees the world like I do. My advice is to expose yourself to as many of everything as you can. If I wasn't so chicken I would have traveled abroad to gain another exposure. Meet people. Don't say no when someone asks you to do something that may sound scary or may not sound like fun because you never know. Sometimes for me when I do something that sounds really awful it turns out to be really fun. So you have to say yes to opportunities. You have to listen to your friends more than your parents. You have to pick good friends and then you have to listen to them. Just don't assume that your parents are right. I feel like I've done things late. If I were to give advice I'd recommend that they explore earlier. Explore as many different things as you can with as many different people as you can."

VOICE OF AMERICA

◆

The US Constitution doesn't guarantee happiness,
only the pursuit of it. You have to catch up with
it yourself.

Benjamin Franklin

We hit DC and everything has changed. We are no longer on the way, we are on the way back. We have made it past the half way mark and all roads now lead back to where we came. Three more months, twenty more states, thousands of miles. But now with the bulk of the trip behind us we find everything is taking on a new tint, a new direction. The weather has swapped seasons to signify the transition for us. The summer is gone and fall is well underway, winter peeking around the corner. We've watched the leaves change colors and fall from the trees and the cool winds of winter begin to blow across New England land-scapes. We have seen both coasts and half the nation, over three months in a Jeep, thousands of miles on the open road. And now we begin the trek south and across the rest of the country.

We had many reasons to pay a visit to the nation's capital. Brian and I both have friends in the area, and both have interest in seeing the sights we hadn't seen since childhood. But most importantly it is an invitation to appear on the *Voice of America* that brings us here. We received an email a couple weeks back inviting us to appear on the world-wide radio broadcast and talk about our quest. An invitation we were quick to accept.

We have received some press already on the journey and each time it has opened doors to meeting new people and letting others know about what we are doing. We find it to be a great help for both our morale and getting the word out and sharing our findings with others. But so far all the media has been in the form of newspaper articles. And always the story was told from the writers' perspective. Now was the chance to offer our own words and ideas in our very own voices.

We settle into the surroundings for a few days prior to the interview, staying with Brian's old college roommates and seeing the town from a resident's perspective. It's one of the advantages to our style of travel. As we stay with locals everywhere we journey we get to see areas of cities and towns we wouldn't see as a normal tourist. We visit favorite spots, local restaurants, and watering holes where the neighborhood hangs out. We get to see the grit and the grime and all the splendor a place has to offer. It's a style of travel I like to call *Resident Tourism*. My friends and family just call it mooching.

We hop around town for a couple of days and then head into the city for our meeting with the world through broadcast voices from America.

Martin Seacrest meets us in the lobby of the VOA building on a crisp Monday morning. Dressed in jeans and a flannel shirt, the tall, lanky man is not at all what I was expecting. Once again I am reminded of how we all have expectations of what certain professionals should be like. For some reason I was expecting the TV anchorman type, with suit and tie and perfectly coifed hair. I knew it was a silly vision, after all this was radio not TV.

Martin gives us the grand tour of the studio, showing us where the news is collected, the bullpen where stories are constructed and edited, and the newsroom where it all takes place on the air. Once again Brian and I are amazed that we are seeing yet another inner-circle, a world we may never have seen if not for this quest.

After the tour Martin leads us to a sound studio and asks us to take seats behind a table laden with microphones. This was it, our time to greet the world. The interview is painless. He asks questions, and we answer. We try to think up pithy quotes and intellectual things to say, wanting to provide the best sound bytes for his piece as possible. But we both leave feeling unsuccessful in this. For some reason everything just seems to come out of our mouths garbled and confused. Or bland. Perhaps we were too conscious of the process and the eventual use for the interview, too excited or too enthralled. We ask Martin how we did and he assures us it went fine. But still we wonder.

With the interview behind us we leave the VOA building bouncing. We were on the radio! Well, we would be sometime soon anyway. We jibber about the interview and what was said and wonder if it was useable and entertaining. We are excited that we will be able to spread the news of our quest all across the globe now, perhaps reaching someone overseas and giving them a bit of support or push in the right direction. I wonder if our friends in Kenya and Greenland will ever hear it.

We finally decide to put the results of the interview out of our minds and instead focus on enjoying the day in the city. There is much to see in our nation's capital just waiting for us.

IT'S AN AGE THING

◆

We shall not cease from exploration
And the end of all our exploring
Will be to arrive where we started
And know the place for the first time

T.S. Eliot

The transition of age has been mercifully kind to me so far on the trip. Perhaps it is the movement, the constant change of environment, the stream of newness I am faced with. Maybe I just haven't had the time to sit back and dwell on the fact that I am now in the thirty-something bracket. Or could it be that it isn't such a big deal after all. But there have been times…

While enjoying a night on the town in Indianapolis with former college roommates and friends the issue did come up and slap me on the face. Thirty is such an awkward age. You're not quite "old" but you're no longer "young". It's the age where you are still looking at the young women of the world but starting to feel guilty about it. Starting to realize that they are forever falling from your reach. The ladies you use to be able to woo are now calling you "sir" and asking your advice.

In Indy we hit Circle Center, a blend of different bars and nightclubs gathered in one area and accessible by one easy admission charge. We figured this was a safe bet, with so many places to choose from there must be something for everybody. We were wrong. There was something for everyone but the thirty-year-old. We walked into one bar and found the clientele far too young. How could these people not be in high school? Are they really of legal age or have the bouncers become lax in checking for false IDs? We sat and watched the scene but felt out of place. Time to move on to another club, another crowd, another scene.

In the next bar called *Flashbacks* we sat and listened to the music of the seventies and eighties. Our music. The music we grew up with that they were now calling "oldies." The music rocked and rolled us with memories of past adventures and conquests. But the room was full of people who, if they were our age were accepting the transition far more easily than I. They seemed so sedate, so old. Surely this crowd must be of an older set. Forty maybe. Maybe older. They were just masquerading in youthful clothes.

We bounced around and found no crowd to suit us. All too old or too young. I felt like I was caught in a bizarre fairy tale, visiting friendly bears and trying bowls of porridge that would never please me. A self-centered little boy not happy with the toys given, always wanting something that is just right.

We left the bar scene that night in a cloud of confusion. Who were we now? Where did we fit in? We let it pass but at times the sensation would come back. Events that would make me wonder when it happened? How did I miss the big event? Was I asleep or out somewhere when the CBS special was on? Did my invitation to the ceremony get lost in the mail? I think back at the other instances and remain confused.

While visiting my old home in Huntington I stopped in for my annual dental check, and after my cleaning I waited for my dentist to come in for his cursory visit. But instead of my usual dentist of many

years his new partner entered the room, reaching out a hand of introduction. I shook his hand and stared up from the dental recliner at him
in awe. He couldn't have been any older than I. There was this guy,
someone my age, looking at my teeth and taking responsibility for my
dental well-being. How did he get there? What happened to my good
old dentist?

And then there was our earlier stop visiting with friends from way,
way back. We went for drinks and were hanging out just like old times
when my buddy got a call on his cell phone. A client wanting some legal
advice. Legal advice from my friend? This guy I've known since the time
of pool parties and roller-rinks was a respected lawyer about town?
Dishing out advice, legalizing and the things attorneys do?

I realized that somehow over night it happened. My friends and peers
became respectable members of their communities. They became lead-
ers and pillars. The torch of authority was handed to us, the world
passed down from the previous generation and left to our care.

And yet I don't remember any ceremony. There were no trumpets or
parades or ribbons or decrees. Just the quiet passing into adulthood. No
fanfare. No prior alert or notice. Here we are, out in the world and told
to make the most of it.

I wonder when I will look at them and see not school chums, or
braces, or awkward adolescents but see the lawyers, doctors, teachers,
and businessmen they have become? When does the picture in the
mind's eye catch up with them and change to reflect their new found
position and stature? The torch has been passed, we're on the clock.

And now another signpost on the road to adulthood. I stand here
faced with the question of when Boba Fett became a cultural icon.
Standing here staring at my favorite of the Star Wars characters, I
wonder if there really is a hidden moral message in Star Wars that is
worthy of a museum exhibit. Or is there something at work here a tad
bit sinister?

Don't get me wrong, I appreciate the "Mythology of Star Wars" exhibit here at the Smithsonian's Air and Space Museum just as much as the next guy (who happens to be Brian) but I do find something about it a little disturbing.

Museums are supposed to be places you go to learn about things of the past. Places you go to hand in hand with parents as they tell you the stories of the relics you see. You listen as they relate personal accounts of seeing the movie, or hearing the person speak at school, or watching as their father used the object in daily life. The museums were jumping off places for the reminiscing of older folk, those that came before. What began with a stroll through the museum usually ended with a story about "walking barefoot through the snow uphill both ways…"

But this is Star Wars! This is my movie, my generation, my memories. My parents probably wouldn't even go to see this exhibit unless dragged by me or one of my brothers. How am I supposed to react to this?

And there in the Museum of American History, whose idea was it to put *those* in there? They weren't there the last time I visited DC. In fact the whole exhibit didn't exist. But there they sat in the display on the history of the computer: a TSR-80 and Commodore 64 personal computers. These dusty relics of the past were still fresh in my memories, and I can easily recall one sitting in my living room back home as I strolled the corridors of the same DC museum over two decades before.

How does one react to the classification and cataloging of his world into the archives of history. Am I supposed to pull a kid aside there in the museum and share with them my memories before cable TV, home satellite dishes, remote controls, CDs, microwaves, and Nintendo? Do I sigh and tell them how tough it used to be and how lucky they are today?

I stare at the displays with a weird sense of mortality. I can't really be old enough to have my world displayed in museums already can I?

What's waiting around the corner, an exhibit of Izod shirts and Steve Austin lunch boxes?

No, Oscar the Grouch behind Plexiglas.

Ouch.

DECISIONS

◆
―――――――――――――   ―――――――――――――

Life is what happens when
you're busy making other plans

John Lennon

When we leave DC and begin the journey south we suddenly feel we've left something more than the first half of the journey behind. The feeling is there, silent and unspoken but so palpable in the confined space of the Jeep it seems like another passenger riding along with us unannounced. Something has changed. A metamorphosis had taken place in DC. Our quest had evolved.

Brian and I sit in silence on the drive through Virginia, both lost in our own thoughts. I can almost guess what he is thinking, but am afraid to broach the silence and ask if I am right. Instead I suggest we continue with our latest audio book, Steinbeck's *Travels With Charlie*. We have been listening to books here and there across the country and knew as soon as we decided to make the trip that this one would be part of our collection. We have already heard most of it, just one tape left. I pull it out of its case and slide it into the stereo and we are once again traveling along with Steinbeck and Charlie, as Gary Sinise reads to us about the back roads of America.

And as we skirt Fort Royal for our junction with 81 Gary reads to us:

Who has not known a journey to be over and dead before the traveler returns? The reverse is also true: many a trip continues long after movement in time and space have ceased...

The words are not from a book, not read to us from a cassette. They are spoken to us.

My own journey started long before I left, and was over before I returned. I know exactly where and when it was over. Near Abingdon, in the dog-leg of Virginia, at four o'clock on a windy afternoon, without warning or goodby or kiss my foot, my journey went away and left me stranded far from home.

They are words of advice from some forgotten old friend. They are words snatched from our own minds. I know as soon as they float from the speakers that that is where we are in our journey. And I know before Brian says anything that his journey is over.

"You know," Brian turns toward me. I guess from the look in my eyes he can tell I did know. He decides not to continue with his comment, so I finish it for him.

"You're done aren't you? Had enough and ready to move on?"

"Yes, I think so. The trip has been great. We've learned a lot. I've learned a lot. But now I think I know what it is that was missing, what it is I wanted. And I guess having that knowledge I'm anxious to get back and get started on the rest of my life."

It comes as no surprise to me. I had expected it for days now. Something had clicked in Brian in the hollows of New England. Or maybe it was even earlier than that, maybe it was back in Pittsburgh where he was surrounded by family and familiar environment. A slow realization, a bolt of lightning, I don't know. But the result was the same. He was a changed man.

"I guess that was one of the big differences between us in taking this trip," I say. "You knew what you wanted and were taking this trip not really to learn anything as much as re-affirm everything. You had a checklist of personal truths and assumptions and were out to prove them right. Which I guess you have."

"Yeah, I think so," Brian says drifting off into thought for a moment. "You're right. And now that I know what I thought was right, I'm ready to jump into a new world with both feet and begin building a life."

"While I, well, I didn't really have any answers," I say, seeing the contrast between us clearly now. "I was seeking and looking and hoping to find. I've learned much, but I still feel there's much to be learned. I guess I'm just not satisfied yet. Not yet satiated. And besides, you have a life to move on to. I on the other hand…"

"What do you mean I have a life to move on to?" Brian asks, looking over at me.

"Well you know where you want to live: Nebraska. You know roughly what you want to do. You know you're ready to settle down and have the house and the dog and the wife and the kids. Me, I'm still not really sure about any of that. I feel like I still need to keep on seeking. I don't know, maybe I'm as confused as ever. I've made some realizations yes, but I feel I'm no closer to any of the answers."

"Maybe that is your answer. Maybe there are people out there, like you, who aren't meant to find clear-cut answers. They are supposed to just keep looking and not settle for anything."

"Intriguing concept. But is sounds like an existence that would surely suck!" I say and lean back in the seat, tossing my feet up onto the dash.

"Would it?" Brian asks surprised. "I thought you enjoyed the motion. Why try to stop all of a sudden. Everything eventually winds down in its own time. Why not just accept that it isn't your time yet. Stop looking for the pat answers through the comparisons to others and what they have, what they want. Look at us, my life wouldn't fit you. Most of the lives of the people we've met on this trip wouldn't fit you. You are you and you have to live up to it!"

I think about this for a moment, knowing he is right. I have thought about it for weeks now, having come to realizations without accepting them. I have been looking for answers that I knew I would never find. Or maybe for answers I had with me all along.

"Well whatever my issues and my problems, we need to deal with the one at hand for now. You're ready to bag it and I'm wanting to go on." I say, putting the life discussion on hold for now.

"It's not that I want to just up and quit. I'm enjoying this, and like I said I am learning a lot. It's just now that we've made the coast and learned as much as we have I'm beginning to wonder if the time and money and resources could be better spent moving into the next phase."

"So where do we go from here. Any suggestions?"

"Okay, how about this," Brian offers a suggestion. "What if we change the pace of the quest a bit. Up to this point we have been actively seeking out information and people and answers. What if we finish the trip as planned but do it in a more personal, free-flowing, relaxed fashion."

"What do you mean?" I ask.

"We finish out the itinerary as planned but we take more time to ourselves. We relax and enjoy the journey more. We see places we want to see and leave ourselves open for more chance encounters and events rather than planned ones." He says.

"And the web site?" I ask.

"We keep it going. I mean, there will still be interviews and such but at the rate we're going it is hard to get them all up on the web as it is. So let's just relax the pace a bit, put less up on the web, and play it by ear more. More fun, less work."

He's right. We currently have a backlog of interviews yet to be transcribed and posted on the web.

"Okay, sounds feasible. And besides, if you are so ready to hit the career track again this could be your last big vacation buddy, I guess we should make sure and enjoy it!"

And just like that part of the quest dies and gives birth to a newness, a fresh outlook, a new genesis. We have succeeded. At least half the team has found what they were looking for. Brian is a new man and is ready for the next challenge. And me?

I feel good about the decision. It feels right, like the right thing to do. The next chapter in our story about to unfold. Maybe I'm just now facing the truths that I didn't want to admit to. Perhaps Brian is right and I am meant to just keep drifting for a while.

It reminds me of a trip I made once while living in Shanghai. After a little coaxing, I agreed to go with a couple of Chinese friends to see a fortune teller. I went initially as an observer but once in the presence of the old, weathered, blind man I was intrigued to hear what he had to say. It was one thing in particular that comes to mind now. He told me that I was currently living as if running through a rain storm, moving quickly and taking shelter here and there to weather out the storm. He said I would keep moving forward, shelter to shelter, never staying at one in particular. But he also said that eventually I would find a place to stay and the storm would clear and my fortune would shine down upon me.

I didn't give it much thought then, and I try not to now. But in light of recent circumstances I can't keep myself from wondering if there wasn't something more to the old man's story than just pure entertainment. It's odd thinking of it now. Why would I keep moving through such a storm? Was I testing fate, trying to move ahead, or could it be I was out seeking to get struck by lightning.

"What are you thinking?" Brian notices me staring out the window.

"Nothing in particular, my mind's just adrift."

I had a lot to consider and much to absorb. All of a sudden the end of our quest looms ever nearer, coming much too soon for me. Although we decide to continue along our path and finish out the trek, the mood has changed. There is a sudden sense of urgency wrapped up in a blanket of suspense. I continue to drift and let it all sink in, words from Steinbeck still resounding in my head:

…my journey went away and left me stranded far from home. I tried to call it back, to catch it up—a foolish and hopeless matter, because it was definitely and permanently over and finished.

LONG ROAD HOME

◆

Life is a great bundle of little things.

Oliver Wendell Holmes

We wind south where we enjoy the first leg of our return trip in the company of family and friends, playing the goofy uncle in Virginia and roaming empty city streets with old high school friends in North Carolina. There is something incredibly scary about a deserted city like the one we see one sunny Sunday afternoon in Charlotte. Just as when in nature you expect to be alone, when in a city built by people for people you expect to see people. But whatever residents make use of the city of Charlotte during the week they are definitely imports, venturing no where near the city on the weekends.

We continue south through the Carolinas and Georgia and trace the contour of Florida, with stops in Daytona, Tampa, Miami, and the Keys. At one point I think our trip will end in Florida. Not due to our arrival at pristine beaches, or the endless sun, or off shore snorkeling, or drinks served by tan waitresses, but by being killed by resident drivers. With over 20,000 miles and most of the nation under our belt we have never seen worse drivers than on the streets of Southern Florida.

I don't know why this is. Some may try to blame it on the retirement set, saying it's the geriatric brigade that takes to the roads minutes before a crucial bridge or shuffle board game. But I can't agree with this. Of the drivers we see turning left across three lanes of traffic, pulling out on a one way street going the wrong direction, cutting off cars left and right, coming to a complete stop on the highway to inspect a road sign a little more closely, and almost running into the divider trying to exit a freeway, few have been elderly. Nope, it's a nice try to blame it on the elderly or the tourists, but it just won't cut it. The driver's disease seems to cross all boundaries of southern Florida residents.

We celebrate Thanksgiving in Miami's South Beach before heading north again and continuing our zag across the country. Savannah, Atlanta, the World of Coke, and the America's best BBQ sandwiches (on either side of the Mississippi). Up through Birmingham and on to Memphis and the lair of the King of rock and roll.

Memphis is a city that definitely has a soul of its own. A soul beating of bluegrass and Rock 'n Roll pulled together and kept holy under the watchful eye of Saint Elvis. The man and his music are everywhere. And turn or twist as you might, all roads eventually lead to Graceland. We can't resist the allure of pink Caddys and sequined jumpsuits and make the trip to Mecca to pay homage to the King. A day in Graceland and a stroll though history in blue suede shoes.

Heading south again we glide through Arkansas and Mississippi, enjoying some time in the rural South before hitting New Orleans. We hit the bayou country and a friend of a friend puts us up for a few days as we explore Bourbon Street and the French Quarter. The town is an electric mix of American charm and European flair, and I find myself more than once forgetting I'm on American soil. Gumbo and hurricanes, beads and balconies, feathers and masks, jazz and Dixieland, it's a bubbling stew of sights and sounds and tasty life. The city has an energy to it that sucks you in and spins you around in a riptide of hedonism. It gives energy as it takes it in a symbiotic cycle of perpetual delectation.

We eventually have to just stand up and walk away, trying hard not to turn back to the call of the music, and quietly drift out of town.

We point the wheel westward and travel though Houston, San Antonio and Austin on a twister tour of the massive state of Texas. Brian and I have toured the state together once before during a break from my summer in Nebraska. We repeat the circuit now, replacing a visit to Dallas with one to Austin. We meet with oilmen and cowboys and gallery owners and high schoolers before making the jog across forgotten roads into New Mexico destined for Carlsbad Caverns, Roswell, and points further north.

We plan on lunch in Roswell and dinner in Santa Fe, but come dangerously close to losing ourselves in-between. After browsing the displays at Roswell's UFO Museum we head back to the Jeep and find it won't start. Thousands of miles across the world and now it decides to break down. Here in Roswell, home of Area 51 and all things eerie and extraterrestrial. On a Sunday afternoon. At 3 o'clock.

But as bleak as it seems, we are very lucky. It could have happened the night before when we drove all night through empty desert roads. Or tonight as we head through more crawling expanses of nothingness. At least here we are parked in front of a Denny's.

A strange calm falls over us as we roam the streets in search of help. I kid Brian about the whole ordeal being orchestrated by aliens bent on delaying our progress in order that we show up at the designated abduction spot at just the right time. It helps a little to cheer up our search for technical know-how.

We find assistance in the form of Mark Fox, a twenty-something backyard mechanic working at a tire shop on the edge of town and just about to leave for the day. The friendly savior drives us back to the Jeep, checks under its hood, discovers a fried distributor cap cable, and has us fixed and on the road in less than an hour and twenty dollars later. Just in time to catch up with the aliens.

As we cruise Santa Fe and Taos, I find myself entering a part of the country I have always wanted to explore. Places of art and mystery. Our glance around the area only proves to show I need to return again and spend more time here. Another area to add to my *More To Come* list.

Our relentless pace continues. It seems the closer we get to the west coast the faster we tend to move through an area as if some giant magnet has caught us in its grip. At one point when we pass through Denver and Boulder I think I may lose Brian. We were dangerously close to Omaha now and it would be easy for him to make the jump via Greyhound. But he declares the show must go on and go on we do.

Through the Rockies, down through Utah and the Arches National Park, across Arizona and north again into Nevada. It is six more weeks in all heading back across America. Six weeks that seem to fly by. We continue to meet people, to talk and to explore, trying our best to live up to our Creed and our quest. The web site continues to grow with new weekly content. I check out possible cities of future residence and explore the myriad of questions that continue to bounce in my head as Brian sees constant reaffirmation of his earlier decisions. But in six weeks we have seen all the places we had set out to see. We have completed the circuit and are almost "back." We pull into our final stop and are ready to celebrate the end of a quest in a fashion only Las Vegas can provide.

PLAYING OUT THE HAND

◆

We have what we seek.
It is there all the time,
And if we give it time,
It will make itself known to us.

Thomas Merton

"Drink?"

It's the waitress again, ready to fill another free drink request. She leans in slowly to take the empty from the table in front of me, her bosoms cleaved inside a tight purple top with one clearly labeled as Cheryl. I consider this and my drink choice and decide I might play poker better if I was a little more liquored up.

"Sure, a scotch on the rocks."

Cheryl simply smiles and moves on to the next player, continuing around the table until everyone has had the chance to get properly sauced. Everyone, that is, except the dealer. Welcome to Vegas.

Cards are tossed across green felt and I take a peek at what I get. Not much; A pair of eights. Gotta bet big to win big, isn't that what they say? I bet two bucks.

I lose. Again. The woman in the seat next to me cashes out and as Cheryl delivers my scotch a newcomer fills the gap. I turn to give him the mandatory welcome nod as I raise the glass for a sip. Instead I drain the glass and peer at the new player through the bottom of the tumbler trying to sort things out.

"How's the game?" The newcomer asks.

"You."

It's him again. From the hill. Dressed in old man's pants and golf shirt and a hat that says *Viva Las Vegas* and screams tourist. A pair of glasses dangle precariously on a nose red with sun or liquor. The Old Man has found me again.

"What are you doing here?" I ask hesitantly.

"You tell me. You're the one who brought me here."

"Me?" It sounds absurd. How could I have brought him here, I was busy playing poker. But slowly a realization came over me. Maybe it *was* me who brought him, looking for someone to talk with on the eve of the end.

"Oh."

"I'm here to help get you all sorted out boy. Your journey ends tomorrow right?" He asks. As he does so he raises a hand and signals to the dealer to count him out of the round. Somehow this ends up excluding me as well.

"Yeah, we'll be back in Los Angeles by tomorrow evening."

"Then we have only tonight." He says.

"Tonight? For what? Why only tonight?" I ask.

"Because that's all we ever really have. Today, tonight, right now. It's all that's guaranteed. We haven't much time at all. A day, a week, a year, a decade or maybe five. So much time or maybe none at all. Take your time. Hurry up."

"You're talking in riddles again Yoda." I say and start to turn back to the table when he places a hand on my arm.

"Life is a riddle boy. And in the end the joke's on you, so you might as well start laughing now." He pulls me in closer and points off at the ceiling in the distance. "It's like a finger pointing away at the moon, don't concentrate on the finger or you will miss all that heavenly glory."

"Hey, Bruce Lee said that in *Enter The Dragon*."

"Oh, so he did. Never mind." The Old Man lowers his arm and looks directly at me again. "Now tell me, you hit L.A. tomorrow and then what?"

"I'm not sure. I don't really know."

"You don't know? After all this traveling around talking with people you still don't know?"

"Not really. But I think maybe I'm okay with that. I-"

"Good!" He slaps his hand on the table and motions for the dealer to give me a hand. She flips cards across the table at me in response.

"Look at them." The Old Man says.

I fold them in my hand and fan them out to see what I got: a five and a three of spades, six of diamonds, three of clubs, and a four of hearts. Nothing.

"Great, another losing hand."

"Is it?" The Old Man asks with raised eye brow. "We all have to play with the hand we're dealt. The problem is we often are just playing it in the wrong game. What if you take this hand over to the black jack table?"

"I'd win. Twenty-one. But I don't think they allow-"

"It's a metaphor you moron. Work with me here. Pay attention. It's one of the keys you've been looking for, what so many people have been saying. You have to find the game that best suits you. Find what makes you happiest and how to best use the hand you're dealt. Isn't that what everyone has been trying to tell you. Life's a game boy. It's a lot of gambling, and beating the odds, and taking chances, and winning and losing. But you have to play, that's the key. Don't rush the game. Don't be afraid to break the rules or make up your own. Have fun with life."

"And when I find the right game to play, that's when the Shamzara hits, right?"

"Ah, so that's it. That's why I'm here is it? Okay then, the Shamzara thing." He sits back in his seat and exhales and long, slow breath. "Ever stop to think that it isn't going to be a sudden bolt of lightning but instead a steady, slow increase in voltage over the years until you are charged and running at full power?"

I hear his argument and know I have heard it before. I tell myself the same thing all the time.

"I've thought about it. That is the way it should be, the way it probably is. But still, in the back of my mind, in the deep recesses of my unconsciousness, I am waiting for the Shamzara to hit. Waiting for that something to just POW! Hit me. Waiting for that perfect world where I say: 'This is it, I have arrived.' Waiting for that moment of complete and utter happiness and contentment. It's a delusional fantasy."

"Well the fantasy isn't necessarily evil," he says. "It depends on how much strength you give it. If you find yourself constantly living while looking over your shoulder for something bigger and better to come along, or keep lifting rocks looking for the bolt of lightning to strike, then that could be bad."

I turn away and look down at the table and my stack of chips. I pick one up and twist it in my fingers, then drop it back to the table. "I know. But how do you reconcile the fantasy with reality? When do you make that decision to give up the dream and just accept what you have or what is headed your way?"

"I can't answer you there. I guess you have to look for the essence of the Shamzara you seek. What is it that will transform your life? What are the key elements there in the lightning. Break it down into the smallest atoms of events and emotions and then find them in daily life, in what you already have."

"You're right. But maybe I'm just not ready for that yet."

"And no one said you should be. Everyone has to come to terms with their own demons on their own time. You can't let anyone else tell you to change. Your problem is you are doing just that. Not directly, but you are looking around at others and holding yourself up to their example. You're expecting yourself to have the life that they have. But face it boy, you're not them and never will be. You have your own path, and if you're still in the lightning-chasing stage then so be it. As long as you are aware of the paradox and problems associated with it and are keeping an eye on it, then what's the harm."

"What's the harm." I repeat, listening to the words slide off my tongue and squeeze between my teeth.

"You *do* know the real problem with your Shamzara theory, right?"

"What?"

"Life. Change. Life is not static, it's flowing. The problem is that the Shamzara is not self-sustaining. Once you have a life-altering event and things are great, life doesn't freeze frame and stay that way. Things change, people change, *you* change. You may find your wonderful world, but life continues to flow and to grow. Soon all that is perfect may not be perfect anymore. Maybe you will grow to a point where you find what was so special isn't that special any more. Then what?"

I look at him blankly, waiting for the answer.

"That's when the Upgrade Factor comes into play. You have the constant need for an upgrade. You are happy and things are going well but you think: Hmmmm, maybe things could be better if only…And then you look for the change, the upgrade that will make everything right again. I'm not saying that the Shamzara isn't possible, I'm just saying that the life changes and effects it brings about are fleeting unless you take them for what they are: temporary. Nothing is going to hit you and forever change your life. At least nothing on the outside. The only lightning that could hit and cause that kind of change can only strike from the inside. You would have to initiate it by making the conscious decision to make the change or to accept the change when it happens, to internalize it. Change how you view the world around you and then your magical event will happen. If you keep waiting for something on the outside to do that you'll constantly be disappointed."

He draws a little closer to make sure I'm paying attention. For me, there is only us in the room now. His words are all I hear.

"I think the after effects of the Shamzara are entirely dependent on a person's personality. Some can welcome the sudden WOW and be satisfied with it and let it last a lifetime. The initial feeling may subside or even vanish, but the fact that it was once there is enough to last forever. Others get the boost from the Shamzara event, and then as it dies down look for another and then another. Of these people there are those that eventually settle for what they have and say: 'It's been great, whatta ride, now here I am to stay.' Then there are those that never settle but keep chasing lightning. I'm not saying any of these are correct. To each their own. But if you are not one to settle, then don't worry over this fact. Accept yourself for what you are and move forward. Maybe you will someday accept life and take what you have and call it your own. Maybe not. Maybe you will always keep looking. But whatever you do, if it makes you happy, then it is right for you. And you can only be happy with what is right for you. Other peoples' shoes just won't fit, so don't even try."

It reminds me of something Brian said to me weeks ago outside of DC: "Maybe there are people out there, like you, who aren't meant to find clear cut answers. They are supposed to just keep looking..."

I guess we're all looking though, aren't we. Everyone we've talked to, no one has really found what they seek yet. Parts of it yes, fleeting moments, stolen smiles and laughter. But no one has said "this is it, here I am." Am I really any different then? Maybe it's just a difference in the degree of cognizance over the search process. Or maybe, as I discovered earlier it's just a matter of where you are in life, at what *stage* you have arrived.

"In the end it's really about the process boy. Quit focusing on the events, the ends, the lightning and enjoy the brewing of the storm and the clearing of the clouds. If the lightning strikes, let it. But don't run around naked swinging a rod and doing the funky chicken rain dance in hopes of Shamzara."

"You've traveled all this way and met and touched so many people, but you've been alone the whole time. No one's been with you boy. Not Brian, not me, no one but you and you alone. It's your road and you have to walk it alone. You will receive help here and there, guidance or friendly gesture, but no one will walk it for you. And while you're enjoying the process you have to try to let others do the same. Help them when you can and when you can't, support them in their triumphs and failures. Ever hear of the crabs?"

I shake my head slowly, a bit unsure how to answer this.

"When you put a bunch of crabs in a boiling pot they will all struggle to get out. They will climb at the walls and try their darndest to escape while all the while pulling down and tugging at the others in order to get out. Each tries to escape and inadvertently prevents the others from escaping in doing so. If they would just work together they could all get out. But instead they clamor and hold each other back on their path to succeed. You must face your own challenges but you have to assist others on the way. Help them climb up as you make the ascent."

Crabs in pots, fingers pointing at moons. They all seem like distant fairy tales or long lost memories. A strange sense of deja vu washes over me. Whether I've heard it before or thought it before I can't say. Or maybe it's all new and I am experiencing the groggy sense of realization.

"Well, that's it. I have to go."

"What? No, wait. Can't you stick around for a while?" I've become very comfortable having the Old Man around, and the thought now of being left alone brings chills.

"No can do. Our time is up. We're finished. I have to leave you to your path and return to mine."

"So what about your path. Why not sit and tell me about it. What about your decisions, thoughts, dreams, regrets?"

"In time. I have a feeling that by the time you're my age you will know more about me and my path than you think. I think I best be getting along now and see about winning that Porsche slot over there and cruising on out of town. Here," he takes a bright red chip from my stack on the table and puts it in my hand. "Keep this one. Always be ready to play another day."

The Old Man stands up and pulls his polyester pants a bit higher on his waist, then straightens his cap. In doing this he reminds me of my grandfather. I begin to protest his departure, but he is already walking away into the crowd of gamblers.

"Wait! Aren't you going to tell me what all that up on the hill meant?" I yell at him standing from my chair.

He halts and slowly begins to turn back around to face me but stops himself halfway. He then turns to go once again and drops his head, shaking it slowly. He disappears into the crowd of gamblers without looking back, without another word. And all I can do is sit and watch. He is gone as suddenly as he arrived.

"Are you in the game?" The dealer asks me from across the green felt.

I stand and watch the crowd of people. Everyone is going their own direction in a flurry of activity. Hundreds of lives making decisions and gambling and taking risks and having fun. Some win, some lose, but everyone is playing.

"Yeah, I'm in."

CHASING LIGHTNING

◆

Be like the bird that,
passing on her flight awhile on boughs too slight,
feels them give way beneath her,
and yet sings, knowing that she hath wings.

Victor Hugo

It is still pitch black in the room when the alarm goes off, but the clock reads eight a.m. I pull myself out of bed and over to the window to open the thick blanket of curtains. Sunlight ignites the room and sends Brian rolling over in his bed.

"Wake up boy, it's the first day of the rest of your life!" I say walking over to his bed and giving it a quick kick. I sit down on the end of my bed and pick up the TV remote control but let the TV remain lifeless. "How'd you sleep?"

"Better than you," Brian says rolling over and trying to adjust his eyes to the new light of day. "You were tossing around and talking in your sleep all night."

"Really? What did I say?"

"Sorry, I didn't take notes."

"Hmm, must have been that all-you-can-eat buffet dinner we had last night. I should have known better than to go back for thirds."

"Speaking of which, I'm kinda hungry. Why don't we hit the breakfast buffet before we hit the road."

"Sounds good. I'll shower first." I toss him the remote and gather my things for the bathroom.

And that's how our last day on the roads of America begins. No trumpets or confetti or news broadcasts. Just two weary travelers ready for home. Or for the end, at least.

We move through the clamor of the casino on the way to the restaurant. Day or night outside, it is always light in here. Neon and flashing lights and singing bells and whistles help you forget where and when you are. It's a man-made Never Never Land. Wonderland with a price tag.

Our stay in Vegas has been just the ending to the quest we needed. Fun, glitz, and excitement. We gambled, we saw a show, we ate and drank in merry fashion. All things Vegas were ours to enjoy. But like our breakfast buffet this morning, there is just too much to consume here. Eventually you are bloated and satiated and need to get moving. Need to work off your excess in motion.

At the Jeep Brian can't resist adding one more notch to our Statistics Page.

"You want to drive or you want me to drive?" It's the 50th time we've asked that question in the 175 days and 23,629 miles we've been on the road.

"I'll drive. Do you have the keys?"

"No, you should still have them from yesterday."

"Oh yeah."

I dig into the pocket of my jeans, the same jeans I had on all day yesterday. They still smell of smoke and casino. It will be nice to get some laundry done soon. I pull out the contents of my pocket instead of trying to fish the keys out alone. There in my hand I see not only the keys but 37 cents in change and a bright red poker chip. Confused, I hold it up for Brian to see and begin to ask him about it. But he's already around the other side of the Jeep so I let it slip back into my pocket and out of mind.

We climb into the Jeep and take one last cruise down the Las Vegas Strip before getting onto I-15 and all points west. Our morning drive has an oddity about it. Perhaps we are too aware of it being our last few hours on the road and don't know how to treat it: be happy or be sad. I think we decide on a mixture of both. Or it could be our exhaustion from six months travel and two nights of Las Vegas living has finally caught up to us. Now in the last steps to L.A. our bodies are just saying "no more."

It will be strange hitting Los Angeles again, now a visitor in my former home. I left thinking I would discover someplace else I wanted to live but ended up with no real contenders. Or maybe too many. The elements of choice have shifted a bit, from geography to people, from what I surround myself with to who, from what I do to what I achieve—for myself and for others. New choices and new decisions to be made.

It's funny that way. All the things I set out to discover seem to be ever elusive. I guess I left chasing lightning, thinking that maybe this trip would produce the sudden realization of sense and answers, that someone somewhere would wake me up to the realities of life. But it didn't happen. There wasn't one voice. There were many. Everyone had something to offer, everything had some sort of meaning. Meaning to me, meaning to Brian, meaning to those who said it. All separate and individual. A vast world of views and opinions and dreams and hopes and experiences.

No bolt of lightning, but the same result nonetheless. It was a life changing event, our quest. One of small steps and little lessons. Everyone learns their lessons at their own pace. These were mine. And maybe that was enough.

I'm not sure what the end of the road will hold for me. I have ideas, maybe even plans, but they could all change between now and then. I let my expectations fall to the wayside like tumble weeds in the desert, blowing around neither here nor there, without substance or import. I am the reed. I am here in the Jeep, right now, and that's all I want to know.

Nevada falls behind us, the last state on our cross country adventure, and the desert highways of California welcome us back. On the side of the road just at the border a rabbit scurries up and stands on its hind legs right as we pass. *Rabbit?* I smile down at it as we drive by, almost wanting to wave, wanting to acknowledge the coincidence of life. A glance backwards in the rearview mirror shows the rabbit running off away from the road and into the desert, choosing a path that will lead him to another day and keep him in the game.

Our journey is over, our quest has just begun.

Shamzara.

Epilogue

◆

Not I nor anyone else can travel that road for you,
You must travel it for yourself.

Walt Whitman

West Virginia, Summer 1999

It's been months since we landed from taking our quest and much has happened. Brian moved back to Omaha, Nebraska within days of hitting L.A. and was with home and new career within a couple of weeks. He took what he learned from the quest and was quick to apply it, entering a world that makes him happy, finding his place, and moving on to the next stage.

As for me, I decided to take some time to put down these words, a process that has proven a quest in its own right. Reliving the journey through writing has help me put things into perspective. And while I continue along the path I had chosen before it seems fuller now, less vacant. The emptiness I felt earlier was a lack of understanding, of myself and the way things are. Or rather the way things could be.

We set out on our journey with the goal of helping at least one person out there in the world to understand a little more of life and their place in it. We ended up helping two. Brian and I both made realizations on the open road that will stay with us forever. Those and the memories of the journey and the fun and challenges we had.

Looking back I can only hope that we were able to help some others along the way. Maybe some of the people we talked to, or someone stumbling across our web site, or perhaps you reading this book. It's a journey we all must take in our own way, but hopefully we have been able to lend a hand. We have a lot to learn from others, things about ourselves and the world and the people next door. I hope these simple stories have offered you some insights into your world.

One question that keeps coming up whenever I tell anyone about the quest is: "Now that you've done this quest and talked with all these people, how would you define successful living?"

It's funny, during all our travels I listened to others defining success and successful living without really trying to define it myself. In part this was because we wanted to be an empty slate for what we would hear. We didn't want to taint what others said with our own expectations or our own pre-defined answers. And maybe in part it was because I really didn't know. But now that we have finished the journey I have had time to think about it and have come to my own conclusions. And for me to define successful living I would refer to a crinkled slip of yellow paper I keep here on my desk beside me that has scribbled in my handwriting:

Listen not just to hear but to understand.

Have a positive impact on the lives of everyone we meet.

Learn and live with passion.

Welcome every chance to meet new people and experience new things.

Embrace each opportunity to have fun on the journey, enjoying the entire trip rather than just the destinations.

Relax, smile, laugh.

Above all else: love, family, and friendship.

Thank you for joining me on my quest, I wish you the best of luck in yours.

Afterword

———————◆———————

This book is a culmination of the efforts of many people. Yes, I authored the book but the tale was written by many friendly faces, from the people we interviewed along the way, to people who encouraged us to make the journey, to friends and family who supported us through donations of food, shelter, full gas tanks, or simple kind words.

First and foremost I'd like to thank Brian Ardinger, my best friend of over 25 years and partner-in-crime on the roads of America. Without Brian the trip couldn't and wouldn't have taken place. It was our mutual decision to make the journey, but it was Brian's enduring optimism that allowed us to make it out the door and to continue when weariness struck.

Likewise, the support of Jeanne Cheng was a godsend during the days when confusion over my life's direction was at its peak. Jeanne was the beacon through my storms of disillusionment. She offered uncompromising love and compassion that I will always be grateful for.

I'd also like to thank our families, Brian's and mine, for all their kindness. They never once called us crazy or told us to think of our resumes. In fact, they were our strongest supporters. We love you guys!

Many of our friends jumped in with buckets of love and assistance as well, especially in the form of constant emails and friendly words sent out to us weary travelers. In particular I'd like to thank the Templetons, David and Cathy, for constantly riding along with us in cyberspace and lending their ear every once in a while. And thanks for the espresso guys!

There were many people—family, friends, and complete strangers—who sponsored our adventures by joining our *Full Tank Club*. These fine people contributed some of their hard-earned money to help us buy a tank of gas here and there as we crisscrossed the country. In fact, we had so many people make contributions that it almost paid for all our gas! Each sponsor got to choose which part of the trip their tank of gas would go toward, and in return received an official Quest-4 Certificate of "ownership" of that part of the road. Our Full Tank Club members include:

Rebecca Allen; Al & Ruth Ardinger; Denny, Terry, & Beckie Ardinger; Nick Ardinger; Rick Ardinger; Csaba & Leah Balogh; Brian Beldon; Nicole & Bill Bien; John Brockwell; the Chengs (Gino, Jeanne, George, Lorna, Bill, & Lilly); Sailaja Cherukuri; Margie Chiang; Gregg Christensen; Communication Skills Department, Columbus State; Kim Dingess & Eric Eckhart; Ruthie, Ron, Kelly & Katie Farquarhson; Mayer Fistal; David Franklin; Jim Howard; Vivian Iwasa; Craig Johnson; Robert Keldsen; Debroah Knott; W.D. Lloyd; Matt Lewis; Susan Moran; Mitch Moreland; Darwin Singson; Stacy & Jeff Smith; Suzanne Snygg; Linda Strohmeyer; Bill Tancer; David & Cathy Templeton; Randy & Shaun Vigil-Brenneman; Walt Wang; Coleman & Mary Willis; Sean & Susan Willis; Mimie Wu; and Kathy Yeung.

The kindness of others wasn't only felt through the sponsorship of gas tanks. We also were fortunate to spend most of our nights on the road in the homes of friends (new and old) and family. Nothing could be better on the long winding highways of American than having a warm bed and friendly face to come home to at the end of the day. For their unbridled hospitality, we'd like to thank:

Neil Sullivan; P.J. McNealy & Rose Riley; Jenifer Mouritsen; Jenny Fearing; Morgan Keldsen & Bindi Klemke; Kristina Taber; Rick & Rose Ardinger; Craig Johnson & Judy Watt; Bob & Monette Keldsen; Gregg Christensen; Diane & Gary Nielsen; Debroah Knott; the Knotts: David, Cindy, Cara, and Chelsea; Al and Sandy Kalin; Eric Eckhart and Kim

Dingess; Alex Ross; the Brueggemans; Eang Ung; Sean & Susan Willis; Beth Kamper & Jeff Waldo; Bruce Ardinger; Ralph & Helen Moeller; Lisa Mann; the Windischs; Al & Ruth Ardinger; Allen Epps; Michelle Jaeger; Terry & Lois Cowen; Ed Feingold; SzeLing Wan; Jimmy Cemprola; Frank & Debbie Moeller; Chad Miller; Alicia & John Beal; Geoff & Joanna Mann; David & Cathy Templeton; David Elmore; John Terovolas; Randy & Shaun Vigil-Brenneman; John Hager; Rodney St. Pierre; Tom & Jessica LeBlanc; David Franklin & Annette Bruno; the Rodrigs: Wayne, Mary, Erin, & Matt; and Liz Paul.

Our trip would have been nothing but a summer excursion had it not been for the generous strangers we met along the way, those that opened their homes and hearts to us and offered us a few moments of their time and a brief glimpse into their lives. Without the kindness of those that afforded us interviews, our trip would have been meaningless. Only a small number of the people we interviewed are mentioned in this book, but the thoughts and feeling of all are represented in the tale as it unfolds. For sharing their wisdom, we'd like to thank:

Dave Arnold; Will Atwater; Scott Behmer; Louann Bebb; David Belitz; Hanif Bey; Kristi Blass; Rick Born; Jenny Bowen; Gordon Brooks; Kaye Byrnes; Al Chartier; Scott Cosco; Stephanie Dowling; Antionettea "Dreadie" Etienne; Joe Femiani; Ryan Fleur; Maureen Goldman; Brian "Squirrel" Hager; Greg Johns; Brendan Kehoe; Mark Tapio Kines; Barry King; Sherry Leigh; Craig Leiser; Todd McElfresh; Traci Muller; Nick Passero; Julie Ponsford; Richard Rhoades; Heather Rizutto; Steve Roberts; Linda Steen; Joe Schmaderer; Mark Sedenquist and Megan Edwards; Marcus Red Thunder; Reuben Troyer; Boris Vatel; Tom Velazquez; Marvin Wengerd; Cindy Wuu; and countless others who made the trip an enjoyable and enlightening experience.

And lastly I'd like to thank everyone who took the time to read this book. I hope you enjoyed it, got something out of it, and maybe even learned a little about yourself along the way. May you find the Shamzara of life in everything you do.

About the Author

◆

Chris Moeller is a writer, painter, and insatiable explorer. His quest for knowledge and new experiences has led him to travel extensively throughout Asia, Europe, and North and South America. Trained as a journalist, Chris is always observing the ways of the world and how people live and enjoy that thing called "life." His "work" roles have included, among other things, creative director, freelance writer, illustrator, and web designer. Though a perpetual nomad, Chris currently lives in Washington, D.C. *Chasing Lightning* is his first book.

0-595-21355-3

Printed in the United Kingdom
by Lightning Source UK Ltd.
121172UK00001B/144